A GLOSSARY

OF THE

DEMETIAN DIALECT.

A GLOSSARY

OF THE

DEMETIAN DIALECT

OF NORTH PEMBROKESHIRE

(With Special Reference to the Gwaun Valley).

BY THE

Rev. W. Meredith Morris, B.A. ("Padarn"),

VICAR OF CLYDACH VALE.

AUTHOR OF

" The Renaissance and Welsh Literature;" " British Violin Makers:
Classical and Modern ;" " The Life of Walter H. Mayson ;"
" The Church Bells of the Diocese of Llandaff "
(in preparation).

First published for subscribers only
at Tonypandy in 1910.
Facsimile reprint 1991
by Llanerch Publishers,
Felinfach.

INTRODUCTION

The turn of the present century was marked by a renewed mature interest in Welsh linguistic studies. John Rhŷs (1840-1915) published his *Lectures in Welsh Philology* in 1877; *A Welsh Grammar: Historical and Comparative* by John Morris Jones (1864-1929) appeared in 1913. The main academic interest of these scholars was for the most part historical, but together with that renowned Celtic historian the Rev. A. W. Wade-Evans (1875-1964) they were also responsible for encouraging and motivating the early synchronic work accomplished in Welsh dialectology.

The Oxford phonetician Henry Sweet (1845-1912) had published a study of the Welsh dialect of Nant Gwynant in 1882-84 and Thomas Darlington (1864-1908) had worked on a series of dialect projects in England before embarking on an investigation of dialect boundaries in mid Wales. The most ambitious work undertaken on the lexicon of a particular locality is undoubtedly *The Welsh Vocabulary of the Bangor District* by O. H. Fynes-Clinton (1869-1941) published in 1913. John Jones (Myrddin Fardd; 1836-1921) published *Gwerin-Eiriau Sir Gaernarfon* in 1909. *A Glossary of the Demetian Dialect of North Pembrokeshire* by William Meredith Morris appeared in 1910.

W. M. Morris (1867-1920) was born in the parish of Pont-faen in Pembrokeshire and educated at the Grammar School and Baptist College, Haverfordwest. In 1891 he was ordained minister of Pisga, Cresswell Quay but soon joined the Anglican communion holding curacies at Treherbert and Llangynwyd before his elevation to vicar of Clydach Vale in the Rhondda. Morris graduated from the University of London in 1900; he received his F. R. Hist. Soc., in 1904, and became M.S.A. (Member of the Society of Arts) in 1906 and F.I.G.C.M. (Fellow of the Incorporated Guild of Church Musicians) in 1909.

Despite a series of valuable published contributions in the fields of language, literature, folklore, campanology and music of Wales, William Meredith Morris is inexplicably excluded from the *Dictionary of Welsh Biography* down to 1940. His valuable lexicon of the Welsh dialect of Cwm Gwaun is, however, included in the significant dialectological bibliography of *Geiriadur Prifysgol Cymru and Llyfryddiaeth yr Iaith Gymraeg.*

Amongst Morris's unpublished works there is an 'Addendum to a Glossary of the Dialect of South Pembrokeshire' completed in 1914 and conserved at the Welsh Folk Museum.

Morris's volume on the Welsh dialect of Cwm Gwaun has always been recognised as an essential reference work for any researcher interested in the Welsh dialects of Dyfed. Copies of the original volume never appear in antiquarian sales catalogues and this new edition from Llanerch Publishers is to be welcomed.

David Thorne,
Department of Welsh Language and Literature,
St. David's University College, Lampeter.

PREFACE.

This Glossary is published in the hope that it may be of some interest and value to those who make a special study of Welsh dialects. Thanks to the splendid efforts of the Guild of Graduates of the University of Wales, persistent and systematic work is now being done in the collecting and arranging of material for what will eventually, it is hoped, prove to be a comprehensive volume on the native dialects of the Motherland. The importance of the study of dialects, alike to the philologist and anthropologist, can hardly be over-estimated. The pity is that in these days of general "levelling down" dialectical distinctions are fast disappearing, making one apprehensive that in another generation all the sub-dialects (at least) will have vanished. Many agencies conspire for the overthrow of the dialect of Dyfed, one is that of imported labour. The sons of the working class migrate in large numbers from North Pembrokeshire to the mining districts of Glamorganshire, where wages are higher and social restraints fewer, and their place is taken by English lads from industrial "Homes" and reformatory schools. The result is bad in every respect, not least in the disturbing effect it has on the dialect.

In collecting the material for this little work, the compiler has avoided the too common fault of attempting too much. It is beyond the power of one who has other pressing work to do to compile a glossary of the dialect of so large an area as the whole of Dyfed—i.e., Dyfed in the older and wider sense of the term. Far better is it for such a one to narrow the limits of his.operations, and to do as thoroughly as possible what lies near at hand. Let those who are interested in this fascinating study do for their native districts what the writer has tried to do for his.

The Glossary contains all the living and obsolescent .words of the dialect of North Pembrokeshire, or at least of that part of the county embraced by the Gwaun Valley extending from Fishguard to the Foel Ery'. In addition to the living and the vanishing, there are some words which may be regarded as almost obsolete. There are also numerous words of English origin, but only such as have by long use become thoroughly incorporated in the dialect. English words which have been introduced since the passing of the Education Act of 1870 have been excluded for obvious reasons. There is no attempt at etymologizing, or at theorizing about the form of words : that is the business of the etymologist. In a few isolated instances only is the derivation given, where the meaning of the word could not otherwise be explained. The part of speech of a word is given in nearly every instance, also the gender and number of nouns. To give the gender of a word is necessary, since it often happens that what is masculine in one sub-dialect is feminine in another.

A word as to the pronunciation. It is assumed that the sound of a word will be readily understood by anyone who can read Welsh at all, and it is not thought advisable, therefore, to burden the work with an elaborate system of phonetics. A simple table of letter-sounds is given at the commencement, which is sufficient to enable the student to utter (with approximate accuracy at least) the word-sounds of the dialect.

All the examples illustrative of the use of words have been taken down from the mouth of the people, and in no case has a sentence or a phrase been " manufactured " for the occasion. Words which show only a slight phonetic departure from the literary forms are not included. Disappearances of sounds-from the beginning of words (aphaeresis), from the body (syncope), and from the end (apocope), occur as frequently in the Demetian as they do in other dialects. There are also additions, mostly at the end of words (epithesis), e.g., *adarn*. If all these were separately noted, the bulk of the work would be increased three-fold. In the case, however, of an important departure from the literary form, the word is included.

Over and above strictly glossary matter there is much that would more properly fall under the head of lore, but it could not very well be eliminated.

Nothing further need be said here except that in the spelling of "Gwaun" the older form of the name has been retained in preference to the more modern "Gwaen." Perhaps "Gwein," the local pronunciation, would have been the best spelling to adopt.

THE COMPILER.

Michaelmas, 1910.

Table of Sounds.

I.—VOWELS.

	SHORT.	LONG.
A	Like *a* in *mat*.	The nearest equivalent is *a* in *lard;* always open and pure. There is never a suspicion of the admixture of the open *o*, or *aw*, nor of the narrow *a* heard in some of the sub-dialects of Gwent.
E	Like *e* in *met*.	Like *a* in *fate*. The open e, like *e* in *there*, is never heard.
I	Like *i* in *pin*.	Like *ee* in *feet*.
O	Like *o* in *not*.	Like *o* in *bone*. Never open like English *au*, nor like the dipthongized *o* heard in the Vale of Dyfi and other parts of Wales.
U	Like *i* in *this*.	Like *e* in *me*. The full, round *u* of Gwynedd is never heard.
W	Like *oo* in *good*.	Like *oo* in *boon*.
Y	Like *i* in *pin*.	Like *ee* in *feet*. The primary sound of this vowel, nearly equivalent to *u* in *fur*, or *e* in *stern*, is never used. The secondary sound, similar to that of *u*, is used in some cases, and this makes it unsafe to write *i* for *y* indiscriminately, as is the manner of some in writing the dialect of N. Pembrokeshire.

II. CONSONANTS.

Ch. This letter is less guttural in N. Pembrokeshire than in any other part of Wales; in fact, it is scarcely more harsh than *ch* in the Scottish *loch*.

Ngh. The aspirate *ngh* is rarely used. *Anghyfiawn* becomes *angifiawn*, &c.

Ll. Like *ch*, this letter is much less aspirated in the dialect of N. Pembrokeshire than it is in the other dialects. The tip of the tongue is pushed more towards the roots of the upper front teeth than towards the side of the mouth, and the "hissing" is consequently less pronounced.

Chw. This combination is rarely used, it is simplified to the aspirated _w_, sounded like _wh_ in _when_.

In addition to the usual consonants we have the following :

J. Like English _j_. It occurs in such words as _jogi, jogel, joni_, &c.

Ch. Like _ch_ in _churn_, in one or two instances.

Sh. Like _sh_ in _shall_, in such words as _Crisht, shawns, shomi_, etc.

PHONETIC CHANGES.

[The enumeration and tabulation of these changes belong to the grammar of the dialect, and the following examples are given here merely as illustrations.]

_ae_ in monosyllables is simplified to _â._ e.g., sâth, trâth, gwâd, etc.

_ae_ accented, in pollysyllabic words is simplified to _ei_, e.g., deiar, cleiar, gweiw, etc.

_ae_ unaccented is simplified to _e_, e.g., areth, arfeth, cwmdogeth, etc.

_au_ in monosyllables is simplified to _ou_, e.g., houl, Iou, brou, etc.

_au_ in the plural ending is simplified to _e_, e.g., minidde (mynyddau), pethe, nedwidde (nodwyddau), etc.

_ai_ unaccented, is simplified to _e_, e.g., effeth, ciwren, llefen, etc.

_ai_ in some monosyllables is simplified to _ei_, e.g., eiff.

_eu_ accented, is simplified to _ou_ (or _oi_), e.g., troulo, etc.

_io_ unaccented, is frequently simplified to _o_, e.g., gweitno, darno, painto, etc.

_oe_ in monosyllables, is simplified to _we_, e.g., llŵer, ŵes, crŵes, nŵeth, etc.

_wy_ in terminations is simplified to _w_, e.g., cowrw (cyfrwy), morwn, pabwr. Sometimes it is simplified to _e_, e.g., trothe, cisbe (cysbwy), istre (ystrwy), etc.

_yw_ is sometimes simplified to _ow_, e.g., bowyd, etc.; sometimes to _ew_, e.g., tewy (tywydd); and sometimes to _i_, e.g., odi (ydyw), etc.

There are numerous other changes, both vocalic and consonantal, to which nothing short of a long chapter could do full justice.

A

Abal   Adj. Rich, well-to-do.

Abasian   N.f.s. The symbol &. (Four syllables, accent on last).

Aca!   Onomatopœic. Crow call.

Achan   A Particle. A corruption of *fachgen*, used as an Expletive, like the Scotch *mon*. The following little picture will illustrate its use. James Shincyn, a celebrated sculptor of D——, is busy carving an angel on a tombstone; a stander-by asks, " Be' chi'n neyd Jâms Shincyn?" The sculptor, a tall, thin, old-world fellow, wearing a leathern apron in front and a peculiar cap on his skull, turning round (depositing a big spurt of tobacco liquid on the ground at the same time) says, " Wn i ddim wir, achan ; wdw i'n treio gneyd angel, ond wir mae e'n myn'd yn githrel ar y ngweitha i."

Achial   N.m.s. Impediment of speech, or rather the defect of uttering the liquid *r* with a guttural quality somewhat approaching that of *ch*.
" Dina druenu fod y crwt bach ag achia! arno!"
What a pity the little boy cannot say *r!*

Achub-y -blan   To steal a march upon.
" Mae e wedi achub-y-blân yn deg arna i."
He has fairly stolen a march upon me.

Achwedyn   [= Ac yna wedi hyny.] And thereafter, afterwards.
" Achwedyn ma rhaid i ni fyn'd i'r cwrdd."
Afterwards we must go to the meeting.

Achwyn [= erchwyn.] N.m.s. The side of a bed.

Adarn [= adar.] N.m.pl. Birds.

Adle [= adladd.] N.f.s. Aftermath.

Adre Adv. Heavily, thoroughly.
" Mae'n bwrw nawr adre, minno."
It rains heavily now, anyhow.

Adwedd Abs. n. The district within which *cardod* was allowed to be solicited. Each *cardotyn* went about to ask for *cardod* within his or her particular *adwedd*, and not beyond. There was a tacit understanding among the poor as to the limits of their *adwedd*. If a *cardotyn* adventured beyond these limits, great indignation was felt among the *cardotwyr* of that *adwedd*.

Adda-ac-Efa Early Purple Orchis. (Orchis mascula).

Afol [= afal.] N.m.s. Apple.
Plur. *fale*.

Agolch [= golchon.] N.m.s. Pig's-wash.

Agosedd Adv. Nearly.
" Fydd y cineua ddim agosedd a bod miwn erbyn gwlengel leni."
The harvest will not nearly be in [i.e., under thatch] by Michaelmas, this year.

Agramwni Agrimony.

Anghni-feri Abs. n. The odd numbers.

Angla [= angladd.] N.f.s. Funeral.
A'i-chorn
    -dani A euphemism, signifying to be dead, used more especially in reference to a beast.

Aing-gou   N.f.s. Gouge.

Aile   [= ail i'w le.] Adv. (1) Near the mark, (2) fairly well.

(1) " Ma gofyn i ddyn fyw yn aile.'
A man ought to live near the mark.

(2) " Shwt y'ch chi Tomos Ifan? "
" O, wdw i'n aile, diolch i chi."
How are you, Thomas Evans?
Oh, I am fairly well, thank you.

Ail-foilyd   V. Intran. To have a relapse after child-birth.

Ail-het   N.f.s. Second attempt.
" Rhaid i ni gwmryd ail-het ati."
We must make a second attempt.

Ail-jo   N.f.s. An old quid of tobacco re-chewed.

Ali   N.m.s. A garden pathway.

Altrans   Abs. n. A change. The word is used in reference to change of weather, or of the condition, for better, for worse, of a sick person.

Allwed   [= allwedd.] N.f.s. A key.

Amal   Adv. As, equally.
" Amal cistal."
Equally good or well.

Amirllid   Adj. Meddlesome.

Amlwgu   V. Tran. To expose.
" O peidwch 'n amlwgu i o flân y bobol hyn i gyd! "
O, don't expose me before all these people!

Am-yr-un
-bowyd
For dear life, at the best.
"Wêdd e am-yr-un-bowyd yn treio penu rhwmo cyn dethe 'i i'r glaw."
He was at it for dear life, trying to finish binding the corn before it came to rain.

Anal
[= anadl.] N.f.s. Breath.

Anfolon
[= anfoddlon.] Adj. and Adv. Unwilling, discontented.

Anles
Abs. n. No good, disadvantage, hurt.

Anlwc
Abs. n. Ill-luck.

Annel
Abs. n. State, condition.
"Ma na annel ofnadwy ar bethe."
Things are there [in the place spoken of] in an awful condition.

Ano
[= anhawdd.] Adj. and adv. Difficult.
"Mae'n ano gneỳd dim ar y tewy hwn."
It is difficult to do anything this weather.

Anriparus
Adj. and adv. Out of repair, dilapidated.

Ansel
N.f.s. The first purchase, which is considered to bring luck to the seller.
"Pwrnwch rwbeth gida fi, i roi ansel i fi."
Buy something of me, to bring me luck.

Anshawns
N.f.s. A mishap, an accident.
"Fe gâs Dafy Tygwyn anshawns ddrwg gida'r cart a'r ceffyl."
David, of Tygwyn, met with a serious accident while in charge of a horse and cart.

Anshwt
[= an-sut.] Adj. and adv. Awkward. Said in reference to the shape of a thing, such as a bundle, which is clumsy to carry; also of a person walking awkwardly.

Anstimogus Part. Having a weak appetite.

Aped [= ateb.] V. and n. To reply, a reply.

Ar [= o'r.] Prep. Of, upon.
"Beth ar glôch yw hi? "
What time is it?
Lit. : What upon the clock is it?

Ar N.f.s. Air. (Pron. *ár*).

Ar-cered }
Ar-gered } Part. (1) Moving about from place to place.
(2) From home.

Archwel N.m.s. The brow or top of anything.
" Ar archwel y storom."
Lit. : On the brow of the storm, i.e., when the storm rages most furiously.

Ar draws [= treisio.] V. Tran. To commit rape.

Ar-dreif " On the go," on the move.
" Ma'r hen rocyn ar-dreif trw'r nos."
The lad is " on the go " all night.

Arfach Adj. Cantankerous, disposed to find fault, ever ready to criticise.
A beautiful word, *ar fach*, literally on the hook, i.e., a man with the hook of destructive criticism always in his hand, ready to catch at the smallest fault.

Arte-hogi N.m.pl. Edged-tools.

Ar glawr Adv. phrase. On record. Clawr = the cover of a book. It was customary before the days of cheap stationery to make entries of all important matters on the cover of the family Bible, or of some other large volume. The covers and fly-leaf of many an old Bible are literally covered with all sorts of curious entries.

B

Ar gownt Prep. phrase. For the purpose of, in order that.

"Dewch i ni gâl stico ati nawr, ar gownt i ni gâl mynd i'r ffair fory."

Let us hurry up now, in order that we may go to the fair to-morrow.

Arian-cam N.pl. (1) Bent coin. (2) Luck.

"Mi gesim saith a whech o lwc, ond wê dim arian cam yndi nw."

I had seven shillings and sixpence for good luck, but there was not a crooked coin amongst them—meaning that good luck did not really attend his purchase.

To receive a bent coin at a transaction is regarded as a good omen. Compare the lines of Gay:

" This silver ring beside
Three silver pennies, and a ninepence bent,
A token, kind, to Bumkinet is sent."

Arian
„ melinion N.m.p. Gold coin.

„ gleishon „ Silver coin.

„ cochion „ Copper coin.

„ papur „ Paper money.

Arian-yr-ys-
pryd drwg Coll. n. Treasure-trove.

There are numerous tales of the whereabouts of hidden money being discovered to people by elves.

Ar'l-arre Adv. phrase. Attending to the call of nature ; evacuating.

Axiod [= erioed.] Adv. Ever.

Arna [= danaf.] Prep. Used in a peculiar sense, as will be seen from the following example.
"Wdw i'n cofio arna i'n cered i'r Hendygwyn lawer gwaith slawer dy, cyn i'r train ddŵad."
I remember walking to Whitland many a time in the olden days, before the advent of the train.

Ar-nail Adv. By-turns.

Arno V. Intran. To owe.
"Wês rhwbeth arno i ti? "
Does he owe you anything?

Arwni [= ar a wn i.] For aught I know.

Arwyddion Signs. Invariably used in the sense of indications of good or bad weather, an abundance of fruit and a good harvest or otherwise. The weather during winter and spring seems to have been narrowly watched by the old North Pembrokeshire farmers, and the chances of a good harvest, a fat pasture, or a loaded orchard, inferred from the experience of previous years, combined with a fair reliance upon fortune. Some of their prognostications show a keen insight on their part into the workings of the laws of nature, and are by no means to be despised in these days of more exact knowledge and extended experience. Some of the old *arwyddion* are interesting, not only as weather lore, but also as giving evidence of the slowly changing climate of this country, and it is not unlikely that at some distant date most of the predictions will be found inapplicable. The following collection of *arwyddion* is a tolerably full one, but it is by no means exhaustive. It includes not only lore which is strictly applicable to the weather, but also observations of a somewhat general character, in so far as they deal with times, seasons, health, and well-being.

Y TIMORE (THE SEASONS).

(A.) Y GWANWYN.

"Gwanwyn llaith, cneua maith."

A wet spring makes a big harvest.

"Os deila y dderwen o flân yr onen, fe fydd cneua teg, ond os deila yr onen o flân y dderwen, fe fydd cneua glŷb."

When the oak comes out before the ash, there will be fine weather in harvest; but when the ash comes out before the oak, the harvest will be wet.

"Crafan mowr ar y ddraenen,
Ddaw a geua mowr ei angen."

An abundance of haw on the whitethorn will be followed by a hard winter.

(B.) HAF.

"Os bydd rhaid rhoi cot fowr ar gefen yr haf, fe fydd yn rhaid i'r geua fynd yn drodnoth."

Lit. : If it be necessary to put an overcoat on the back of the summer, the winter will have to go barefooted.

"Hâf côch, geua du."

A red summer makes a black winter, i.e., when the land is burnt by the heat in summer, there will be much suffering in winter, owing to the scarcity of provender.

"Os bydd blode mwyar yn Mihefin,
Fe fydd cneua cinnar, cinnar wedin."

If the bramble blossoms in June, there will be a very early harvest.

"Pan ddeila yr onen o flân y dderwen,
Eith llawer i gwsgu yn nghesel yr iwen."

When the ash comes out before the oak, many will fall asleep in the bosom of the yew tree.

"Hirddydd a glaw, trwmddydd a ddaw."

Rain at midsummer will bring misery.

(C.) HIDRE.

"Fe fydd eishe têl o farlish a llwyth o dwarch ar gifer pob winshin o fês."

It will be necessary to provide a sack of barley and a load of turf for every bushel of acorn.

(D.) GEUA.

"Geua glâs menwent fras."

A green winter makes a fat churchyard.

"Trwste yn y geua, a llifogydd yn yr hâf,
Mowr fydd y gofid a'r ffwdan a gâf."

Thunder in the winter and floods in the summer will bring disaster.

"Os na fydd eishe un got yn y geua fe fydd eishe dwy yn y gwanwyn."

If the winter will not require one coat, the spring will require two.

"Sheced o eira ar gefen y geua,
A ffedog o galch-gwyn ar gwel y gwanwyn,
Rydd iechyd i ddyn a phawr i anifel,
Hâf dan 'i lwyth a chneua ar 'i uchel."

A coat of snow in the winter, and of lime in the spring, will give health and abundance to man and beast.

"Os bydd porfa las yn Ionor,
Dilit gloi ar ddrws y scubor."

If there is green grass in January, you ought to lock the barn door,—meaning that there will be a scarcity of grass later on, when the corn will be required.

Y GWILIE (SAINTS' DAYS).

"Os gwena'r houl ar ddwgwl Bôl,
Fe rêd y flwyddyn ar 'i ôl."

If the sun smiles on S. Paul's Day, the year will run after him, i.e., the year will be a bright and cheerful one.

"Drwg yw gwynt y dwyre'
Ar ddwgwl Fair Ganwylle."

To have an East wind on Candlemas Day is a bad omen.

"Pan ddaw Dewi ar farch gwyn,
Fe ddaw Mair ar fuwch gôch."

When S. David's Day is rough, Lady Day will be fair; literally, when S. David comes on a white horse, Mary will come on a red cow.

"Os bydd dwr ar ruddie Swiddyn,
Deugen dydd o ddwr fydd wedyn;
Os bydd gwên ar wmed Swiddyn,
Deugen dydd o wrês a ganlyn."

If there are tears on S. Swithin's cheeks,
There will be forty days of rain;
If there is a smile on S. Swithin's face,
There will be forty days of heat, or sunshine.

"Hâf bach Gwlengel,
Iglan sych ddiogel.'

S. Michael's little summer gives a dry, safe haggard.

"Dwgwl Seintie—mowr eu breintie;
Dwgwl Neidie—rhwydd bidere;
'S esgeuluswn neyd erfinie,
Garw dewy fydd yn Hidre."

Lit.: All Saints' Day—great their privilege;
All Souls' Day—easy paternosters;
If we neglect our intercessions,
Rough weather will ensue in Autumn.

"Gwynt dwgwl Domos gwynt tri mis."

The idea is that whence the wind blows on S. Thomas's Day, thence it will blow for three months for the most part.

" Windolig gwyn ddaw
Gwanwyn gwyn ddaw."

Snow on Christmas Day will be followed by
a beautiful Spring.

" Sulgwyn ar adyn,
Suldu ar dda."

Lit.: Whitsunday on man,
Blacksunday on cattle—the idea is that
ill-luck happens to cattle on that holy day.
They are more apt to fall into a ditch or to get
stuck in a quagmire on that than on any other
day of the year. Men are told off to watch the
cattle on Whit Sunday, even at the present
day. Benny, of Twcwr, was wont to reason
thus: " I chi'n gweld; ma'r Ispryd Glân yn
gneyd i ore dros ddyn ar y dwarnod hwn, a
dyw'r Ispryd Drwg ddim yn folon, a mae e'n
minnud dial ar rewun. All e ddim dial ar ddyn,
ond mae e'n dial ar dda."

" Ar y Pasc dod bilyn newy'
Rhag i'r hen frân ddu i ddomi."

Wear something new on Easter Day, to pre
vent the black crow voiding excrement upon
you.

O BOB MATH (GENERAL).

" Bŵa-ràch y bore,
Glaw yn y godre ;
Bŵa-ràch prynawn,
Tewy têg a gawn."

A morning rainbow indicates rain, an afternoon rainbow indicates fine weather.

The following (which need not be translated)
are indications of rain :—

Fŵel Ery yn gwishco 'i gapan.
Ffrŵd Cwmdu yn canu 'i chrŵth.
Mŵg Pencnwc yn gorwe ar yr wrglo.
Y gwynt yn whithu o Bwlchwiniad.

Y wanol yn hedfan ar y llawr.
Y gwŷdd-corn yn hofran.
Y ci yn pori.
Y gâth yn golchi 'i gwmed dros 'i chluste.
Dail y cŵed yn dangos 'u bòlie.
Pêll yn agos, a bâch yn fowr.
Indications of fair weather :—
Yr houl yn gôch yn mynd lawr.
Mŵg Pencnwc yn seithu 'r owyr.
Y dwrydd yn dŵad gatre.
Y wanol yn hedfan yn uchel.
Agós yn mhell, a mowr yn fâch.
Gwlith trwm yn y nôs.
Y crechy yn mynd gida'r afon.
Gwynt Carn Ingli.
Y sêr yn siriol ganol nôs.
Yr hwch yn gorwe yn y llaid.
Arwyddion marwoleth :—
Y cŵn yn wbeñ yn y nôs.
Deryn yn ffusto yn erbyn y ffenest.
Clôch yn y glust.
Breuddwydo fod dyn wedi colli 'i ddane.
Seren-dân [a meteor] yn cwmpo ar dir yr hwn a'i gwelo.
Cwrdd a drichioleth [spectre funeral.]
Gweld canwyll gorff.
Dafad yn dwad miwn i'r tŷ byw.
Clŵed swn llais heb fo neb 'na.

Sefyll ar dir côch pan gliwir y gwcw ginta sy arwydd y bydd y person farw cyn daw'r gwcw 'to.

Ci yn dilyn dyn i'r cwrdd sy arwydd o fendith, ond câth o felldith.

Lladd neidir yn mish Mai sy arwydd y bydd i'r dyn wntrechu [conquer] ei elynion.

Rhoi gwenwn i ast dorrog ddaw a melldith ofnadwy.

There are endless other *arwyddion* of a superstitious character, which would fill a volume by themselves, but they are outside the scope of the present work.

Ase   [= aswy.] N. The left side. Also adj. in *llaw ase*, left hand.

Asto   A term of endearment spoken in fondling a bitch.
"Yr asto fach!"
Poor little bitch!

At-'i-law-e   In his power.
"Mae at-'i-law-e i neyd ffafar i fi."
It is in his power to do me a favour.

Awen   N.m.s. Often used metaphorically for a leader, or one who is the moving spirit in anything.

Awffus   Adj. Covetous.

Awr-deilwr   The twilight; literally, a tailor's hour. The time between two lights (natural and artificial), when it is too dark to do such work as that of tailoring, and too light to light candles. The term has a wider application now and signifies any idle hour.

B

Babi [= baban.] N.m.s. Baby.

Bac A word of command addressed to a horse when it is required to move back. It is curious that nearly all the words addressed to a horse are of English origin.

Bacar Adj. and adv. Awful, exceedingly, bad, &c.
(1) " Mae'n dewi pacar."
It is awful weather.
(2) " Ma pethe wedi myn'd yn bacar yn Pontgam ys llawer dy'."
Matters are unsatisfactory at Pontgam this long while.

Bacco N.m.s. Tobacco.

Bacco-main N.m.s. Twist tobacco.

Bacco-melus N.m.s. Ship tobacco.

Bacse N. pl. Feet.

Bacso and bacsan Intran. Verbs derived from the above Noun.

Bacse bach A term for a baby.
" Ma bacse bach wedi dwad i Treddol."
A baby has arrived at Treddol.

Bache N.m.pl. Hands.
" Gad dy fache 'n llony."
Keep your hands still.

Bach-'l fam   N.m.s.   Mother's spoilt boy.

Bach-'i-fangu   N.m.s.   A boy spoilt by his grandmother.

Baglan   (1) To walk about in a limp manner.
(2) To walk till one is weary.

Baglu   Part.   Entangled.
" Mae e wedi baglu yn y rhwyd."
He has become entangled in the net.

Baglyn   N.m.s.   A bandy-legged fellow.

Baginet   N.m.s.   Bayonet.

Balc   N.m.s.   A piece of earth accidentally left un-
turned by the plough.

Ball   N.m.s.   A peak.   Nearly obsolete.

Bambocs   N.m.s   A bandbox.

Banc   N.m.s.   A meadow near the farm-buildings
which slopes towards the water-edge, or which
has the appearance of a magnified mound.

Bando   N.m.s.   A game, also the stick with which
the game is played.

Bara brith   N.m.s.   Cake, especially currant cake.

,, **planc**   N.m.s.   Bread made on the bake-stone.

,, **dan cil**   N.m.s.   Bread baked under a kettle in the
old-fashioned way.

Bara tene   Bake-stone barley bread.

Bare pare Bake-stone barley bread (i.e., the flat thin cakes or loaves so called) made in batches of six, ten, or a dozen at a time. To make them in this way required great skill and practice, and few were masters of the art. The lumps of dough were piled one on top of the other, and the loaves kneaded at the same time. There was a celebrated *pobreg* at Treclyn, in the parish of Llanychllwydog, named Lydia Fach, who could make thirty loaves together. She was considered the champion of the county, and her fame had spread far and near. A farm lass had reached the summit of her ambition when she was commended by her mistress with the words—" Da merch i, wyt ti'n pobi gistal a Lydia Fach! "—There's a good girl, you are a match to Lydia Fach at making bread.

Bara crou [= croew.] N.m.s. Unleavened bread.

Bara-chaws -y-gwcw N.m.s. Wood-sorrel.

Bara-gwellt -'l-hunan Bread made of corn that had been dried with its own straw, in the old time kiln. The old people held strongly to the belief that no bread was absolutely healthy unless it had been so dried—" Os na fidde fe wedi 'i grasu ar 'i wellt 'i hunan."

Bara-iach In the expression, "Fitodd e fara iach fyth wedin "—He was never well, or like himself, thereafter.

Bara llafan Laver bread, made of sea liver-wort.

Baraf [= barf.] N.f.s. Beard.

Baraf-lwyd N.f.s. Long, hairy mildew; a kind of fungus.

Barco   V. Tran. and Intran. To bark. Many women earned their living formerly in the Gwaun woods by barking timber, in the days when oak bark was used in the preparation of leather. The wages in 1850 were eightpence a day.

Barferwi   V. Intran. To boil over, to boil furiously.

Bariad   N.m.s. A fence across a stream.

Bariets   N.m.s. A gate, or rather a stop-gap consisting of two upright posts and slip cross-bars.

Barlish -barian   N.m.s. Barley imported from Barbary.

Basarn   N.m.s. A sieve, used for the purpose of sifting flummery.

Baser-rhawn   A horse-hair sieve for sifting *sucan*, *vide* also above.

Basged -dandis   N.m.s. A child's rattle, made with rushes, with small pebbles inside to produce a noise.

Basned   N.m.s. A basinful.

Batal   N.m.s. A mole catcher's tool for cutting a hole to set a trap in.

Beching-galw   Exp. What-d'-ye-call-it. This phrase does duty on all sorts of occasions, and fills up all kinds of gaps. It is what is significantly described in local parlance a *gair llanw*—a fill-up word. Cf. *bethma* in N. Wales.

Bedydd-arch   The old custom, not quite forgotten yet, of baptizing an infant over the corpse of the mother who had died in giving it birth. Undoubtedly a survival of a species of vicarious baptism.

Beili   N.m.s.   Bailiff.

Beilied   N.m.pl.   Burdock (Arctium lappa).

Beltin   N.m.s.   Used metonymically for the stomach.
" Yn Hwlffor bu tirfa am llona y lle,
Wrth agor y railroad wych hinod i'r dre ;
'R'wedd pawb yn giffredin a'u beltin yn dyn,
Fe gadd y tilodion eu digon am ddim."
                —(Old ballad).

Bel-toper   N.f.s.   A silk hat.
' Bel-toper hen ffeshwn."
An old-fashioned silk hat.

Bena   [= bynag.]   Indef. Pron.   Soever.

Ber   Equivalent to the vulgar exclamation *dickens!*
" Mae e wedi whare'r bêr ag e."
He has played the dickens with him.

Berem   [= burym.]   N.m.s.   Barm.

Bermu   [= burymu.]   V. Intran.   To froth.

Berris   N.m.s.   Burrows, sand dunes.

Biafio   V. Intran.   To behave.
" Biafiwch, blant ! "
Behave, children !

Bic   Inter.   Peep O!   A term used by mothers in
playing with their infants. (Pron. *bic*).

Bic   [= mic.]   Abs. n.   Spite (Pron. *bic*).

Bicne   N.m.s.   A beacon.   Variants are *becn, bicnin.*

Bicnin   N.m.s.   A prominent `spot, elevated ground.
No doubt a corruption of *beacon.*

Bidloni [= boddloni.] V. Tran. To satisfy.

Bidlonus [= boddlonus.] Adj. Contented.

Bidren-y
    -dwr N.f.s. The water-bug. An insect living in water, belonging to the genera Belostomatidae.

Biddin
    bisgota N.f.coll. An organised gang of salmon peachers, trained under a " Captain." The gang had its code of rules, method of initiation, &c. It would be interesting to give a detailed account of the *biddin*, but it is impossible to obtain particulars—such is the secrecy with which they guard their movements.

Bietin N.m.s. Turf that is pared and burnt. That which is termed in S. Pembrokeshire and some parts of the North of England *bratland*. When mountainous land is brought under cultivation the turf is first pared with the breast-plow and burnt in heaps. The ashes thus obtained is considered first-class manure.

Bigwth [= bwgwth.] V. Tran. To threaten. *Bigwyth* is a variant.

Bipsan V. Intran. To jeer, sneer.
" Mae'n bipsan am ymhen i."
She is sneering at me.
Bips is the corresponding noun.
" Mae'n llawn hen fips i gyd."
She is very sarcastic, or disposed to sneer.

Binheddig [= boneddig.] Adj. Proud; frequently used in this sense.

Birwen N.f.s. A maiden of from seventeen to twenty summers.
" Birwen bert yw nghariad i."
My sweetheart is a lovely maiden.

Biscis N.f.pl. Biscuits.
Sing. *biscisen*.

Bise N.m.pl. Fingers.
Enwe bise (1) Bis mowr.
(2) ,, buan.
(3) ,, cosi.
(4) ,, y galon.
(5) ,, bâch.

Bishtogedd Adj. Obsequious, servile.
A dog that comes on wagging his tail and crouching on the ground is addressed *bishto bach*—hence the term *bishtogedd* as applied to an obsequious person.

Bisnesgar Adj and Adv. Fussy, officious.

Bita [= bwyta.] N.m.s. Itch.
" Ma bita ar y nghefen i.''
My back is itching.

Bita-'i-eire Chopping his words, speaking indistinctly.

Bithawnos [= bythefnos.] N.f.s. A fortnight.

Bitholi V. Tran. To immortalize.
" Ma Washington wedi bitholi 'i hunan wrth riddhau'r slâf.''
Washington has immortalized himself by liberating the slave.

Biwch-goch
-y-foreu N.f.s. The lady-bird—the small coleopterous insect so called.
An old inhabitant of the parish of Pontfaen called it *biwch-goch-Duw*.

Biwch hir   A hired cow. Poor people often hire a cow from the time of its calving until it becomes dry. If the animal is kept for more than one season, the next calf becomes the property of the hirer. The fee paid for one season is twenty-five shillings.

Biwti   Adv. Correctly, perfectly.
" O, wdw i'n gwbod yn biwti, gistal a thithe."
Oh, I know that perfectly, as well as you [do.]

Blaced   N.f.s. A black-lead pencil.

Blaenon
-hoilon   Coll n. Nail-tips broken off by the blacksmith in shoeing horses. These are eagerly collected by farmers when they visit the smithy, who make use of them for sprigs.

Blan-a-bona   A term applied to an arrangement of anything, such as sheaves, thatch, &c., heads and tails alternately.

Blanced   N.m.s. Blanket.

Blandrwch   N.m.s. The stubble under the swath; the stubble at the point to which the scythe is carried in cutting corn.

Blawdo   Part. That condition of ploughed land when it breaks up readily into small particles with the harrow, and rises in fine dust with the smallest gust of wind. The land is then considered to be in ideal condition for sowing.

Bleino   [= blino.] V. Intran. To be tired.

Bleins
Pl. bleinsis   N.m.s. Blind bridle. The bridle which is used with ordinary cart harness, never a part of a riding outfit. when the ffrwyn is used.

c

Blewina   V. Intran. To graze a little. An animal that has been sick, on being turned out to a field, picks a few blades of grass, but does not graze eagerly: it is said to *blewina*.

Blewyn   N.m.s. A small bit of anything. Sometimes the word is used in an abstract sense, as in the sentence:

" Dyw e ddim blewyn gwell."

He is not a whit better.

Blewyn -cwta   N.m.s. A method of drawing lots. Pieces of stick, or of straw, of varying lengths, are hidden in the hand, and the parties drawing lots are made to pick out one piece each. The lot falls on the one who gets the shortest.

Blidd   Adj. Noble, generous.
" Dyn blidd."
A generous man.

Blith   Often used as the equivalent of *enllyn*, obsonium. Not at all restricted to milk.
" Popeth sy'n dwad o'wrth y fiwch."

Bliw   N.m.s. A pot, a measure somewhat less than a pint.
" Bliw o ddiod."
A two-penny mug of beer.

Blode-gini'r -owns   A tiny red flower which grows abundantly in cornfields.

Blode'r -mansh   The " mansh flower."

Blodyn-y gelen   N.m.s. Deadly nightshade.

Blodyn-y widdig   N.m.s. Honeysuckle.

Bloigi, Fem.   N.m.s. A noisy, rude person.
  Bloigast

Blotyn   N.m.s. Lot.
Tinu'r blotyn, casting lot.
This was the term used formerly for drawing or casting lot in the days of impressment.

Blwthog   Adj. Full of blossom.
" Perllan flwthog."
An orchard full of blossom.
" Parc blwthog."
A field covered with blossom.

Bo !   Inter. Hm! Umph!
" Ddwad e ddim ' bo!' wrthw i."
He never said even ' hm!' to me.

Bobol-bach   N.c.pl. The common people. Small farmers, labourers, and the poor are all alike designated by this name.

Boced, y   N.m.s. The man who carried the salmon caught by the *biddin bisgota* (q.v.). He was armed with a club made of well-seasoned whitethorn. and was well known for cunning and desperate bravery.

Boddran   V. Tran. and Intran. To bother.

Boi !   Inter. Adieu!
" Boi, boi! "
Adieu, adieu!

Boichen   V. Intran. To bellow, to roar like a bull.

Bois   Coll n. The male inhabitants of a district, with reference more especially, perhaps, to the younger element, and generally in a disparaging sense.

"Bois Cwmgwein"—the fellows of Gwaun Valley.

"Bois Casmâl"—the fellows of Puncheston.

Bola lawr — Rupture of the abdomen. Also *bola wedi dwad lawr.*

Bolas-y-binc — N.f.s. The blue-bottle fly. The word is practically obsolete.

Bolbocs — N.m.s. Culm box; the box in which mixed culm is held ready for use.

Bolen — N.f.s. The marten.

„ **-y-cwed** — „ The wood-marten.

„ **-y-garreg** — „ The rock-marten.

Bolon — [= boddlon.] Adj. Willing, contented.

Bolsen — N.f.s. A hit on the head, an angry blow.

Bolo'r-tan — V. Tran. To make up the fire, to put balls on the fire. Small anthracite coal is mixed with clay till it attains the consistency of mortar, and then worked by the hand into balls something in the shape of an egg, only larger, and put on the fire.

Bomp — Onomatopœic. Loud, noisy.

"Wil y romp
Yn trawo bomp o rêch,
A ninne 'n bump neu whech yn grondo,
A'r pump arall
Tudraw'r cwm
Yn clwed y drwm yn taro."

—(Old Saw).

Boncernen — N.f.s. A box on the side of the head.

Bondrweh N.m.s. The stubble at the point where the scythe enters in cutting corn.

To leave too much *bondrwch* and *blandrwch* (q.v.) earned for the reaper the character of an inferior workman.

Bon-y-gwynt N.m.s. The direction whence the wind blows. " Bôn Bwlchwiniad "—the wind that blows from the direction of Bwlchwiniad, i.e., the S.E. wind.

Gwynt Bwlchwiniad (S.E.)
Dẁr yn 'i ligad ;
Gwynt Trellwyn (N.W.)
Sìch y crwyn ;
Gwynt Fŵel Ery (E.)
Dyr y deri.   —(Old Saw).

" Gwynt trâd y meirw " (East).
Lit. : The wind of the feet of the dead.

" Gwynt y cinheua mowr " (N.W.).
Lit. : The wind of the big harvest.

Bor [= ebo'r.] An exclamatory particle.
" Bôr hen fuwch arni! "
What's the matter with the cow !

Bord-adea N.f.s. A folding table.

Bord-fowr N.f.s. The long table, usually placed in the *rhwm-ford*, at which farm hands eat.

Bord-rownd N.f.s. A small, round, or polygonal table, invariably found in a N. Pembrokeshire parlour, and round which a few privileged guests are put to sit at an afternoon tea.

Boreddi [= bore heddyw.] This morning. (Pren. bòreddi).

Borier N.m.s. A butter merchant's instrument for testing a cask of butter.

Borio V. Tran. To test a cask of butter with an instrument called a *borier*.

Botsn-fowr N.f.s. The alimentary canal.

Bowlyd [= bawlyd.] Adj. Dirty.

Bracso V. Intran. To walk through a river without boots and stockings, and with the trousers turned up.

Bradwr N.m.s. The pin of the old Welsh mole-trap. Poetically so called because the mole touched it with its nose, thus releasing the string holding down the spring and compassing its own death. It was truly the "kiss of death," and the little piece a real "bradwr." In shape it resembled an inverted V.

Brag V.n. Boasting. (Pron. bràg).

Bragaldian Part. Bragging, boasting.

Brago V. Intran. To boast, brag. (Pron. bràgo).

Bragod N.m.s. Small beer. The modern equivalent is ginger beer. This was formerly retailed at village fairs at a penny per glass, and was the favourite beverage of feminine gossips. It was palatable and non-intoxicating.

Brancor N.m.s. Land bordering on a river and divided into small enclosures.
Query, Is it from a proper name?

Bran-diddyn N.f.s. The tenement crow; a crow that settles down on a certain farm or in a particular field, where it remains, and to which it becomes attached. The belief obtains that the *brân diddyn* is both a harbinger of good-luck and also (in some mysterious way) a sure-defence against ill-luck. No farmer would knowingly or willingly destroy a tenement crow ; indeed, he would rather lose a valuable cow or a dozen sheep than do so. Among other wonder-ful virtues, this crow is said to possess the power of scaring birds as well as that of defending the crops from its own tribe. Farmers believe it religiously to-day that other crows will never attack the crops of a farm in the vicinity of the tenement crow's habitat.

Branol N.m.s. Awl (carpenter's tool).

Bran-y-gors N.f.s. Raven.

Bras Adj. Proud, high-minded.

Brasder Abs. n. Pride, in a more offensive sense than *mowrder* (q.v.).
" Ma llond i grwen e o hen frasder drewllyd."
His skin is full of stinking old pride.

Brasgamu V. Intran. To walk with long, brisk strides, to walk very hurriedly.
" Mae e'n i brasgamid hi shag adre."
He is walking towards home hurriedly.

Brat N.m.s. Pinafore.

Brathu V. Intran. To insinuate.
" Brathu wêdd e ma fi wê'r euog."
Insinuating he was that I was the guilty party.

Brawl Abs. n. Idle talk, tattle.

Brecwast N.f.s. Breakfast.

Bredich N.c.s. A weakly, sickly person.

Bredyn N.m.s. Braid.

**Brethyn
-brocloth** N.m.s. Broadcloth.

**Brethyn
-plod** N.m.s. Plaid, homespun cloth.

Brichgai V. Tran. To ride, to go a-horse-back.

Bridich Abs. n. Doubt, misgiving.
"Sarna i [nid oes arnaf fi] ddim bridich am hiny."
I have no doubt as to that.

Bridi-enw A Part. phrase. Discovering the name of a future husband—a method of divination adopted by a young woman who was anxious to enter the married state, and who was desirous of ascertaining the name of her fated spouse. The *modus operandi* was as follows. She stole (the Eighth Commandment despite) a turnip from a neighbour's field, washed it in salt water, and peeled it in one continuous strip, beginning at the apex and finishing at the podium or foot. Great care was taken that the peel did not crack and break off, otherwise the charm would be broken. The turnip thus cleaned was hung up behind the kitchen door, and the peel buried in the garden. The person of the opposite sex who next entered the kitchen bore the same name as the maiden's future husband.

Bridlyn N.m.s. An unstable fellow.

Bridyll N.m.s. A trout.
The classical form *brithyll* is never heard.

Brichnau — N.m.s. A surety, bail. (Pron. brichnân, accent on last syllable).
"Ma Dafy'r Wern wedi myn'd yn frichnân dros Sheci 'r Ddôl."
David, of Wern, has become surety for John, of Dôl.
The verb "brichneuo" is sometimes heard, but rarely.

Bridwn — N.m.s. Prognostication.
"Taw! wyt ti a rhyw hen fridwn neu gily gida thi o hyd! Gad y difodol yn llony."
Hush! you have some prognostication or other always to communicate. Let the future alone!

Brigellu — [= briallu.] N.m.s. and pl. Primrose.

Brigo — V. Intran. To put furze or thorn bushes on a fence for the purpose of making it more secure.

Bripshin — N.m.s. A small bit of anything.
"Rows e ddim bripshin o ddim i fi."
He did not give me the least bit of anything.

Brith — Adj. and Adv. (1) Faint, (2) Fairly.
In the phrase brith cof—faint recollection.
"Ma brith cof gen i am rifel fowr Crimea."
I have a faint recollection of the great Crimean war.
" Brith iach "—fairly well.

Brith — N.m.s. A begging book. Sometimes the word is used for the act of going round with a begging book. " Pan fidde diuion bach yn colli nifel slawer dy, we nhw'n myn'd a papur neu lifyr mâs i gâl help i bwrnu nifel yn 'i le fe. ' Brith ' we hyn yn câl i alw." (Beny'r Twcwr).

Broga N.m.s. (not feminine). The noise heard in the belly of a horse when running.

Broifad [= brefu.] V. Intran. To bellow, to bleat.
"Y fuwch yn broifad."
The cow bellowing.
"Y ddafad yn broifad."
The sheep bleating.

Brou [= bran.] Adj. Brittle.
Brown-'r
-adar Groundsel.

Brua [= truan.] Exclam. Poor thing!
"Yr hen brua bach!"
Lit.: Poor old little thing!

Brwsh N.m.s. Brush. Used in connection with various words, such as brwsh-shafo, brwsh-scubo, brwsh-scrwbo, brwsh-danne, etc.

Brwtshis N.m.pl. Breeches.
Brwtshis
-pen-glun N.m.s. The old-fashioned breeches, which were worn to the knee.
Buwch-goch
-Duw N.f.s. Lady-cow, the insect so called. Regarded among children with superstitious awe, and never killed or wilfully injured on account of its supposed special sacredness to the Deity.

Bw! Onomatopœic. The buzzing sound of bees. (Pron. bŵ, with emission of breath).

Bwarach N.m.s. Rainbow. (Accent on rách).

Bwbach-wal An almost obsolete name for a scarecrow. This particular species of scarecrow consisted of an effigy holding a scythe—hence the latter element of the word, wai = gwae.

Bwci-Bal   N.m.s. A bogy, the bogy-man.
"Mae'n dangos houl a bwrw glaw,
Ma'r Bwci-Bàl yn ochor claw."
—An old Saw.

Bwci-bo   N.m.s. Hobgoblin. (Accent on *bô*).

Bwco   Part. (1) Backing; said of a horse that will not pull.

(2) The word is used also in describing the condition of cream that will not yield butter, or that is slow in yielding butter at churning. If over heated, or gaseous, it is said to be *yn bwco*.

Bwch   One who is made to answer or suffer for another's crime. This points, of course, to the scapegoat of Holy Writ. The goat lore of Dyfed is both abundant and interesting: some of it we give here. The old farmers generally kept a goat with the rest of the stock, because they said "it was healthy for the cattle." It was also said that goats (more especially he-goats, cleared the land of poisonous herbs left by horned cattle and sheep. Cheese made of goat milk was considered to be the richest food man could ever procure, and the milk itself was believed to be a cure for consumption and many other diseases. Goat excretum was a specific for gall-stones.

Benny 'r Twcwr, of Pontfaen-fach, Pontfaen, said that when the *dwymyn-ddu* attacked the inmates of a house, it was customary to burn the horns and hair of goats in the sick chamber, "nes wê nw hyd at fogi" (till they, i.e., the sick, nearly smothered). The fumes were believed to expel the fever.

"Pob un wê a bwch dâg e slawer dy, wèdd e'n 'i glwmu e dros y nos rwle yn agos at y tŷ-byw, at gadw'r Bwci-Bàl bant." (Benny 'r Twcwr).

The old people of the neighbourhood of Dinas believed that ill-luck would never befall any of the Raymonds, of the Island, on account of the large number of *bwchod* they kept on their farm.

Bwch danas   N.m.s. Stag.

Bwchyn   A term applied to a person who, by cunning and craft, outwits his neighbours, or who, by superior ingenuity, frustrates any design or plan. It is not applied in a depreciatory sense, on the other hand, a person endowed with more than the ordinary share of worldly cunning is often regarded with something like superstitious awe.

Bwdlac   N.m.s. Filthy mud, and sometimes a stagnant pool.

Bwdlan   V. Intran. Working a little at leisure, or according to strength.

A person recovering from illness, who is unable to do his usual work, but who does the little he can, is said to *bwdlan*.

"Ma Shams yn gwella 'to, mae e'n dachre bwdlan tipyn."

James is getting well again; he is beginning to do a little.

Bw dram   N.m.s. Thin flummery.

Differs from *iwd*, which is thick and served with milk.

Bwdram is of the consistency of gruel, and is taken alone, with the addition of a little sugar or golden syrup.

Bwell-gaib   N.f.s. A hatchet and mattock combined.

Bwl   N.m.s. The hip-bone, the socket of the thigh bone. (Pron. bŵl).

Bwla Inter. A call term, addressed to horned cattle.

Dewch, dewch, bwla bach,
Bwla! bwla! bwla!

Bwlen N.m.s. Pl. = *bwle* or *bwlod*.

The *bwle* were pear-shaped brass or iron nuts screwed on to the points of the horns of a vicious bull to prevent his doing injury.

Bwmbwr N.m.s. Blind-man's-buff.

" Whare bwmbwr," a game at blind-man's-buff.

Bwmp Abs. n. Lash, slander.
" Ma'r hen Ddeio a'i bwmp ar bawb."
Deio slanders everybody.

Bwmp-y-pys N.m.s. Yellow-bunting.

Bwadel N.m.s. A pack, with special reference to a pedlar's pack.

Bwrgetsh N.m.s. A small field, usually about ½-acre in extent, situate near the out-buildings of a farm, into which calves are turned when they leave the *cetsh* (pen).

Bwrlwm N.m.s. A sore point, the cause of dispute, &c.
" Dina beth yw y bwrlwm i gyd, eishe 'i fod e'n càl y ffarm ar 'i enw 'i hunan."
The cause of the dispute is that he wants the farm on his own name.

Bwrn N.m.s. A bundle of straw.
It differed from *sopen o wellt* in that the straw was cleaned and " pulled " into lengths for thatching purposes. The word is, therefore, used in a specific sense.

Bwrnar   [= braenar.] N.m.s. Fallow land.

Bwrnaru   V. Intran. To plough, turning into fallow. " Ma'r gweishon yn fishi iawn yn bwrnaru." The servants are busy ploughing, or turning into fallow.

Bwryn   N.m.s. A small field near to or adjoining a house. Nearly obsolete.

Bwrw
  -pladur   V. Intran. To reap with scythe and *cader*. It is the same as *taro pladurie*—an expression heard in certain parts of the county.

Bwtach   N.m.s. A well-to-do but rude person; the vulgar rich.

Bwti   Abs. n. Home, in the phrase *dwad bwtu*, to come home.
" Ma bechgyn Pengegin wedi dwad bwtu am dro."
The young men of Pengegin have come home on a visit.

Bwtwn   [= botwm.] N.m.s. Button.
Bwtwn-dyn
  -ifanc   A flower of the species *scabiosa*.
Bwtwn-'rhen
  -ddyn   N.m.s. A garden flower of the species *scabiosa*.
Bwtwn-yr
 -ispryd-drwg   Devil's-bit, *Scabious* (Scabiosa succisa).

Bwyd-imbor   N.m.s. Food taken by workmen in the field.

Byng   A carousal held at the time when farmers brought their *penwent*, or load of grain, to the mill to be ground and hulled. The Rev. D. Jenkyn Evans has the following note upon this obsolete custom: " The *Byng* would last all night, and the young of both sexes would con-

gregate to the mill from far and near, and
would indulge in harmless sport till the morning.
They dressed up a horse's head and carried it
about from place to place during the night,
and if there was a man or woman in the neighbourhood of the mill more disagreeable than
others, the 'penwentwyr' would cause him or
her as much annoyance as they possibly could."

Byti Adv. Nearly, almost.
"Mae byti fod yn bump ar glôch."
It is nearly five o'clock.

Byth-a
.hefyd Adv. phrase. Lit.: Ever and also.
" Hen rocyn diwerth yw Twm, wdw i'n gorffod
gweyd yr un peth wrtho o hyd o hyd, a'i drin
e byth a hefyd."
Tom is a worthless fellow. I am obliged to
tell him the same thing several times, and to
lecture him constantly.

Bythwiredd Abs. n. Eternal verity.

Byw na-bod Lit.: Living or existing. A phrase frequently
heard.
" Stim byw-na-bod gida'r hen grwt."
" Stim byw-na-bod gida Ann eishe bod hi 'n
càl myn'd i'r dre i fyw."
" Stim byw-na-bod gida'r hen nashwn."

e

Cacen N.f.s. A bun.

" Cacen ddime "—a halfpenny bun.

" Cacen geinog "—a penny bun.

" Cacen fach "—a small bun specially made for *dy' calan.* (Pron. *càc-en*).

Caci N.m.s. Human excreta.

Caca is the variant heard in the district extending from Casmid to Tyddewi.

Caci V. Intran. To attend to the call of Nature, to excrete matter from the system ; to evacuate.

Cadno N.m.s. A fox, a metaphorical way of describing a deceptive day; a day which promises too well in the morning and ends up in heavy rain.

Cadno N.m.s. A bundle of straw used for constructing a funnel or air passage in a stack of corn when the corn is not well seasoned. The *cadno* is pulled up through the " chimney " as the *helem* is being made.

Cadw'r -mish Lit.: Keeping the month.

This refers to the custom of providing dissenting preachers with hospitality on Sunday. The principal families of a country chapel volunteer to become responsible by turns for a month's entertainment.

Caerdroia   N.m.s. A puzzle.
The schoolmaster of the author's early days was wont to relate to his scholars that the plan of ancient Troy was as shown in the accompanying drawing. The puzzle was to get into the citadel at the centre of the city.

Cafaltri   Coll. n. Cavalry.

Caff   N.m.s. Dry weeds gathered out of ploughland, which are heaped together and set on fire.

Caffern   N.f.s. A sort of dung-fork, with two or three prongs bent at right angles with the handle. Nearly obsolete.

Cafflo   V. Tran. To confuse, to entangle.
" Peidwch a nghafflo i."
Don't confuse me.
" Peidwch cafflo'r dafe."
Don't entangle the thread.

Calch-slac   N.m.s. Slaked lime.

Calenig   N.m.s. A Twelfth-Day gift.
Dy' Calan is held in many parishes on the 13th of January, and not on the 12th. In olden days children went about carolling in the early morning for coppers and cuce bach and tablen. During the day the poor went about from farm to farm soliciting calenig, which was never refused.
Can Dy' Calan is as follows:—
" Deffrwch ben teili,
Dima flwyddyn newi,
Wedi dŵad adre
O fiwn eich drwse,
Drwse yn nghâ
Yn nghlo dros y nos.

D

Drwy'r baw a thrwy'r llaca
Daethon ni ima,
Drwy'r eithin weithe
Dan bigo'n coese.
Dima'n bwriad nine,
Mofyn bobo ddime;
Bwriad trwy gariad
Rhoddwch heb genad.
Paste nas torwch,
Cwrw nas spariwch;
Plant ifenc i ni,
Gollingwch ni 'r tŷ,
Gollingwch ni 'n gloi
Te tima ni 'n ffoi!"
This is ouly a fragment of a much longer song.

Calofnus   Adj. Faint-hearted.

Camfarch   N.m.s. A canal, larger than a *penfarch* (a leat).

Campo   V. Intran. To frisk, to gambol.
" Ma'r wyn bach yn campo 'i chalon hi."
The little lambs are gamboling.
Lit.: " The little lambs are gamboling the heart of it."

Camshengyd   V. Intran. To step falsely in walking, so that the foot is twisted or sprained.

Canan   N.m.s. Cannon.

Canel   N.m.s. The stop-pin of a brewing vat, used in lieu of a tap.

Carne   N.pl. Numbers, heaps; a multitude.
" We carne o ddinion yn yr acshon."
There was a large number of people at the sale.

Can-eslls   N.m.s. A big tin jack; so called, possibly, from the manner of its being carried, when full, with the bottom resting against the side. (Pron. càn-èslis).

Can-cnapyn   N.m.s. A medium sized tin jack.

Can-grot   N.m.s. A small sized tin jack. So called from its price.

Canolig   Adj. and Adv. Indifferent, middling.
" Iechyd canolig "—Indifferent health.
" Mae e'n lled ganolig."
He is only indifferently well, i.e., he is only middling.

Canolwith   Abs n. Average.
" Shwt gnidie sy' leni? "
" O, rwbeth yn ganolwith 'ma."
What sort of crops are there this year?
Oh, something about the average.

Cansen   N.f.s. A cane.
" Ffòn gansen "—A cane walking stick.

Cansen
 -ganswllt   A term half-humorously, half-sarcastically applied to an " old maid."
" Dysg di wers fy machgen ffamws,
Gan hen gadno ffalst yn gwmws ;
Paid a gneyd yr un gyfeillach
A hen gansen ganswllt mwyach."
                    —(Old ballad).

Cantreg   N.f.s. A songstress.

Cantwll   Adj. and Adv. Riddled with holes.
" Ma'r badell yn gantwll."
The pan is riddled with holes.

Canwyll
 -bren   A wooden candle.
On old S. David's Day, March 12th, it was customary to place a wooden candle instead of

the ordinary tallow one in the candlestick on the table. This was the signal that the time for partaking of the evening meal by candle light had passed. Henceforth, till the ensuing autumn, farm hands were to sup without artificial light.

" Nos dwgwl Ddewi fe gaiff Ben,
Fita swper gida'r ganwyll bren."

These were days when candles were a rare commodity, and when people retired for the night at reasonable hours.

Canwyll-fold　N.f.s. A large moulded candle, made of mutton fat. The mould was usually made of lead, and was about as long as the barrel of an old-fashioned fowling-piece, with a bore an inch and a quarter in diameter. The candle was used at wakes.

Canwyll-yr-yspryd-drwg　Mud Horsetail (Equisetum limosum).

Capel　Used peculiarly in the sense of " traps " or belongings.

" Peidwch termo llawer ar yr hen roces, te fe gwyd 'i chapel a bant a hi."

Don't scold the old girl much, or she will pick up her " traps " and be off.

Capseiso　V. Intran. To lose balance, said especially of a person on a load of hay, a rick, etc., losing his balance and falling over.

Caran　N.c.s. Poor thing, the dear one, &c.
" Ma Deio Shors, 'r hen garan. yn sâl iawn."
David George, poor fellow, is very ill.
" Fe fu farw Hannah Hŵel, 'r hen garan."
Hannah Howell, poor thing, is dead.

Caran　N.m.s. Carrion.

Carbel   Adj. Absolutely, outright, &c.
"Mae e'n garbel ddwl."
He is perfectly silly.

Carchni   Abs. n. Fidgetiness.
"Ma rhyw hen garchni arno, all e byth a bod yn llony."
He is so fidgety that he cannot be still.

Careg-aped   N.f.s. An echo-stone. It was formerly believed that an echo was caused by a particular kind of stone, or by some mystical quality inherent in a particular kind of stone.

Careg-aped   Used metaphorically for a preacher who plagiarizes, or who preaches another man's sermon.

Careg-bowl   N.f.s. A stone that is dressed for building purposes.

Careg-eithin   N.f.s. A large flat stone for pounding furze upon, and in use before the introduction of the modern chaff-cutter.

Careg-goitan   N.f.s. A cromlech. The word *cromlech* is rarely or never used in the neighbourhood of the Gwaun Valley, but always *coitan*.

Careg-gopa   N.f.s. Cope-stone.

Careg-leifi   N.f.s. A thin chip of stone, usually of flint, kept by farm labourers in their pocket for the purpose of cleaning or scraping dirt off their tools with.

Careg-nadd   N.f.s. A bath stone.

**Careg-y
-ginddaredd**   The stone of hydrophobia.
This was a celebrated stone in the possession

of one Miss Bowen, of Weinifor, in the parish
of Llandyssul, Cardiganshire, said to possess
the properties of curing hydrophobia. Its fame
had spread as far as the Gwaun Valley. The
superstitious resorted to it from all parts.

Cargo N.m.s. Lumber. Used metaphorically for a
person. It is a significant word, implying that
a man carries in his body a lot of rubbish and
not a living thing.

"Hen gargo digon gwâl yw Twm Penfigyn."
Thomas, of Penfigyn, is a useless fellow.

Cargwchdod Abs. n. Cumbrousness.

Cargwen V. Tran. To lug a lot of useless things.
(Pron. car-gŵen, accent on gŵ).

Carlad A tea leaf floating on a cup of tea is said to
indicate that a young man or woman is about
to have a fresh sweetheart. Several leaves
floating show that he or she will have a number
of possible sweethearts to choose from. The
length of the leaf indicates whether the sweetheart will be tall or short. The leaf is picked
up and placed on the back of one hand, whilst
the back of the other hand pressed on it
attempts a transfer. If the leaf passes from
one hand to the other at the first attempt, it
shows that the sweetheart will "come" within
a week; if at the second attempt, the event
will happen within a fortnight, and so forth.

Cario-'nghyd Gathering sheaves together at harvest, for
the purpose of making the *deise* of corn. This
task is assigned to children, usually the poor
children of the neighbourhood, or of the
labourers, who receive a copper or two for the
work nowadays, but formerly received two meals
a day as their hire.

Car-llwye

N.m.s. A wooden spoon rack, an article of primitive furniture never absent in a N. Pembrokeshire farm or cottage Usually made to hold 24 spoons.

Side View. Front View.

Carsi

Adj. Corded or ribbed, a term applied to homespun cloth that is of a ribbed pattern.

Cartws

N.m.s. Carthouse.

Carthad

N.m.s. The manure obtained from a stable or a cow-house at one cleaning.

Cas

Abs. n. Condition.
" Ma càs da ar yr anner."
The heifer is in good condition.

Cascen-fenyn

N.f.s. A cask of butter.

Casgal

[= casgliad.] Collection, offertory.

Castil

N.m.s. Steel. (Pron. cas-til, accent on last syllable).

Castithad

N.m.s. Herring-bone stitch, a sewing term. The verb is *castitho*.

Caton

[= cantwn.] Adv. All to shivers.

Catw

Adj. Conceited, over-wise.
The term is applied to anybody, whether male or female, who is very wise in his or her own estimation, such as " Jack Catw," " Rachel Catw," &c.

Catw-ffwrn
·fach

A game played on *Nos Glingeua*, the 12th of December. A small piece of candle was lit and placed on the floor, when two strong lads or young men would stand on either side, back to back, bending forwards, and with a long pole between their legs, would contend, the one for the extinction of the candle, the other for its

preservation. The defender repeated aloud the
words : —

Catw ffwrn fach!
Catw ffwrn fach!
Beth bennag a ddelo,
Yr anwyl a'i cadwo,
Catw ffwrn fach!

The struggle went on sometimes for half-an-
hour together, when both parties would have to
give up contending through sheer exhaustion.
The game caused roars of laughter, and if either
party won he was hailed as the hero of the
evening, and treated to an abundance of home
brewed and *pasteiod bach.*

Catah-y-lloi   N.m.s. Calf-pen.

Cathbwl   N.m.s. A silent, sly fellow ; a sneak. (Pron.
càth-bwl, accent on first syllable).

Cath-mish
-**Mai**   N.f.s. A May cat. Believed to be more apt
than cats born in other months to carry vermin,
especially adders, into dwelling houses. Metaphorically, the word is used for a woman who
has several illegitimate children.

Cathren   V. Trans. To lead a horse or ox at ploughing.
Cathren was defined for the author by an old
relative of his—a farmer of the old style—thus :
—" Arwen pen yr îch (ox) slawer dy' pan yn
rhedig a'r arad Gwmrâg. Wê rhaid câl pedwar
o ddinion at y gwaith o redig pryd hiny, un i
drin yr arad, un i ishte ar y cawell wch ben y
swch i neyd pwyse i chadw hi yn y ddeiar, un
i ddreifo a'r prica, a'r llall i gathren. Nid
bisnes bach wê rhedig 'r amser hiny, fachgen,—
tipyn cletach nag yw hi nawr a'r fenshwns
[inventions] newy' ma,—ond howyr f'argol,
dina pryd wê llafurie i'w câl."

Cath-tri-lliw   N.f.s. A tortoise-shell cat.

Cauad   V. Intran.   To put up a fence, to repair a hedge.

"Ma'r gwrŵod wedi myn'd i gauad heddy."

The men have gone to repair the fences to-day.

Cauedig   Adj.   Compact.   A term applied to a farm that is compact and well fenced.

Cau-'i-gilleth   Part. phrase.   Shutting his knife; metaphorically it means finishing a thing or bringing a thing to an end.   Formerly servant men used their own pocket knives at table, for none were provided in the olt-time farmhouses. When the foreman's knife went click! it was a signal to the rest that the meal was over, and whether they had finished or not they were obliged to follow suit, and click! went a dozen pocket-knives in rapid succession.   All this is changed now, but the expression *cau-'i-gilleth* lives.

Cawdel   Adv.   Higgledy-piggledy.

Cawed   [= cawod.]   N.f.s.   A shower.

Cawl-cwta -berw   N.m.s.   Broth that has been prepared in a hurry and which is consequently not well " done."

Cawl-llath   N.m.s.   A meal of boiled milk and oatmeal or grits.

Cawlo   V. Intran.   To be entangled, said especially of corn that has been beaten down by wind and rain, and become so entangled that it is difficult to cut.

Cawl-shir -Bemro   N.m.s.   The celebrated Pembrokeshire broth, containing a little of everything from the garden. The word is used metaphorically for any hodge-podge affair.

Cawl-twmo N.m.s. Broth re-heated, called also *cawl-ail-dwym*.

Cawn -pengrych N.pl. Shaking grass.

Cawr Mowr The devil, the mighty giant.

"Galw ar y *Cawr Mowr*" is the euphemism for "tyngi a rhegi." The principal swear words of Dyfed are:—Ar fen'd i, byth-na-chwmpw-i, byth-na-chiffrw-i, byth-na-fidw-i, daro, dancio, damo, diwedd-anwyl, drato, deio, diwch-afion, jawl, jawch, jawl-a-ngoto-i, mowcedd, mowredd, myn-Mair, o'r-grimwedd-anwyl, o'r jiwbil, tawn-i-heb fido, tawn-i-marw.

Most of these are merely mild expletives.

Cawalet [= cawsellt.] N.m.s. Cheese vat.
A variant is *coslet*.

Cecial Part. Stuttering. (Pron. cèc-ial, two sylls.).

Cedor-y -wrach N.m.pl. A kind of weed that grows in corn, causing much trouble to the farmer.

Cedrued [= creaduriaid.] Animals, limited to the domestic kind.

Cefen In the phrase *ar gefen heddy'*. The usages are :
(1) Ar gefen heddy' bu farw'r Gwaredwr.
The Redeemer died as at this time.
(2) "Peder bline ar gefen heddy' bu'r trwste mowron."
This day four years the great thunder was.

Cefnent N.m.s. Depth, middle, darkest part.

" Wdw i wrthi drwy'r dydd hyd gefnent y nos."

I am at it all day long, even to the depth of night.

" Yn nghefnent y nos ma'r lleidir wrth 'i waith."

During the darkest hour of night the thief is at his work.

Ceffyl-heiarn   N.m.s. Bicycle.

Ceffyl-tan   N.m.s. Locomotive.

Ceffyl-shaff   N.m.s. The shaft horse of a team.
Metaphorically used of a person who, in connection with religious or other work, is willing to bear the " brunt of the battle "—the downright hard and obedient worker.

Cegyrn   N.f.pl. Hemlock.

Ceibo   V. Tran. Said of a furious bull pawing or scratching the ground; also in the expression *taw ni heb geibo*, literally, " if I did not dig," equivalent to English " if I never move."

Ceiled   N.m.s. Cheese after it has been dry-pressed and made ready for the final process of moulding.

Ceinog -owns „ Ffrensh   N.f.s. The big penny cast in 1797, in commemoration, it is said, of the landing of the French at Fishguard.

Cel   N.m.s. Horse. An abbreviation for *ceffyl*. (Pron. cèl).

Celen-eni   N.f.s. Caul. Also called *gweren-eni*.
The following interesting paragraph appeared in the " Western Mail " for August 9th, 1910:—
" Dr. W. Wynn Westcott, at the Hackney

Coroner's Court on Saturday, delivered himself of an interesting little address on the subject of olt-time superstition regarding cauls. At one time, he said, cauls were considered of great value, and were carefully kept, dried, and preserved. Sailors would hardly think of sailing without one. They were advertised in the papers, and fetched from 20s. to 30s. each. He had a case at that court some time back of a sailor who had carried a caul for forty years, and it was found in his pocket when he died. But he did not die of drowning—he hanged himself."

At Fishguard, as late as the year 1878, £5 was paid for a caul by a sailor who was bound on a first voyage for the South of America. Children that are born with a caul are believed to be under the influence of the luckiest of stars.

Celent   N.f.s. A heap of carcases.

Celshib   Inter. Villain! Ah you cur!
A term of reproach addressed to a dog, and to no other animal.
" A'r celshib ag e! "
Ah you brute!

Celwrn   N.m.s. A large, shallow tub in which butter is dressed. The word is restricted here to this sense.

Cender   [= cefnder.] N.m.s. Cousin.

Cenin-shifyn   Coll. n. Chives.

Cered -piseshwn   Beating the bounds of common lands. In N. Pembrokeshire formerly the Lord of the Manor, Sir Marteine Lloyd, of Bronwydd, used to beat the bounds of the Commons once every seven years. The event was celebrated with great festivity, and the days of *cered piseshwn* were always regarded as holidays.

Cernap   Adj. Coquettish.

Cerndopi and Cerndwpan   V. Intran. To sleep and nod on one's feet.

" Beth wyt ti'n cerndopi fan na, es; cer i'r gwely."

Lit. : Why dost thou nod there, girl; go to bed.

Cernicill   N.m.s. A decoy. The person whose business it was to mislead the water-bailiff when the *biddin bisgota* (q.v.) was engaged on its depredations. The *cernicill* was the most cunning fellow of the gang—one who had graduated in the art of trickery, in fact. It was his business to keep the water-bailiff under strict surveillance, and to report his movements to the *pentrifwr* (q.v.). On the night of poaching the *cernicill* paraded the road, always within hailing distance of the *biddin*, and at the approach of danger he blew his whistle, when the *pellen* was at once plunged into the river, and the gang dispersed orderly in the direction of the nearest cover.

These desperadoes, who cared little for the laws of the realm, were not altogether unobservant of the laws of Nature. They frequently manifested a respect for the order of Nature, and showed an acquaintance with her subterfuges. The name *cernicill* is witness to the fact that they had observed that bird's manner of luring an intruder away from its nest by its comical feints.

Cernwigil   N.m.s. Peewit.

This variant of the word is heard at Llangolman and surrounding district.

Cerig-camud   N.f.pl. Stepping stones. Stones placed on their ends for the purpose of crossing a brook or shallow water.

Cerig-cant   N.f.pl. Stones placed on their ends on a wall as a cope.

Cerig-cawse   N.f.pl. The stones that are dug up from what was anciently a Roman causeway. Metaphorically used for obstacles.

Cerig-defed   N.f.pl. Stones placed in a paper bag to charm away worts. As many stones were selected as there were worts on the hands—each wort, in fact, had its own particular stone; these were rubbed on the worts and then put in paper made up to resemble a packet of sweets. The bag was borne to the nearest cross-road, where it was thrown down in a careless manner, as if it had been lost by someone on his way from the local shop. A passer-by would find the bag, open it, and discover to his chagrin that he was cursed with somebody's worts—" Wedi i ribo a defed rhewin." The " defed " now departed in a body from their present pasture, and sought fresh grass on the hands of the unfortunate discoverer of the bag.

Cerig-Llantwd   An expression signifying " great stumbling blocks," or " a rough time in store," &c.

Cerig-y-drewin   N.f.pl. Druidical stones.

Cesel   N.m.s. A cloak, a covering, now used only in a metaphorical sense.

"Dyw un weithred dda ddim yn ddigon o gesel i guddio'r drwgionu nâth e'n i fowyd."

One good deed is not a sufficient cloak to cover the evil he did in his lifetime.

Cesim   [= cefais.] V. Intran. I had.

Cetsh   N.m.s. Calf-pen.

"Faint o loi bach sy gida chi leni yn y cetsh?"
How many calves have you in the pen this year?

Cetyn
In the phrase "tyn iawn at 'i getyn." Keen on getting on in the world. Also N.m.s., a considerable length or piece. "Cetyn o ffordd." A considerable length of road.

Cether
N.f.s. A clan. Never used in the classical sense of a *friend*.
Cether Casnewy—The clan of Little Newcastle.
Cether Casmâl—The clan of Puncheston.

Cewn
N.m.s. The back.

Cewnog
Adj. Well-to-do.
"Ma Dafis, Trellwyn, yn ffarmwr cewnog."
Davies, of Trellwyn, is a well-to-do farmer.

Cewndid
Abs. n. Substance, goods.
"Dyn a chewndid."
A man of substance.

Cewnoctyd
Abs. n. Encouragement.
"Wdw i'n câl pob cewnoctyd gida mishtir i wella'r tir."
The landlord gives me every encouragement to improve the land.

Ci-aden
N.m.s A setter (dog).

Cidled-cidid
Adv. phrase. As broad as it is long.
"Pwlffyn o fustach cidled-cidid," said of a fat, short man, who is almost as broad as he is long.

Cidyn-gafar
N.m.s. Whiskers on the lower chin, trimmed in billy-goat or Yankee fashion.

Cifer N.m.s. A turn, or a day of work.

"Hala cifer" is to drive out manure from the farmyard till time of "gillwn," i.e., the time when the horses should be unharnessed for a feed.

"Cifer o 'redig" is a "turn" of ploughing, from about 9 a.m. till 3 p.m.

Cifor N.m.s. A cover (of a book). A lid.

Cig-coch N.m.s. Lean meat. Lit., red meat.

Cig-gwyn N.m.s. Fat meat. Lit., white meat.

Cig-mharen N.m.s. Mutton of any kind, including the flesh of lambs.

Cingel N.m.s. (1) A band, a hoop, put around anything to prevent it from splitting. (2) The belly-band of a saddle.

Cingron N.m.s. (1) A long-stalked fungus, sometimes called the stinking mushroom. (2) A stinking fellow.

"Mae'n drewi fel y gingron."

It stinks like the stinking mushroom.

The following bit of characteristic lore is taken down from the mouth of Benny'r Twcwr, of Pontfaen Fach, near Fishguard, who died in 1898:

"Glwest ti, fachgen, shŵt dâth pwrs-y-mwg, bwyd-y-barcud, a'r gingron i'r byd. Fel hyn: fe gwrddodd y barcud, y lliffan, a'r coryn a'u gily un tro, i scêmo shŵt wê porthi'r gâm yn well, wàth wê'r adar yn dene, y malddod yn sich, a'r cilion yn fân anŵeth. Fe ffeindiodd y barcud flawd, fe ffeindiodd y coryn ferem, a fe gimisgodd y lliffan y twes. Fe gwmro pob un o honi nw lwmpin o'r twes a'i bòbi e'n i ffwrn 'i hunan. Tortne'r barcud y;w bwyd-y

barcud, torthe'r lliffan yw pwrs-y-mwg, a
thorthe'r coryn yw'r gingron. Oddar hini ma'r
adar yn tewau ar fwyd-y-barcud, ma'r malddod
yn sleimo ar bwrs-y-mwg, a'r cilion yn dŵad yn
fwy o faint wrth smilo'r gingron."

Cil   N.m.s. A cauldron.

Cil cawl—the kettle or cauldron used for
boiling broth. (Pron. cil).

Cil   In the phrase *ar gil* = having disappeared.
" Mae e wedi mynd ar gil o'r wlad."
He has fled the country.

Cil   Adj. Slender, graceful.
" Lodes gil lanwedd."
A slender, lovely maiden.   (Pron. cil).

Ciler   N.m.s. A vessel of exactly the same shape
as the *celwrn*, but of much smaller size.

Cilion-caci   N.m.pl. Dung-fly, the yellow fly.
Often called also *cilion-y-dom*.

Cilion-cneica   N.m.p. Spanish flies.
Cilion-tin-bweth (Maenclochog).

Cilion-llidnod   N.f.pl. The flies which attack sheep, depositing their ova in their skin and wool at the
fly season. Sing. *Cilionen lidnod*.

**Cilion
-tingron**   N.f.pl. The ox-fly.

Tingron is probably a corruption of *tan-
groen*, seeing that this fly is hatched under the
skin of cattle. Sing. *Cilionen-dingron*.

Cilogod   Coll. n. The seed of the ribwort plantain.
Children play at cross-swords with the long-
stalked seed of the ribwort, the point being

to cut off the head, or the seed: this is called *whare cilogod*. The victor acclaims his victory with *cock-a-doodle-doo!*

Cils   [= ceilys.] N.m.p. The game of nine-pins.

Cilwc   N.m.s. (1) A shy, sheepish look, a side glance; and (2) as an abstract noun, anger, malice.

Cilyn   N.m.s. A small piece of anything, but generally of cheese.
"Cilyn o gaws a chwlff o fara."
A bit of cheese and a slice of bread.

Cillegi   V. Intran. To belch, to break wind through the mouth.

Cilleglad   N.m.s. A belching.

Cilleth
-gasneiff   N.f.s. Table knife. *Cilleth ford* is never used by the generation now passing, and only rarely by the rising one. Farmers' daughters who have had boarding-school education affect new terms now and again, and the old dialect stands in some danger of modification through the inoculation of modern ideas. *Cilleth-gasneiff* is a very curious hybrid, the second element being, no doubt, a corruption of *cast-steel knife*.

Cilleth-goden   N.f.s. A pocket knife.
Cillith-a
-ffircs   In the phrase:
"Mae'n bwrw cillith-a-ffircs."
It is raining very heavily; equivalent to the English "It is raining cats-and-dogs."

Cimercyn   Adj. Unwell, unfit.
"Digon cimercyn yw Deio 'n paro o hyd."
David still keeps unwell.

Cimmalo   V. Intran. To bend to work, to put all the joints of the body into action, and work for all one is worth.

Cimun-angen   N.m.s. Extreme unction. The word is quite obsolete, but I have seen it in an `old Pembrokeshire ballad.

Cimro   [= Cymro.] Often used as the equivalent of *home-made*, especially in reference to tools. such as *picwarch Gimro, arad Gimro,* &c.

Cindron   [=cynron.] N.m.p. Maggots.

Cindronni   V. Intran. To breed maggots.

Cinllwyn   Prop. n. (1) The wicked one, or the Father of Cunning.
Also (2) a mischievous, cunning fellow.

Ciuogwarth   [= ceiniogwerth.] N.f.s. A pennyworth.

Cino-pen
-medi   The harvest-home dinner.

Cinsarns   Abs. n. Dealings.
" Diw Tomos Penrhiw ddim yn gneyd un cinsarns o gwbwl a Benny'r Fwel nawr."
Thomas, of Penrhiw, has no dealings at all with Benjamin, of Foel, now—i.e., they are at variance.

Circh-du
-bach   N.pl. Old Welsh black oats.

Circh
-tantarian   N.pl. Russian oats.

Cirddad   [= cyrhaedd.] V. Tran. To reach.
" Wdw i'n rhy fyr, alla i ddim cirddad pen y wàl."
I am too short, I cannot reach the top of the wall.

Cirlaw   N.m.s. Driving rain.

Cirnhoifa   (1) An asesembly.
(2) A store, especially of water in a pond or river.

Cisarns   Abs. n. Connection, dealings.
" Dyw e'n gneyd un cisarns o gwbl o heni nawr."
He has no dealings at all with her now.

Cisen   N.f.s. A swede, i.e., the tuber so called.
This is often used instead of *swedjen*.

Cisled   [= cystal.] Adj. As good as.

Cithrel-gwyn   N.m.s. A row in a chapel.
" Ma'r cithrel gwyn finicha yn dangos 'i ben yn y côr canu."
Chapel rows generally start in the choir.
Probably there is a connection between *cithrel gwyn* and a surpliced choir.
" Cithrel gwyn y canu " is an expression frequently heard.

Ciwco   Part. Peeping, casting a furtive glance.

Ciwpi   N.m.s. The parting of the hair. The fashion of parting or dividing the hair and brushing it down neatly was severely denounced by the Puritans of a generation gone by. (Pron. ciw-pi, two accents).

Ciwt   Adj. Crafty, subtle, and deep. More significant than the English *cute*.

Chas   Abs. n. A turn at work.
" Dewch i fi gâl châs nawr."
Let me have a turn now. (Pron. tshâs).

Chas-y-ffenest   N.f.s. Window-sash. (*Chas* pron. tshàs).

Clabiach   Abs. n. Gossip, in the phrase *erlid clabiach*, to go a-gossipping.

Clacwiddi   N.m.pl. The iron stays of a reaping cradle.

Clacwy   N.m.s. A gander.

Cladd-gwallt   N.m.s. A place where hair is buried. Hair that is cut is never destroyed or thrown away, but is carefully buried in a hole or crevice in a stone wall—usually a garden wall. The person to whom the hair belonged gathers it together and religiously deposits it in the hirsutical mausoleum. Above all must the hair never be burnt, or thrown into a stream, unless the person wishes to challenge all kinds of fearful calamities. It is no exaggeration to say that many an ancient garden hedge is gorged with human hair.

Claddu -clecer   V. Intran. To evacuate, to ease nature—a euphemistic expression.

Clap   N.m.s. Tales, gossip.
Pl. : *Claps.*

Clapian   V. Intran. To bear tales, to commit a breach of confidence, to " split " upon one.

Clapgi   N.m.s. A tell-tale, an informant.
Pl. : *Clapgwn.*
I have never heard the corresponding feminine. A girl who is addicted to tale-bearing is called *yr hen gartws* (the old carthouse).

Clasgu   [= casglu.] V. Trans. To collect.

Claspo -garddwne   Part. n. Wrist-clasping.
Great rivalry exists among young farm servants as to who possesses the thickest wrist.

It is considered a mark of superior worth to possess an exceptionally thick wrist. That wrist is considered to be the finest which cannot be clasped by the one possessing the longest hand in a company.

Clatsh
Adj. Right in the head.
"Dyw e ddim yn eitha clatsh."
He is not quite right in the head

Clatshan
Part. Flapping.
"Clatshan 'i adenydd."
Flapping its wings.

Clatshan
Part. Making a loud report.
"Fe gauodd y drws gida'r gwynt nes bod e'n clatshan."
The wind closed the door with a bang.

Clatshen
N.f.s. A slap, especially with reference to the face, or the bare skin of any part of the body. It is never used of a slap or hit on a covered part of the body.

Clau
[= glanhau.] V. Tran. To clean.
"Cer nawr, merch i, a gna hàst i glau'r parlwr cyn daw'r pregethwr."

Go now, my maid, make haste to clean the parlour before the preacher comes.

Cleco
V. Intran. To affect, impress.
"Stim yn y byd yn cleco arno."
Nothing in the world affects him.

Cledrwyth
N.m.s. Starch, or that which formerly did service for starch. The word is nearly if not quite obsolete.
"Dillad cledrwyth" = starched linen.

Clefer Adj. Kind. Signifies the same as the N.W. *clên.*

"Dyn clefer anghiffredin yw Griffi Penbanc."

Griffith, of Penbanc, is a very kind man.

Clefyd-y
    -pwd Abs. n. Miff, pique. Used specially in reference to a choir or of a member thereof who has taken offence and stays away.

"Ma Ianto Penfedw,
Ardderchog ei ddawn,
Wedi digio yn groulon
Wrth gôr Pantycawn;
Ma eishe ar y bachgen
Gâl ledo ei hun,
A eishe ar y côr
Roi cic yn 'i din.
Hen glefyd-y-pwd, hen glefyd-y-pwd !
Hen glefyd ofnadwy yw clefyd-y-pwd."

Clem Abs. n. A notion, idea. In the plural it means grimaces.

"Sta'g e ddim clèm shwt ma gneyd dim."
He has no idea how to set about anything.

"Paid a gneyd hen glème fel na."
Do not make grimaces so.

Clepsin N.m.s. A clasp.

A variant is *clasbyn.*
"'Clepsin clocs."
The clasp of a clog.

Clerchen N.f.s. An old hag, a miserly old woman.

Clers N.f.p. Gad-flies.
Sing.: *Clersen.*
The word *clêrs* is strictly limited, in Gwaun, to the species gad-fly.

Cletsh   Adj. Agglutinative, mouldy.

Cletsh   In the expression *bara cletsh*, i.e., bread made of heated wheat, or wheat that has been spoilt at harvest. Called in S. Pembrokeshire *reemy* bread, and in Glamorganshire *bara ropin*. The year 1866 is called in N. Pembrokeshire *blwyddyn y bara cletsh*. The harvest of 1865 had been a wet one, and the wheat and barley were heated, so that the bread was of the quality known as *cletsh*. There was great distress and sickness, and the generation now passing speak of the event as *barn Duw ar ddrigionu dyn*.

Clid   Coll. n. Dried cow dung, formerly used for fire material. Poor people fifty years ago were allowed to go over the land of the neighbouring farms to gather *clid*. This was about the only kind of fuel the poorest of the poor could afford to get, and very wretched stuff it was, for its fumes and smoke not only tanned the skin, but also told on the health.

Clifer   Adj. Generous, hospitable. Never used in reference to calibre or ability.

Clinsho   V. Trans. To bruise the flesh by hitting it with a hammer or other tool.

Clip   Adv. At once, in a twinkling.
"Dewch miwn clip."
Come in a trice.

Clipad   Abs. n. Twinkling.
"Miwn clipad lligad."
In the twinkling of an eye.
A variant is *clipiad*.

Clipo V. Intran. To blink, twinkle.

C'lo [= coelio.] Used enclitically after expressions.
"Ma eishe mynd i'r farced arna i, dewch chi? Dewa i c'lo," and numerous other instances.

Clobyn N.m.s. A plump, good-conditioned fellow. Fem. *cloben*.

Cloc N.m.s.
An instrument shaped thus: placed around the neck of horned beasts to prevent trespassing. (Pron. clòc).

Cloc N.m.s. Dandelion clock (Taraxacum officinale). (Pron. clòc).

Clocs N.f.pl. Clogs.
Sing. *Clocsen*.

Clocsan Part. Walking about in clogs so as to produce the "clatter". peculiar to that footwear.

Clochangla N.f.s. "A bell in the ear." The sound which one sometimes hears in the ear somewhat resembling that of a bell tolling in the distance is believed to be a foretoken of death in one's family.

Clochened N.f.s. The passing bell; lit. the soul's bell.
Benny'r Twcwr remembered the *clochened* being tolled in the parish of Pontfaen. This would be somewhere back in the early thirties of last century. The word lives, but the beautiful old custom itself is dead.

Clochtran   V. Intran. To cackle.
"Clochtran giar ar ol didwy," said of a man who blows his own trumpet after he has done what he conceives to be a wonderful deed.

Clomen-yn -yr-arch   A species of garden flower.

Cloncen   N.f.s. An empty-headed woman.

Closhwns   N.f.pl. Goloshes.

Closo   V. Intran. To make love to.
"Ma Tom Pantybrwyn yn clòso tipyn ar Ann y Wern."
Tom, of Pantybrwyn, is making love to Ann, of Wern.

Clwmlys   N.m.s. The dodder.

Clwsho   Part. Scraping, said of a hen sitting on an ash heap and scraping or wallowing in the ashes.

Clwt   N.m.s. A slice.
"Clwt o fara menyn."
A slice of bread and butter.

Clwto   V. Trans. To patch or mend clothes.

Clwyd   N.f.s. A gate which is not a fixture, or made to hang. Iet is the word for a gate that hangs on hinges.

Clyndardd -ant   N.m.s. A small spring of water.
Plur. Clarddante.

Cnaf   N.m.s. A knave. Never used in the feminine.

Cnafichdod   Abs. n. An evil penchant; an itch for mischief.

Cnapan   An old game, which has been termed "the royal game of Dyfed." Too well known to need describing here.

Cnappo   Part. To become lumpy; a term applied to flour when it has been standing in the *garnesh* (q.v.) for some time and is becoming mouldy.

Cnecs-y-cwn   N.f.s. The foxglove. (Pron. cnècs-y-cŵn).

Cnidyn   N.c.s. A little child, in fond language. Pl. *Cnidynod.*
"Y cnidynod bach!"
The dear children!

Cniferi   Abs. n. The even numbers.

Cnoco   V. Intran. To go a-courting; lit. "to knock." The N. Pembrokeshire manner of wooing is too familiar to need describing here. Saturday night is the orthodox night to go a-knocking. The prince of Welsh bards describes how he went on a Saturday night to his fair one and
"Mi a roddais dri chnippws,
Er ei mwyn ar drwyn y drws."

Cnwbyn-o -grwt   N.m.s. A strapping fellow.

Co   [= acw.] Adv. There, yonder.

Cocer   N.c.s. The Yorkshire breed of pig, a pig with ears erect. (Pron. còc-er).

Coco   V. Trans. To gather into a heap. Used in combination with *gwair, twarch, mate,* &c. (Pron. còc-o).

Coco-'i-glust   Pricking up his ears. Said of a horse, or of any other animal which has muscular control over his ears.

Cocrell N.c.s. A hermaphrodite.

Coeh Coll. n. Conservatives.

"Y Côch we 'n arfer bod grifa yn Shir Bemro, ond ma nw wedi colli tir nawr."

The Conservatives were at one time the stronger party in Pembrokeshire, but they have lost ground lately.

Cochion-bach
-y-gors N.m.pl. Cranberries, sometimes called *manna'r gòrs.*

Cochyn N.m.s. A male crab.

Coden N.f.s. A pocket. The word *llogell* is never heard in N. Pembrokeshire.

Codi V. Intran. To swarm.

"Ma'r gwenin yn ddweddar yn codi leni."

The bees are late swarming this year.

Codi-a
-chwmpo Knitting terms, meaning widening and narrowing the stocking; literally, rising and falling.

Codi-cefen V.n. To cease work.

Codi-'l-grefft To set up and practise a craft or a calling on one's own account.

"Ma Dafi wedi penu 'i brentisheth, mae e'n myn'd i godi 'i grefft nawr."

David has completed his apprenticeship, he is going to start on his own account now.

Codi-mas Part. n. The service held at the house of the dead previous to starting for the church or chapel, i.e., previous to the funeral procession. (Pron. còd-i-mâs, with accent on first and last syllables).

Codl
N.m.s. A sort of gruel or caudle given to women after childbirth. The ingredients are rhynion (shelled oats), old ale, gin, ginger, spices, and sugar.

Coiled
[= coflaid.] An armful, a lapful.
" Coiled o danwent."
An apronful of twigs for the fire.

Colddu
Adj. Dark complexioned.
" Merch golddu gywrain gain."
A dark-complexioned, cunning, lovely maiden.

Colo
[= coeliaf.] V. Intran. I believe.
A variant is *c'lo* (q.v.).

Colsyn
N.m.s. A live cinder.

Colten
V.n. A beating.
" Mi roisim i'r eitha golten iddo."
I gave him a good beating.

Colli-ar-'l
.hunan
V. phrase. To lose control of onse's-self ; to be frantic, especially with grief.

Combador
N.m.s. Gaffer or foreman. (Pron. com-ba- dôr, accent on last syll.).
No doubt from *commodore*.
Said especially of a man in charge of the rick at haymaking, and of the man who undertakes to see that the field is scraped clean.

Commins
N.m.pl. Common lands.

Constant
N.m.s. The heel or part of the scythe fitting into the handle.

Constrowlad
Abs. n. Correction.
N. com. A beating.
The following illustrates the latter use : —
" Be sy ar yr hen gi wr ? Cer di ona, te mi roia i 'r eitha gonstrowlad i ti ! "

What is the matter with the dog? Go thou hence or I'll give thee a good beating!

Copish   N.m.s.   The fly or flap of a breeches or trousers. There are two kinds of *copish; copish tarw*, a fall down flap, and *copish buwch*, the fly of the ordinary trousers, i.e., the style in vogue to-day. Formerly the *copish tarw* (lit. *bull's fly*) was the fashion for men and lads from their teens on, and *copish buwch* (lit. *cow's fly*) for small boys. It was a proud day for a lad when he first disported his *copish tarw:* it was as great a day as that on which the Roman youth assumed the *toga virilis*. From this day on he looked down upon his quondam companions of the *copish buwch* with sublime contempt. (Pron. còp-ish).

Copit   Adj. Haughty, defiant, strictly, it means to carry the head high. (Pron. còp-it).

Copsi   N.m.s. The cope of straw put upon a hay stack, &c.

Copsien   N.f.s. A small cope, sometimes put on the larger cope for ornamentation.

Copsych   Adj. Dry and speechless. A term applied to a person who keeps aloof from everybody and will not converse.

Cor   N.m.s. A pew or seat in church or chapel; not at all restricted to a choir stall.

Corach   N.m.s. A big bundle of branches or twigs tied together like a sheaf of corn and placed at the door of a dwelling to break the keenness of the blast. The *corach* is rarely, if ever, seen now.

Corclaw   N.m.s. A low hedge.
A hedge that is not above two or three feet in height, and bare of growth.

Cordo   V. Intran. To harmonize.
" Lleishwr da yw Dafi Owen, ond y gweitha arno yw, mae e'n canu bâs o'i ben, dyw e ddim yn cordo."
David Owen has a good voice, but the worst of it is, his bass is of his own making, and does not harmonize with the other parts.

Cordroi   N.m.s. Corduroy.

Corddad   N.m.s. The butter made at one churning.

Corffyn   N.m.s. A droll fellow.

Cor-giar-a-cheilog   A mixed Church choir, consisting of women as well as surpliced men and boys, all sitting in the choir stalls. Such a choir is half-humorously, half-contemptuously referred to as " côr-giar a-cheilog."

Corgwed   Coll. n. Stunted trees.

Corlac   N.m.s. A long, wooden, how-shaped instrument used in turning and moving about corn on the kiln.

Corlan   [= ceulan.] N.f.s. River-bank.

Cornel   N.m.s. Colonel.

Corn-y-fedel   N.m.s. The harvest horn or trumpet.
This was made of cow's horn, and blown at harvest-tide to call the reapers to their work in the morning. Old Benny'r Twcwr remembered the call, which was: —

Coryn N.m.s. The boy who received the "Welsh-not" (q.v.) at the master's hand.

Coryn N.m.s. The foundation of a mow of corn, constructed with four sheaves so arranged that the top of each rests on the stem or stock of the other. This arrangement prevents the grain coming in contact with the ground.

Coryn-y-llyn The water-fly.

Costen
-wenyn N.f.s. A home-made straw bee-hive.

Cotofarms C. ll. n. Utensils, implements, especially the implements used by farm labourers, such as the mattock, how, breast-plow, shovel, &c. (Accent on last syllable).

Cowir [= cywir.] Adj. Correct.

Cownti-crop N.m.s. Haircutting in jail. Formerly all prisoners on being discharged had their hair cut very close. Metaphorically the term is used for serving time in jail.

"Wỳt ti'n shŵr o gâl y cownti-cròp os na fiâfi di'n well."

You will be sure to find yourself one day in jail if you do not behave better.

Cowrw [= cyfrwy.] N.m.s. A saddle.

Crab N.m.s. A small iron trivet or stand used with culm fires, and placed thereon for the purpose of holding kettles.

Crabachlyd Adj. Miserly.

Crabwtshyn N.m.s. A puny fellow, and metaphorically, an insignificant fellow.

Crach N.f.pl. Grievances—metaphorically so used in the saying, *codi hen grâch*—raking up old grievances.

Crachen N.f.s. An ox-shoe.

There is no plural, but the cardinal *un, dwy, tair*, &c., is used to denote the number implied. The term *pedol ich* is never heard, but *crachen ich.* The *crachen* was made much in the shape of the claw of the hoof—one *crachen* for each claw, with three slender nails to attach them, as shown in the accompanying drawing.

Crach-y
  -pentan N.f.pl. Fireside gossips. A term of contempt applied to old women who gather together around the fire to discuss their neighbours.

Crafan-y
  -moch N.m.pl. Haw.

Crafi V. Trans. To clean, to peal.

In the phrase *crafi tato*, cleaning, or peeling potatoes.

Crafishcyn
  -starfo N.m.s. A phantom; a thin, lean, unreal thing. Often said of a mere skeleton of a man.

During a recent General Election, some local wag described the Tariff Reform movement as " hen grafishcyn starfo," and raised a great laugh at the expense of the Conservative candidate.

Craflon Coll. n. Hay or corn that is gathered in a field with the small hand rake after the bulk has been taken away.

Crafu V. Intran. To crawl.

" Fe grafodd 'rhen garan mor belled a phont Gotty, a man 'ny marw hi.''

The poor old thing crawled as far as Cotty bridge, and there she died.

F

Cramansh Coll. n. The sediment which forms at the bottom of the pan in the process of making candles. (Pron. cra-mànsh).

Cramen-y -cerrig N.f.s. Lichen.

Crantin N.m.s. A dwarf.
Fem. *Cranten.*

Crapach N.m.s. The benumbing of the fingers with cold.

Cras Adj. Rough or metallic, applied only to the timbre of the voice. (Pron. crâs).

Crasen N.f.s. Crest for building purposes.

Crasfa N.f.s. A thrashing, a beating.

Cratshan Part. Creaking.
" Gweitho nes bod 'i esgyrn e'n cratshan."
Working till his bones are creaking.

Crec N.m.s. A trice, a moment.
" Dewch miwn crèc! "
Come in a trice!

Crecwil N.m.s. An insignificant, delicate fellow. Often said of a puny, good-for-nothing child.
" Yr hen grecwil bach! "
You insignificant little thing!

Crechi-din -don N.m.s. A crane,—the bird so called. (Accent on *din*).

Cregin N.f.pl. Broken bits of crockery scattered about, or collected together in a heap.

Creignor N.m.s. A magician, or one who, versed in black art, by craft and cunning is able to induce the Devil to have a conversation with him.

Creso

V. Intran. To multiply, to increase. Said of weeds multiplying in a garden.

" Dina hen wreidde drwg i grêso yw rhain."

These are roots bad to increase, or spread.

Cresten

N.f.s. A riff: the wooden riff used for sharpening scythes. There were two kinds, *rhip gresten* and *rhip sand-o-fán* (q.d.). The *cresten* was encrusted by means of alternate layers of hog's lard and sand, till it attained a depth of about four inches, when it was considered the ideal thing for edge. There are specimens in the Welsh Museum.

Cretsh

N.m.s. The tail-board of a cart.

Cretshen-yr
-afon

N.f.s. Water-parsnip.

Crenog

Adj. Full-blooded, applied to a person with a red, bloated face.

Crib-ddadris

N.f.s. A dressing comb.

Crib-fan

N.f.s. A small tooth comb.

Cribion

Coll. n. Combings, i.e., hair which comes off in the comb in dressing the hair.

Crib-y-cerrig

N.m.s. Stone moss.

Cric-y-berth

N.m.s. The blackcap, the bird so called.

Cric-y
-pentan

N.m.s. Cricket, i.e., the insect so called.

Crigwen

V. Trans. To gather together, to accumulate, to store. (Three sylls., accent on *gw*).

" Crigwen cifoth "—to amass riches.

" Crigwen moddion tŷ "—accumulating 'furniture.

Crimpen N.f.s. Oaten-meal cake or bread baked crisp.

Crimpo V. Tran. To air before a fire.
"Crimpo dillad y gwely."
To air (before a fire) the bedclothes.

Crino Adj. Neat, prim and prop. Often used in the much wider sense of energetic as to worldly advancemerft, striving, &c.

Crinshal Part. Crunching, with the teeth; producing a sound with the teeth in chewing anything hard. It is used also of the gritty sound produced by crushing rubbish under the feet.

Crinhail N.m.s. A small bundle of rushes dried for the purpose of making shackles, cord, &c.
The following is the *mesur brwyn* of Dyfed:—
Douddeg ugen o frwyn neith un grinshil,
Dwy grinshil neith flân a bôna,
Douddeg blân a bôua neith isgub.

Crinshon Adj. Dry and powdered.

Cripil N.m.s. A cripple
Adj. Cripple.

Criplyn N.m.s. A cripple.
Fem. *Criplen.*

Crishpin N.m.s. A clog-maker.
"Ma'n rhaid i fi fyn'd at crishpin."
I must go to the clog-maker, i.e., I must have new clogs, or have my clogs repaired. It is never used of a boot-maker.

Crithi Part. Trembling with fear or anger.
"Mae e'n crithi gida'i natur."
He is trembling with passion.

Criws Abs. n. A boose.

Crochon
-medl N.m.s. The big kettle or cauldron in which broth was made at harvest-tide. It contained about 20 gallons. Sufficient broth would be boiled on Monday to last over Wednesday, and on Thursday to last over Sunday. The *cawl cineia* was a celebrated dish, containing an example of pretty nearly everything of an edible nature that grew in the garden. A whole ham, or half a flitch, together with a big piece of dried beef, would be put in the cauldron, and form a solid basis for the appetising meal.

Crochon-y
-gweir N.m.s. Lit. the pot-of-pain.

This was a crock, or earthenware vessel, concealed in a hole dug in the garden, made to contain tallow candles, in the days when this latter necessary article was taxed.

Crongol [= cronglwyd.] N.m.s. Roof.

Croishi-
-gwddwg A euphemism for "cutting the throat," suicide.

"Druan a Shecci'r Gelli, mae e wedi croishi 'i wddwg."

Poor John of Gelli, he has cut his throat; lit.: he has crossed his throat.

Cropyn
-eithin N.m.s. A furze bush, or a single branch of furze or whin.

Croth-y-
-fesen N.f.s. Acorn-cup. This word, still retained in the Demetian dialect, would seem to point back to the time when the acorn in its cup was an emblem of fecundity in phallic worship.

Croulon [= creulawn.] Adj. Cruel.

Crowner   N.m.s. Coroner.

Crwen-dene   Adj. and adv. Sensitive, easily offended.

Crwen-gwydd   N.m.s. A term applied to a condition of the human skin in cold weather, when it resembles goose skin.

Crwes-dibieth   N.m.s. Prejudice.
" Dyn parchus yw'n ffeiriad ni, sta ge ddim crŵes-dibieth yn erbyn un enwad."
Our parson is a respected man—he has no prejudice against any denomination.

Crwgwd   Abs. n. A crouching posture.

Grwn   Indef. Pron. All.
" Ma nw wedi dwad bwti yn grwn nawr."
They have all come home now.

Crwshed   A good quantity of anything.
" Ma crwshed o lâth da'r fuwch hon."
This cow has a large quantity of milk.

Crwth   in the phrase " canu-'i-chrŵth "—the purring of a cat.

Cryfdwr   Abs. n. Strength; nearly always restricted to strength in reference to numbers.

Cwafars   N.m.pl. Ornamentals, especially ornamental lettering.
" Ma John Jâms yn gallu tori llithrene cwafars."
John James is able to make ornamental letters.

Cwal   N.c.s. Quail—the bird so called. (Pron. cwâl).

Cwan   [= cywion.] Chickens. (Pron. cwân).

Cwanen N.f.s. A pullet.

Cwartar N.m.s. Neighbourhood, frequently used in this sense.

Cwato V. Tran. and Intran. To hide.

Cwcen N.f.s. A small cake, about the size of a penny bun, made with flour, milk, and lard. Plur. *cwcod*.

Cwdwm-coler
,, -gwasg
,, -penlin } N.m.s. Different styles of wrestling.
,, -ahiglo
,, -towlu

Cwdwmo [= codymu.] V. Intran. To wrestle.

Cwel N.f.s. A lap. (Pron. cŵ-el).

Cwen [= cywain.] N.m.pl. Chickens. (Pron. cŵ-en). A variant is *cwdn*.

Cwesta V. Intran. To go about begging alms at the time of a death ; to beg money to help bury the dead.

Cwffins N.f.pl. Cuffs.
Sing. *cwffinsen*, and sometimes *cwffsen*.

Cwibir [= crwybr.] N.m.pl. Honeycomb.
The sing. *cwibren* is feminine.
(Pron. cwi-bir, consonantal *w*).

Cwilo V. Tran. (1) To iron with a particular iron the border or frills of the old-fashioned Welsh cap.
(2) To coil a rope.

Cwilsen N.f.s. A quill.
Cwilsen
·screfenu A writing quill.

Cwilsen-fran A writing quill procured from a crow's wing. Documents were formerly engrossed with this kind of quill, which was preferred to goose quill on account of its greater toughness and finer point.

Cwilsen -wydd N.f.s. A goose quill, for writing.

Cwiltreg N.f.s. A female quilt maker. Many young women used to earn their livelihood at this occupation formerly.

Cwinten N.f.s. A rope covered with thorns used for throwing across a road at weddings, to stop the wedding party on their way from church, for the purpose of extracting a *ffwtin* (q.v.) from them.

Cwiro and Cwro V. Trans. (1) To make, (2) to prepare, &c.
" Cwiro gwair "—haymaking.
" Cwiro menyn "—to make butter.
" Cwiro dillad " — to mend clothes.

Cwlffin N.m.s. A slice of anything, but especially of bread.

Cwlwm N.m.s. Culm, small anthracite coal.
" Tân cwlwm "—culm fire.

Cwlwm N.m.s. A knot. Here are the chief kinds in use : —
Cwlwm llinglwm—a single knot.
,,   *dolen*—a loop knot.
,,   *rhedeg*—a slip knot.
,,   *morwr*—a sailor's knot.
,,   *penglwm*—a double knot.
,,   *lligad*—an end knot put into a slip knot. Cattle are tied in this way to the post.
,,   *bach-a-lligad*—a hook-and-eye knot.
,,   *dolen-ddwbwl*—a double-looped knot.

Cwlwm *doupen*—a knot made by putting both ends of a string through one loop.

,, *esglwm*—a double twisted knot.

,, *pôs*—a puzzle knot.

,, *hèr*—a peculiar knot. This is used when it is not desired that the knot should be untied. If made tightly, it is almost impossible to untie it.

Cwm-bwlet   N.m.s. A popgun.

Made of the same material as *cwm-dwr* (q.v.) and in the same way, except that the piston had no yarn tied around it. The " shot " consisted of paper chewed into a pulp, and the " powder " was the air compressed in the barrel.

Cwm-cwilsen   N.m.s. A popgun made of goose-quill, with sliced potato for " shot." *Cwm-cwils* were the " arms " used by the " pistol-brigade " at a school fight.

Cwm-dwr   N.m.s. A syringe, a whistrel.

Made of a piece of elder rod, with the pith cleaned out. The piston was made of, willow, with yarn wound around the end in lieu of indiarubber. School children formerly used to range themselves on either side of a brook and play at war with *cwm-dwre* for cannon, and *cwm-bwleti* for rifles.

Cwmffwr -ddus   Adj. Comfortable.

Cwmpassol   Adj. Of moderate size.

" Dâs bach cwmpassol."

A moderate sized stack [of hay or corn.]

Cwmpassu   V. Tran. and Intran. To complete, to hurry, etc.

" Cwmpassu'r gwaith "—to finish the work.

"Dewch i ni gal cwmpassu nawr, i ni gal mynd i'r isgol gân heno."

Let us hurry now that we may go to the singing practice this evening.

Cwmpni [= cwmni.] Abs. and c.n.

(1) Company, i.e., the quality regarded *per se*.

(2) Two or more together.

Cwmpo-mas V. Intran. To quarrel.

Cwmryd [=cymmeryd.] V. Tran. To take.

Cwmwle N.m.pl. Clouds.

Local names of different clouds are:—

Cwmwle cawn—Clouds with parallel flexuous or diverging fibres, extensible in any or all directions.

  ,, *boliog*—Cirro stratus.

  ,, *coprog*—Bronzed cirro stratus. These are said to indicate thunder.

  ,, *caws a maidd*—The cirro cumulus, commonly called mackerel sky.

  ,, *duon*—Rain clouds.

  ,, *torgoch*—Dusky clouds with red fringes, said to indicate rough weather.

  ,, *minidde*—Clouds that appear in the distance like mountains.

  ,, *piscod owyr*—Long stripes of clouds which have the appearance of large fish.

Cwmwys Adj. Perpendicular, level, hanging evenly.

"Dyw'r pictwr 'na ddim yn gwmwys."

That picture does not hang evenly.

Cwnsaint Abs. n. Suspicion.

Cwnsaintlyd   Adj. Suspicious.
"Dyn cwnsaintlyd."
A suspicious man.

Cwnsela   V. Intran. To talk privately.
"Beth i chi'n cwnsela a'ch gily fanâ yn y cornel?"
What are you talking about privately there in the corner?

Cwnsel-y-claw   N.m.s. A soliloquist, a man who talks to hedges.

Cwnsheri   V. Tran. To conjure.

Cwnsherwr   N.m.s. A wizard.

Cwnstaff   N.m.s. Constable, i.e., of the olden days, when one of the parishioners was "sworn in to look after the peace," by the Lord of the Manor at the old Court Leet. He was chosen from among the more respectable of the people "amid a not inconsiderable degree of sway and ceremony"—so observes an old writer. If he refused to act a writ of mandamus was served upon him, and if he still declined he was fined or imprisoned.

Cwpla   [= cyplysu.] V. Tran. To tie two together.

Cwpwl   N.m.pl. Two tied together.

Cwrcwd   Abs. n. A bent position. A person that is bent with age is said to be yn 'i gwrcwd.

Cwrdeb   N.m.s. Rennet.

Cwrdo   Part. Writhing.
"Own i'n cwrdo gida'r bŵen."
I was writhing with the pain.

Cwrdd [= cyffwrdd.] V. Intran. To touch.
"Paid cwrdd ag e."
Don't touch it.

Cwrdd-bach Abs. n. (1) An entertainment. (2) A cottage meeting.

"Ma cwrdd-bach i fod yn Isgol-y-Cwm nos Iou nesa."

There will be an entertainment in the Cwm Schoolroom next Thursday evening.

Cottage meetings are invariably called *cwrdde-bach*.

Cwrdd-mowr N.m.s. The monthly Communion Service of Nonconformists, usually held on the first Sunday in the month. It is never called *Cwrdd Cymundeb*.

Cwrdd -partoad N.m.s. A preparatory meeting. The meeting held by Dissenters once a month preparatory to the Communion Service. Usually held on a Friday afternoon at 3 o'clock.

Cwrdd -whech N.m.s. The Sunday evening meeting at dissenting places of worship. The meeting is usually supposed to commence at 6 o'clock— hence the name. As a matter of fact it rarely commences till 6.30, my countrymen being proverbial for their unpunctuality. Whatever the hour, the meeting is always called *cwrdd-whech*. (Accent on second element of word).

Cwrens Coll. n. Currants.

Cwrlin N.m.s. A curly-headed one.
Fem. *cwrlen*.

Cwro V. Tran. and Intran. To heal, to mend, to be healed, cured, mended.

"Fe dorres ynghlin, ond mae wedi cwro."
I broke my leg, but it has set.
"Cwrwch y rhacca."
Mend the rake.

Cwrpin   N.m.s. The fello of a wheel.

Cwrpno   Adv. Very tired; i.e., so tired that one cannot stand erect, but is bent up like the fello of a wheel.

Cwrt-bach   N.m.s. Court of petty sessions.

Cwrt-mowr   County Court.

Cwrtshwns   N.m.pl. Blinds, curtains.
The word is used indifferently for blinds, window curtains or bed curtains.

Cwrwm   To be in a double, a bent position, a stooping.

Cwsno   V. Tran. To coax, to stimulate.
(1) "Ma rhaid treio cwsno'r tân ma, te fe ddiffodith."
This fire must be coaxed, or it will go out.
(2) "Cwsnwch dipyn arno, mae e'n bur bengam."
He is very stupid, coax him a little.

Cwt   Used in a peculiar sense in the following expression: "Ma cwt gida'r ddiod," literally, the beer has a tail, meaning that the liquid has a sort of unpleasant after-taste.

Cwta   Adv. Abruptly.
"Fe âth rhai geire rhwnt Deio Blanffwes a finne, ond fe drows bant yn gwta cyn i ni fyn'd at fôn y peth."
David, of Blaenffoes, and myself had words, but we could not get at the root of the thing, for he went away abruptly.

Cwta   N.m.s. A lot.
" Tini blewyn cwta "—Casting lots. Several pieces of sticks or grass of various lengths were concealed in the hand, their ends only protruding; these were drawn in rotation, and the shortest was called *y blewyn cwta*. The lot fell on the person who drew this.

Cwtloni   Part. Wagging the tail in a friendly manner, said of a dog.

Cwtshin   Abs. n. Courtesy, an act of civility made by women and girls towards their superiors.

Cwtsho   V. Intran. To crouch, to stoop.
" Cwtshwch lawr."
Stoop down.

Cwt-yr-wyn bach   Hazel catkins.

Cwthwm   in the phrases
Cwthwm o wynt = a puff of wind.
Cwthwm-tro = a whirlwind.

Ɖ

Da   [= gyda.] Prep. With.
"Dewch da fi."
Come with me.

Dablin   N.m.s. A pointed piece of steel fixed on the end of a walking stick, or of a *pren bugila*, to help grip the ground.

Dab   N.m.s. A kind of fence placed on the top of a clod hedge, at either edge, and obliquely to the perpendicular of the hedge. It consists of slender branches, which are wattled together something after this fashion.

Dach   [= gyda chwi.] P. Prep. With you.
"Dewch ag e dâch.'
Bring it with you.

Dadmodd   Abs. n. Something laid by against need—"for a rainy day." as is expressed in common parlance.
"Dadmodd rhwnt dyn a'r gweitha."
Something between a man and the worst.

Dadris   V. Trans. To comb.
"Dadris gwallt."
To comb hair.

Dafetwr   N.m.s. One who rears sheep, also one who is a good hand at managing sheep.

Dagre-Mair   A garden flower, with a spotted leaf. Lit.: The tears of Mary.

Dail-brenig Rose of Sharon (Hypericum calycinum).
Much used as a preservative against the clothes moth.

Dailcawl N.pl. Rape.
" Parced o ddailcawl."
A field of rape.

Dail-dringol N.pl. The sour dock. Much used formerly in dyeing stockings and other woollen wear black. The juice was extracted by steeping the leaves in *Ueishw* (human urine).

Dail-llosc
   -tan N.m.pl. The water-wort, an aquatic plant of the genus elatine.

Dail-trad-yr
   ebol N.f.pl. The herb colt's-foot.

Dail-y
   -geinog Pennywort (Cotyledon umbilicus).

Dal Abs. n. Reliance, trust.
" Stim dàl ar y tewy."
There is no trusting the weather.
" Stim dàl ar yr hen Wil Shams."
There is no reliance [or confidence] to be put upon William James.

Dala V. Intran. To harness horses, to turn out with a team.
" Mae'n bryd dala, onte chewn ni ddim cifer cifan heddy."
It is time to turn out with the team, else we shall not put in a full turn to-day.

Dala V. Intran. (1) To ask. (2) To bet. (3, To read signs.
   (1) " Be chi'n ddala ar y ŵyn? "
      What price do you ask for the lambs?
   (2) " Mi ddala i swllt a chi."
      I will bet you a shilling.

(3) " Dala ar arwyddion y tewy."

Reading [or watching] the signs of the weather.

**Dala-pen
-rheswm** Having a confab, talking together on matters of interest.

Dale N.f.pl. Leaves. *Dail* is used here in a collective sense, and *dale* in a distributive sense.

**Dalen-y
-crwman** N.f.s. Plantain leaf, i.e., the – ribwort plantain.

**Dale-surion
-bach** N.f.pl. The wood-sorrel.

Dal-trwyne Adv. phrase. Holding or maintaining the price, to be stiff in the price.

" Pan weles i fod cistal prishodd am yr wyn, mi ddales i 'i trwyne nw finy."

When I saw that the price of lambs was good, I held stiff to my own figure; lit.: " I held up their noses."

Dallgipio V. Tran. To waylay.

Dampo V. Tran. and Intran. To damp.
(1) " I chi wedi dampo 'ch dillad? "
Have you damped your clothes?
(2) " Odych chi wedi dampo? "
Are you damp?

Damprwydd Abs. n. (1) Dampness. (2) Timidity.

Damshil V. Tran. and Intran. To tread, tread upon. A variant is *damshel*.

Daran [= hytrach.] Adv. Rather, somewhat.
"Mae'n daran llaith i fynd i rwmo."
It is rather damp to go to bind (corn).

G

Darfod
Part. A euphemism for " being dead."
" Ma Shanw 'r Ddôl, druan, wedi darfod."
Poor Jane, of Dôl, is dead.

Darlwgu
V. Intran. To be parched with thirst.
" Bron a darlwgu 'n lân o eishe diferyn o ddwr."
Nearly parched with thirst for the want of a drop of water.

Darllis
-bentai
N.f.pl. The house-leek.
Sing. *Darllisen.*
These were regarded as a specific for the *rhwden* (ringworm).

Darrig
Adv. Briskly, quickly, strongly.
" Ma gwynt cryf 'da 'i, mae 'n sichu 'n darrig."
There is a strong wind, it is drying quickly.

Daru
[= darfu.] It happened, it fell out, &c.
" Pan ddaru nw fynd."
When they went.
In a number of instances the word cannot be translated.

Dambwyll
Adv. (1) Slowly.
(2) V. Imper. mood. Take time, go slowly.
(3) Inter. Hold! (Accent on last syllable).

Damper
N.m.s. A tot, a measure smaller than a pint, holding twopenny-worth of beer. It is often called a *bliw* (q.v.).

Damshil
[= damsang.] V. Tran. and Intran. To tread, to tread upon.

Dandis
N.m.pl. A game played with marbles and shells or small round stones.

Dane   in the phrase *ar weitha 'i ddane fe* = in defiance of, in spite of; literally, on the worst of his teeth—a very peculiar idiom.

Dane-bargod   N.m.pl. Projecting teeth.
"Merch escirnog a brichni,
Dane-bargod a chrichni,
Shidan glas ar war 'i chefen,
A mil neu ddwy yn i choden."
—(An old Saw).

Dansher   Abs. n. Danger. *(Sh* like in *shall).*

Dansherus   Adj. and adv. Dangerous; dangerously.

Danto   V. Intran. To be daunted, discouraged.
"Wdw i wedi danto 'n lân nawr."
I am quite discouraged now.

Darlimpo   V. Tran. To swallow hurriedly.

Darlwncu   V. Intran. To make the motion of swallowing with the throat; to pretend to swallow.

Daro   Inter. Bother!
Daro i! and *daro fach* i! are expressions frequently heard.

Dat   N.m.s. Date.
" Mâs o ddât."
Out of date.

Dawch   [= da i chwi.] In the phrase *nos dawch!* = good-night!

Dawn   N.f.s. In Pembrokeshire the word has the same signification as the word "hwyl" elsewhere; it never refers to ability, gift, or talent. By " dawn bregethu " in N. Pembrokeshire is meant, not the gift of preaching, but the ability to preach with the inflexion of voice called "hwyl." *Dawnus* and *doniol* are Adjs. referring to the same thing.

Decon-pren   N.m.s. Lit.: A wooden deacon. A deacon in a dissenting chapel who will not take part at extempore prayer meetings. Old William Havard, of Penbank's definition of a *deconpren* was—"Dyn sy fel pòst ièt, yn dda iawn i glwmu peth wrtho."

Delalti   N.m.s. An ointment used for cows' udders.

Deiareb   [= diareb.] N.f.s. A proverb. The North Pembrokeshire folk express themselves frequently in proverbs and other trite sayings. Following is a list of *deiarebion*, which will serve to show that Dyfed is virgin soil as far as the proverb hunter is concerned, as well as illustrate the use of some curious words:—

"Gwỳna gwỳn po nesa du."
"Yng ngene'r sàch ma tolio."
"Ma campunt miwn llawes [merch] yn well na campunt miwn llogell."
"Houa dy gwnsel yn yr hwyr, ti gei fedi o hono 'n y bore."
"Talu'r rhent i flân 'i drwyn." (Said of a drunkard).
"Yn nhrâd 'i sane ma dewish gwraig."
"Nid wrth 'i big ma nabod cwffwlog."
"Nid wrth 'i chòt fowr ma nabod crefydd."
"Crifa taro, peido taro."
"Hir pob aros ond ange."
"Ma llawer ffordd i ladd ci heb 'i grogi e."
"Fe gwsg galar, ond ni chwsg gofid."
"Dihuna pob diawl pan gwsg cidwibod."

" Y cinta i'r felin bia'r mâl."

" Gwalch all gwrdd gwalch."

" Rhoi cingor merch y crydd " (i.e., giving
a kick).

" I'r môr y rhed yr afon " (meaning that to
him that hath shall be given).

" Ma cân bert gan dderyn du."

" Gwell brichgau march gwyllt na thimer
ddrwg."

" Angel pen stôl a diawl pen ffair."

" Nid a bladur ma hollti blewyn."

" Ni fyn drewgi ddrewi neb ond 'i hunan."

" Minwared medd y ffeirad, minwared medd
y clochy."

" Twlc mochyn fydd twlc mochyn er 'i wyn-
galchu."

" Myn'd o'r ffreimpan i'r tân."

" Mae fel dŵr ar gewn whiaden."

" Mae'n mesur pob un a'i lathed 'i hunan."

" Ffrinsieth ci a chath yw ffrinsieth lleidir
ac ispeiliwr."

" Stim eishe'r ffinon cyn iddi sichu."

" Croga di leidir neu fe groga lleidir di."

" Hwch yn myn'd i Llenden a hwch yn
dwad gatre."

" Iscawn pob baich ond 'i faich 'i hunan."

" Llincu cawr ac esgor ar goryn."

" Hès da'r ci a how da'r cadno."

" Rhoi'r cart o flân y ceffyl."

" Hwch fud fyt y swêg i gyd."

" Dŵeth fydd dwl tra taw."

" Hai o hyd y ceffyl parod."

" 'Dwes neb mor droidnoth a phlant y crydd."

" Gwell rhanu punt rhwnt dou na rhoi 'i
mhentig hi i un."

" Gwell pwrnu'n ddrud na gwerthu'n rhad."

" Nid a rhaw ma rhwyfo cwch."

" Trech dysc na diddysc, ond trech dawn na dysc."

" Nid wedi i'r ebol jengyd ma cau drws y stabal."

" Nid a mwrthwl pren ma girru hŵel."

" Gwell cingor y da na chimorth y drwg."

" Ma côf maith gida hen gi."

" Gore moithyn whant bwyd."

" Cyn gneyd drwg ma bod yn edifar."

" Nid yw cimmeriad da yn gwella wrth 'i gamol, ac ma un drwg yn gwaithigu."

" Myn'd i'r ffair i mofyn neges." (Said of a man who goes to a fair on no particular business, and who returns with a pair of blackened eyes).

" Goreu barn, barn gifiawn."

" Uchaf llis [llys], llis cidwibod."

" Cynt rhed birgam [byr gam] at ofid na hirgam oddiwrtho."

" Erlid baw rhai erill a dwyno 'i [dirty] bilyn 'i hunan."

" Newidir dim anian asyn wrth gropo 'i gluste."

" Anhawdd cario dŵr miwn gwagar."

" Wrth ddilyn drwg y daw mowrddrwg."

" Anhawdd twyllo hen dderyn ag us."

" Plant Deio'r twyllwr geith 'u twyllo ginta."

" Mae'n hawddach cwato rhag cawed na'i stoppo hi."

" Nafel a gwin i niflyd y gofid." (Drinking wine to drown sorrow).

" Gwell heb esgid na bod wrth un."

" 'Run seis yw iet parc bach a iet parc mowr."

" Haws holi pwnc [q.v.] nag aped."

" Nid mewn ffair y codir ffeirad."

" Gellir pligu'r gangen, ond rhaid tori'r goiden."

" Ma pidere ar wddwg Rhagrith, a wîc-wâc yn 'i thrâd hi."

" Nid a bach-a-lligad ma midrwyo mochyn."

" Blewyn dagodd y deryn, nid mwydyn."

" Bola llawn sy'n hollti, nid bola gwag."

" Ma crefydd dyn, fel nerth shain [chain], i'w phrofi yn y man gwana."

" Yr iglan [q.v.] ar gefen y ceffyl heddy, a'r ceffyl ar gefen yr iglan fory."

" Y mae gan hen oson [q.v.] lawer o berthnase."

" Gweithaf taro, taro'r gwàn."

" Goreu llôg, llôg gonestrwydd."

" Gwell salw na sâl."

" Wedi i ddiogi ddachre cripial, fydd hano 'n hir cyn cered."

" Ma dou fath o ddigon : digon bach a digon mowr."

" Ni chân aderyn ar ei nyth."

" Ni raid girru buwch i bori, ma agor y ièt yn ddigon."

" Ma whỳn yn tiddu heb 'u gosod na'u trin."

" Gida Tad y Celwy ma'r teulu mwya."

" Y gwendid mwya yw ofon."

" Lloged [q.v.] y diwyd yw lligad y dydd."

" Cered lwir-i-din, fel diawl yn mynd at râs."

" Ma man gwỳn yr anfodlongar o hyd man draw."

" ' Pob un ar 'i ffèns 'i hunan,' ys dŵad y diawl wrth 'i fam."

" Eith baich ddim yn llai wrth newid isowydd, ond fe eith yn fwy wrth beido."

" Penrheswm eboles yw penwast."

" Crefydd Balaam : whant byw 'n ddŵl a marw 'n dduwiol."

" Sheci'r holi mwya
Gliwith gelwi amla."

" Siwra cwlwm, cwlwm tafod " (i.e., matrimony).

" Trecha treished, gwana gweidded."

" Rhaid i'r sawl gano'r gloch odde'r swn."

" Nês penelin na garddwn."

" Wen man hyn a mharen man draw." (Said
of a burden which becomes heavier the further
it is carried).

" Sawl nâth y cawl raid i ifed e."

" Gwaith binewyd yw torri twll, gwaith
hoelen yw 'i lenwi e."

" Ma dyn fel dwr a'i fryd ar fyn'd."

" Nid ar gais gwr y cwyd y gwynt."

" Ma cistal piscod yn y môr ag a ddalwd."

" Ma cistal cŵed yn yr allt ag a dorrwd."
(These two are spoken to console a man who
has lost his sweetheart).

" Gwerth peth yw 'i brinder ac nid 'i brîsh."

" Torri'r gwir i gwro celwy." (The idea is
that if you want to cure a liar, you must not
believe him when he speaks the truth).

Os cregin gweigon fydd yn y sâch, cregin
gweigon ddaw mas o hani."

" Gall newy drwg hedfan heb un aden."

" Picleryn [q.v.] y defed yw ŵen swcci."

" Ma broga blwydd yn lladd broga dwy-
flwydd."

" Mofyn gordd i gnoco gwïbedyn." (Said
when a deed accomplished is not commensurate
with the energy expended).

" Ffusto'r heiarn tra fyddo'n gôch."

" Taro'r hŵel ar 'i chlòpa."

" Gweyd celwy fel ci yn ifed cawl."

" Anodd cal oaws o fola ci."

" Cistal gan gi garan a chawl."

" Esmwyth cwsg cawl erfin."

" Mwyaf golud yw gras."

" Gall cwmmwl bach guddio'r houl, os bydd
e'n gwmmwl agos."

" Gwell ffrwyn na ffòn at nâd ddrwg."

" Rhaid torri r pilyn yn ol y brethin."

" Hir y daw celwy' adre, ond pan ddaw fe
ddel a i dilwyth gidag e."

" Coched gwâd y tlawd a gwâd t'wysog."

" Difal donc a dor y gareg."

" Anhawdd gwaith gweidu careg."

" Gall pob hen geilog wmla ar 'i ddomen 'i hunan."

" Y bore bia'r dydd."

" Hirach nôl na mlân, fel rhiw Tredin " (q.v.).

" Gneyd melin âg [ac] Eglws o hani."

" Dala twsw o flan y ffrwyn." (Often used for dissimulation).

" Prin caiff amser sichu a wlîch ei grys dros arall."

" Unwaith yn hènddyn, dwywaith yn ddwlyn."

" Unwaith yn hen, dwywaith yn blentyn."

" Taith bell yw byth."

" Gwell hwyr na hwyrach."

" A geir yn rhad gerdd yn rhwydd."

" Fe aped carreg, ond prin y daw." (Vide carreg aped).

" Ma barn gan ffwl, ond barn ffwl yw 'i."

" Hwnnw ddiawl ato githrel."

" Ma tafod llym yn dala hawch heb 'i hogi."

" Cuwch cŵd a ffetan."

" Trêch gwlad nac Arglwydd, ond trêch gwir na'r ddou."

" Rhwnt dwy stôl yn cwmpo i'r llawr."

" Brawd mogi yw tagu."

" Taith hoilen ŵyth, o'r blân i'r bôn."

" Ni chyll y gwir 'i bwyse."

" Dina pryd ceir hufen heb gâl llâth, pan eith y byd yn bedyll."

" Talu fel cibydd, trwy din 'i ddwrn."

" Llawer o fŵg a 'chidig o dân."

" Bâch, ond nid digon bâch, fel pigad whanen."

" Morgrugyn miwn oson a whanen miwn clust." (Said of a cantankerous person).

" Ni chyll 'i nabod yn mhig y frân."

" Mofyn 'i anal o'r pridd." (Said of an old man on his " last legs ").

" Mae'n hawsach cinu tân ar hen eilwd nag ar un newy."

" Ede rhy dyn a dor."

" Iach dreni pen cachci."

" Taith henddyn o'r pinwyn i'r pentan."

" Try yn llawen poen a lwydda." (The meaning would appear to be that pain is joy in the making).

" Diwedd y gân yw y geinog."

" Digon dawr digon."

" Brawd pengam yw gwirgam."

" Ma'r bobol sy'n rhoi wedi marw."

" Swydd heb barch, swydd heb ddiolch."

" Swydd heb arch, swydd heb barch."

" Y ci a gerddo geith asgwrn i bilo."

" Talu diled 'i âch yn echraint."

" Towlu 'i ddiled dros bont ange."

[Perhaps these two proverbs are an echo of the Druidic belief that debts contracted in this world could be repaid in the next.]

Deimwnt
N.m.s. Diamond. A glazier's tool for cutting glass.

Deir
Adv. Slow, tedious.

" Pethe deir iawn i'w clasgu yw llise duon bach."

Picking winberries is very tedious work.

Deiro
V. Tran. To slander.

" Hen griadur dansherus yw Shanw, mae'n deiro pawb byth a hefyd."

Shanw is a dangerous creature, she is for ever slandering people.

Deis
An expletive.

" Deis i fach i, mae'n bryd mynd."

Goodness me, it is time to go.

Del Coll. n. Deal trees.
Sing. *delen*.
"Plantashon dèl."
Deal plantation.

Delers Coll. n. Dealers, cattle drovers. There is
not a singular; when one dealer is spoken of,
he is termed *pwrnwr*.

Delff } Adj. and Adv. Stupid, dull, slow of compre-
Delffedd } hension. Same as " daft " in Provincial English.

Delffo V. Intran. To dote upon.
"Mae e'n delffo ar y plentyn."
He dotes upon the child.

Denfydd [= defnydd.] (1) Material. (2) Use.
"Pwy ddenfydd yw e? "
What material is it?
"Dyw e o un denfydd yn y byd."
It is of no earthly use.

Dere Irreg. V. 2 Sing. Imper. Come thou.
"Dere ma."
Come here.

Derinod [= adar.] Birds.

Deryn-corph The death bird. "A bogle which a little
over a generation ago helped to keep in good
behaviour at night time the young people of
those days."

**Deryn-glas
-yr-afon** N.m.s. Kingfisher.

Desim [= deuthum.] V. Intran. I came.

Dest [= daethost.] Thou camest, didst come.

Dewan   [= deuant.] Irreg. V. *Dyfod*.
The various dialect forms of *dyfod* could be given only in a grammar.

Dewe   [= deuai.] Irreg. V. Subj. mood, also the Interrog. form of *dyfod*.
"Fel y dewe fe."
"Dewe nw?" &c.

Diarebi   V. Trans. and Intran. To scandalize, to speak offensively about one, to condemn, &c.
(1) "Ma' nhw'n diarebi y pregethwr yn ofnadwy."
They scandalize the preacher awfully.
(2) "Ma' nhw wedi mynd i ddiarebi am dano."
They have begun to speak offensively about him.

Diar-i-bono-i   Inter. Gracious me!
A variant is *jâr-i-bono-i!*

Dibal   That which is ruined.
"Hen ddibal o le."
A ruined old place.
[Query. Is it connected with Fr. *debâcle?*]

Dibendod   Abs. n. Untidyness, slovenliness.
Used interchangeably with *annibendod*.

Dibin-doben   Topsy-turvy. Onomatopœic.

Dibinu   [= ymddibynu.] Part. Depending upon.

Dibrish   Adj. Reckless.
"Hen griadur dibrish."
A reckless old fellow.
This is the only sense in which the word is used here.

Dic-doc   The ticking of a clock.

Dici-doca-do   A game. A number of inter-
secting lines are made on a slate,
and the players, two in number,
place a X and an O alternately
in each square.   One tries to get
three X's or three O's as the case
may be, to stand in line, whether
vertically, horizontally, or diagonally, and the
other tries to prevent it.   When one succeeds he-
cries *dici doca do*, and scores a point.

Dico   [= dacw.]   See yonder, see there.

Dichlyn   V. Intran.   To separate, to loosen.
" Ma'r coce gwair wedi myn'd yn stecs gida'r
glaw, stim ffordd 'u dichlyn nw."
The hay tumps have become a mass of jelly
with the rain, it is impossible to loosen and
spread them.

Dichmigieth   Abs. n.   Idea, conception.

Didaro   Adj. Nonchalant.
" Mae e'n hollol ddidaro; tae'r wibir yn
mynd yn bedyll, simide fe ddim gam yn nghynt
na'i gily."
he is quite nonchalant [or cool]; if the
firmament became pans, he would not move one
step the faster.

Didol   Adj. and Adv.   Extravagant, unsparingly.
(Accent on second syll.).
(1) " Criadur didòl iawn yw hi."
She is an extravagant creature.
(2) " Mi roisym i bryd o dafod yn ddidòl
iddo."
I gave him my tongue unsparingly; lit. " I
gave him a meal of tongue unsparingly."

Didoreth   Adj. Extravagant.

Diddal

Adj. Unstable.
" Mor ddi-ddal a cheilog-y-gwynt."
As unstable as a weathercock.

Didditod

N.f.pl. The nipples of a man's breast. Never used of a woman's nipples, and there is no Singular.

Diddos

V. Intran. To doff hat or cap at meal. It is regarded as a sin against Providence for a male person to eat with hat on.
" Diddos, bachan, rhag dy gwily di ! "
Take your hat off, lad, for shame's sake !

Diddownu

V. Intran. To be sobered, tamed, toned down, &c.
" Ma 'rhen grwt wedi diddownu llawer ddàr mae e wedi myn'd i Tycanol yn was."
The fellow is considerably toned down since he went to Tycanol as servant.

Diddownus

Adj. Happy, contented.
" Plentyn diddownus."
A happy child.

Dierth

[= dieithr.] Adj. and Adv. Strange, exceedingly.
(1) " Dyn dierth "—A strange person.
(2) " Ma'r tewy wedi oeri yn ddierth i'r byd."
The weather has become exceedingly cold.

Dietrid

[= dihatru.] V. Intran. To undress.
A variant is *datrid*.

Difarn

[= edifarhau.] V. Intran. To repent.

Difeishlyd

Adj. Inventive, always in a bad sense.
" Hen griadur difeishlyd, câs."
A nasty, inventive old fellow.

Difirio
V. Tran. and Intran. To reprimand, to chide.

Diflad
Adj. Barren, strictly in reference to a woman.

Diflasder
N.m.s. Procrastination.
"Diflasder bob tamed yw na fisèn ni wedi talu'r trethi miwn pryd."
That we have not paid the rates in time is simply due to procrastination.

Diflasu
Part. Growing tired.
"Wdw i wedi diflasu aros am dano."
I have grown tired of waiting for him.

Diflasu
V. Intran. To loiter.
"Cer i'r shop, merch i, i mofyn shwgir a thê, a paid ti a diflasu ar y ffordd."
Go to the shop, my girl, to fetch tea and sugar, and don't loiter on the road.

Diffeth
Adj. Unkind, ill-willed.

Diginig
Adv. Exceedingly.
"Pregethwr da diginig."
An exceedingly good preacher.

Digon
Part. To be cooked—said of anything boiled.
"Ma'r tato wedi digoni."
The potatoes are cooked.

Digownt
Adj. and Adv. Not appreciated; of no account.

Digwydd and Digwyddad
Adv. Hardly, scarcely.
"Digwydd iddo ddwad nawr."
He will hardly come now.

Dihowlt
Adj. and Adv. Unreliable, unstable.

Dilif   Abs. n. Type, image.
"Ma Deio bach yr un ddilif a Deio mowr."
David junior is exactly the same type as
David senior.
Dilif is stronger than *shedrem* (q.v.). The
latter refers more especially to similarity of
accidents, the former to similarity of properties.

Dimbwch   Abs. n. Oblivion.
"Mae wedi myn'd i ddimbwch."
It has gone into oblivion.

Dim-byd   N. phrase. Nothing at all.
"Cheith e ddim byd am 'i drafferth."
He'll get nothing for his trouble.

Dime-bren   N.f.s. Wooden half-penny. Said in local
legend to be the coin with which the devil pays
his agents.
"Dyw e'n hido dim dime bren am neb."
Equivalent to the English, "He cares not a
brass farthing for anybody."

Dimewa..h   [= dimeuwerth.] N.f.s. A half-penny-worth.
Dim-o-un
-craff   N. phrase. Nothing of any account.
"Stim-o-un-crâff ar iol nawr."
There is nothing of any account left now.

Dim-o-un
-gwerth   N. phrase. Nothing of any significance,
nothing much.

Dim-un-wan   Pron. phrase. Not a single one; lit. *not one
one*. (Accent on last element).

Dim-yw-dim   N. phrase. Absolutely nothing. (Accent on
last element).
"Rows e ddim-yw-dim i'w ferch pan briododd hi."
He gave his daughter absolutely nothing on
her marriage.

Dinad   [= danadl.] N.f.pl. Nettles.

Dincod   N.f.s. Teeth on edge.

Dipendod   Abs. n. Reliance.
Dipèns is a variant of this word.
" Dwes dim dipendod i roi ar 'i addewidion e o gwbwl."
There is no reliance to be put on his promises.

Direini   V. Intran. To change countenance, to be displeased, &c.
" Pan wedes i'n neges wrtho, mi gweles e'n direini bob tamed."
When I delivered my message, I saw him change countenance altogether.

Dirfalch   Adj. Very proud, over-bearing; used more especially in reference to a person who is over-proud of his attainments.

Dirin-coden   N.m.s. A piece of steel formerly carried by farm labourers for the purpose of striking a light, used in conjunction with a flint and touch-paper.

Discwrs   N.m.s. A confab, a talk between two.

Disen   [= dwsin.] Num. A dozen.

Diserch   Adj. Dry and abrupt. The word is never used in reference to the affections, but only to manner.

Dish   N.f.s. A teacup. The word " cwpan " is never used, nor is the word " dish " often used for any ware other than a teacup.

H

**Dishgil-pont
-Mene**
The old willow pattern dish or plate; literally, the plate of Menai Bridge. This is a Welsh version of the Chinese legend of Chang and his daughter Koong-see.

Dishmol
Adj. Mirthful, funny.
"Dyn dishmol iawn yw Tomos Penfigin."
Thomas, of Penfigin, is mirthful.

Dison
In the phrase *disôn am 'i bèn*, said of a man of irreproachable character.
"Druan a'r hen Ddafis Treyet, mae e wedi marw. Un disôn am 'i ben ariod wêdd e."
Poor old Davies, of Treyet, he is dead! He ever was of irreproachable character.

Dissenters
Coll. n. This is the name by which the Independents, or Congregationalists, are known in N. Pembrokeshire. The word is never applied to any of the other dissenting bodies.

Diwardd
Adj. Unruly, forward. (Accent on last syll.).
"Plant diwardd"—Unruly children.

Diwc
Inter. An exclamation. Other similar exclamations are: diwch! diwc-i-fach-i! diwch-anwyl! diwc-i! diw-campo! &c.

Diwch
N.m.s. A thin layer of fine black dust. The word, evidently derived from *du*, is pronounced as one syllable.

Diwedwst
Adj. Speechless, diffident; said of a person who has little or nothing to say to anyone.

Diwedd
Adj. Abundant, teeming. (Accent on last syllable).
"Ma circh diwêdd yn y parc hwn leni."
There is an abundant crop of oats in this field this year.

Diwel   V. Intran. To rain heavily.
"Mae'n 'i diwel hi."
It rains heavily.

Dodi-a-dithe   "Thou and thee," a degree of familiarity
which admits of the use of the second person
Pronoun.
"Ma nw mor ion ar 'u gily a ' dodi-a-dithe '
gan nad beth."
They are as free with one another as to admit
of their using the " thou and thee," anyhow.

Doin   N.m.s. A proud one.
" Y doin dwl fel ag yw e."
The silly, proud one that he is.

Dolian   Part. Dangling one's legs whilst sitting on a
high seat.

Dollwr   N.m.s. The measure used in taking the toll
at a mill.

Dotlyd   Adj. and Adv. Confused, feeble-minded, with
special reference to the mental infirmity of old
age.

Douddribwl   Num. Adj. Sextuple.

Doupen   [= deuben.]   Lit. the two heads, meaning
the head and the feet.
" Mae e a'i ddoupen ynghyd."
He is doubled up.—said of an aged or an
infirm person who is unable to stand erect.

Drabe   N.m.pl. Pieces, Shreds.
Sing. *drabyn.*
" Stop yr ast fynd ar iol y llwdwn. te fe'i
dragith e'n ddrabe."
Stop the bitch to go after the sheep, or it
will tear it in pieces.

"Wdw i wedi rhico'n ngown yn ddrabe."
I have torn my dress in shreds.

Drabets-i
-gocs-i   Inter. Botheration it!

Drabin   N.m.s. A part, a section, a piece.
Pl. *drabie.*

Draenogllyd   Adj. Peevish, spiteful.
Drainen
-frich   N.f.s. The thorn-bush on which the after-
birth of a cow was put to hang for three days
after calving, for the purpose, it was said, of
clearing the milk of blood—" Er mwyn clirio'r
gwâd o'r llatn." This curious superstition is
not quite dead yet.

Dreial   Adv. Quite, completely, splendidly.
" Y'ch chi wedi gwella, Shôn? "
" Wdw i, diolch i chi, wedi gwella'n dreial."
Have you recovered, John?
Yes, thank you, I have recovered completely.

Drewl   N.m.s. Cow's drivel, specially applied to the
long strings of drivel sometimes floating from
cows' mouths.

Drib-drab   Adv. Bit-by-bit, in driblets.

Dribli-drabli   [= driphlith-draphlith.] Adv. At sixes-and-
sevens.

Dribwith   Adj. Awry.
" Ma'r cifan yn dribwith."
It's all awry.

Drichid   [= edrych.] Part. Looking.
" Drichid trw'r ffenest."
Looking through the window.

Drichidus   [= echrydus.] Adj. Shocking, horrid.

Dridwns   N.m.pl. Starlings.

Sing. *dridwnsyn.*

Dringad   [= dringo.] V. Tran. and Intran. To climb.

Drillhuan   [= dylluan.] N.f.s. An owl.

Drisu   Part. Demented; lit. confused, a euphemism for mental derangement.

Drith   Adv. Unctionless, dry.

"Ma'r achos wedi myn'd mor ddrith a Gilboa."

The cause has become as dry as Gilboa, meaning that a religious " cause " is in an unflourishing condition. The word is nearly obsolete.

Driwc   N.m.s. A crank, crane, handle.

" Driwc y fidde "—The crank, or turning handle of the churn.

Droitol   [= dryntol.] N.f.s. The ear or handle of a jug, cup, &c.

Dropas   N.m.s. Soot, especially the thick coat of grey-black soot formed in the large chimneys of old farmhouses, by the burning of " twarch a mate.'

In the Mathry district *dropas* signifies the droppings of the chimney during a rainstorm.

Dror   N.f.s. A drawer.

Drors   N.m.pl. Pants.

Drost   [= dros.] Prep. Over.
"Drost yr hâf."
Over the summer.

Druens   [= druain.] N.c.pl. Poor things.
"Druens bach!"
Poor little things!

Drwa   [= draw.] Prep. Yonder, over.
"Drwa 'co "—Yonder.
"Drwa man draw "—Over yonder.
"Wdw i'n myn'd drwa i Ma'nclochog."
I am going over to Maenclochog.

Drwge   Abs. n. Harm, injury.
"Odi 'r mwg dibacco ma 'n gneyd drwge i chi?"
Does this tobacco smoke do you harm?

Drwge   N.pl. Lightnings without accompanying thunder; called also *gole tewy têg* = fair weather lightning.
"Mae'n bwrw drwge."
It is lightning (without accompanying thunder).

Drwm   Adj. Foul, in the phrase *anal drwm* = foul breath.

Drws-mas   N.m.s. The front door.

Du   Adj. Unforgiving, in reference to temper.
"Ma natur ddu iawn indo."
He has a very unforgiving temper.

Duryn   N.m.s. The length of a swath of corn.
"Duryn sawl hogad yw e?"
How many whettings long is this swath?
The meaning is: How many times shall we

have to whet our scythes in one length of swath in this field? The size of the field was gauged by the answer.

Dwad   [= dyfod.] V. Intran. To come.

Dwad-at   In the phrase *dwad-at-'i-stumog* = to regain his appetite; lit. " coming to his stomach "—a very peculiar idiom.

Dwad-o-hyd   V. phrase. To find, to discover.
" Wdw i wedi dẃad-o-hyd i'r gilleth golles i."
I have found the knife which I lost.

Dwarnodyn   N.m.s. A single day, one brief day.

Dwblon   N.c. Pairs.
" Myn'd yn ddwblon."
Going in pairs.
A variant is *dwble*.

Dwbwl   Adj. Double.
The verb is *dwbli*.

Dwe   [= doe.] Adv. Yesterday. (Pron. dẃe).

Dwetha   [= diweddaf.] Adj. Last.

Dwgu   V. Tran. and Intran. To steal.
A stronger word than *dwyn* (q.v.).

Dwgwl   [= dydd gwyl.] N.m.s. A saint's day.
Dwgwl Fair—Lady Day.
Dwgwl Dewi—S. David's Day.
Dwgwl Stephan—S. Stephen's Day; &c.

Dwl   Adj. Demented.
" Ma Dafi Pendre wedi mynd yn ddwl."
David, of Pendre, has become demented.

120

Dwli Abs. n. (1) Nonsense. (2) Great affection.
(1) " Ma'r hên Ann Pantygors yn llawn hên ddwli i gyd."
Ann, of Pantygors, is full of nonsense.
(2) Ma nw bron a dwli ar y babi."
They dote upon the baby.

Dwmp-di -damp Adv. phrase. Topsy-turvy. (Onomatopœic).

Dwmpriach N.pl. Lumber, old articles of furniture, implements, &c.

Dwnshwn N.m.s. A hollow or sudden depression of the ground.

Dwr-coch Red water : a disease of animals.

Dwrfogl V. Tran. To catch trout by putting lime in the river. The word is nearly obsolete.

Dwr-'l -hunan One's own urine. This was formerly prescribed as a remedy for many ailments, and is even now applied in cases of sore eyes.

Dwrlwncu V. Tran. To swallow one's spittle.

Dwrn-fedi Part. n. Fist reaping. A very laborious method of reaping formerly employed before the introduction of scythes, exceeded in tediousness only by the old Eastern method of plucking the corn by handfuls from the roots. In fist reaping the corn was cut in handfuls at a time by means of a sickle.

Dwr-y-mor N.m.s. Sea-side, sea air; lit. sea-water.
" Myn'd am fish i ddwr-y-môr."
Going for a month to the sea-side.

Dwst　Abs. n. A whit.
"Dyw e ddim dwst gwâth na newy'."
It is not a whit worse than new.

Dwyn　V. Tran. and Intran. To steal.
A milder word than *dwgu* (q.v.).

Dwyno　[= diwyno.] V. Tran. To soil, to be soiled.
"Peidwch dwyno 'ch dillad."
Don't soil your clothes.
"Ma'r llifir wedi dwyno."
The book is soiled.

Dydd-Iou -Gilbid　Prop. n. Maunday-Thursday.
Also termed *Dydd-Iou'r-Gofid*.

Dyn-shengel　N.m.s. A bachelor. The term *menyw shengel* is rarely used, the terms *merch ifanc* and *hen ferch ifanc* being preferred.

Dy' Sul-dy' -bach　The Sunday next before Christmas Day.
(Accent on last syllable).

Dd.

Ddar　[= oddiar.] Adv. Since.
"Mae'n rhewi ddar hechdwe."
It is freezing since the day before yesterday.

Ddi　[= hi.] Pron. She, her, it.
"Ble mae ddi?"
Where is she?
"Wdw i'n 'i hofni ddi."
I am afraid of her, or it.

Ddrittod　The Tertian ague.
Drittod (with the radical *d*) is never used.

122

E

E   P. Pron. 3 Sing. He.
This is the person of direct address among
acquaintances. The 2nd person sing. is used
only between members of the same family, or
old acquaintances; the 2nd person plur. is used
only by people of reserved manner, or by
casual acquaintances.
" Ble mae e'n mynd? "; literally, " Where
is he going to? " but equivalent to the English
" Where are you going to? "
Hi = She, is similarly used among women-
folk.

Ebill   A bradawl. A word used metaphorically for
a man who worms himself into the confidence
of another for the purpose of getting possession
of an important secret.

Ebrwn   [= hèbrwng.] To accompany, to send.

Ecstri   N.m.s. The axletree of a cart.

Ech   An exclamatory word used as a warning to a
child not to touch, or put in its mouth anything dirty or unpalatable.

Echifi   [= ach fi!] Inter. Ah me! Fie upon it!

Edi   [= eddi.] N.pl. Thrums, fringe.
" Brethyn edi "—Fringed cloth.

Efrith   [= llefrith.] N.m.s. Skimmed milk.

Ei Inter. Pron. What?

Used when one person has not understood what another has just said. It is not considered a mark of good breeding to use this word; *nàn* (q.v.) is used by people who affect etiquette.

Eidlpac N.m.s. An idle, good-for-nothing fellow. Not infrequently it means an immoral man. (Pron. eid-l-pac).

Eidon-du In the expression " Mor sâff a banc-yr-eidon-du "; As safe as the bank of the black ox, said of any person whose credit is good. The reference is to a well-known bank now defunct.

Eirin-meirch N.m.p. The berries of the white brier.

Eirw N.m.s. Tether, neck-collar.
Mostly used in the latter sense, like the classical word *aerwy*.

Eis N.f.pl. Ribs. Pl. of *asen*.

Eitha In such phrases as " Dyw e ddim yn eitha peth "; It is not quite the thing.
" Mae e'n eitha da nawr "; He is quite well now.

Eithin-pwno N.f.pl. French furze, furze for chaffing.

Eli-penelin Hard work, perspiration; expressed by the English colloquialism " elbow grease."

Enill-'i-wres Verbal phrase. To get one's heat; to walk so as to set the blood in circulation.

Enwe-gwartheg The names of cows.
Until recently the custom obtained of giving a name to every cow on the farm, but it is now falling into desuetude. Anciently the naming

was accompanied by a great deal of ceremony. Benny, of Twcwr (an authority often quoted in these pages), told the author that his grandfather used to relate how a young she-calf that was intended for a milch cow was " christened " (surely a most profane use of the word) when it was turned out for the first time from the *catsh* (the pen). The farmer, or more often his eldest daughter, would give grass to the calf, over which salt had been sprinkled, at the same time as she named it. It is noteworthy that the names of cows were almost invariably Welsh, whereas the names of horses and dogs were nearly always English, as is the case to-day. Following is a list of all the names of cows in use in the parish of Pontfaen in the year 1885 :—Braithen, Pincen, Penwen, Cochen, Llwyden, Rhodd, Rhosen, Bwtwn, Brigwen, Pwlen. Ceinwen, Pwythen, Moelen, Gwenno, Pigen, Seren, Mwynen, Merfen, Cossi, Crichen, Pica, Taith, Peren, Blacen. There were many duplicates, of course.

Enwyn-a-dropas Butter-milk and soot.

This used to be the sovereign remedy of the old Pembrokeshire farmer for the sheep-fly. The wool was shorn, and the remedy, being of the consistency of thick paste, spread on the affected parts.

Erbyn V. Tran. To meet.
" Wdw i'n mynd yn 'i erbyn e."
I am going to meet him.

Erod (yr) Shingles.

The correct form *erryrod* is never heard. There is a popular belief that the disease originated with Herod, who killed S. John Baptist.

Es and Les   Particles.
Frequently heard at the end of expressions in addressing a female.
" Ble ti'n mynd, ès? "
Whither bound, woman? "
" Taw sôn, lès! "
Hush, woman!

Esim   [= euthum.]   V. Intran.   I went.

Estro   N.f.s.   A link in a chain shaped something like the letter S, and probably named *estro* (tro fel S) on that account.

Estro   [= ystod.]   N.f.s.   A swath of hay.
This is the word used in some parts, but *ystod* is also used.

Ethon   [= aethant.]   Perf. of *myned*.
" Ethon nhw? "
Have they gone?

F

Fale-bwci   N.m.pl. The seed of brier or horse-bramble.

Falen   N.f.s. Melancholia.
"Ma'r ràlen felen bron a lladd Tomos."
Lit.: The yellow melancholy is almost killing Thomas.

Fale-tato   Coll. n. The fruit of the potato. Never used in the singular.

Falle   [= fe allai.] Adv. Perhaps.

Farnod   N.m.s. A red-lead mark put on sheep for identification. Each farmer had his own particular mark on the body of the sheep in addition to the *nôd-glust:* this was for identification at fairs and markets.

Feidir   N.f.s. (1) A narrow lane overmantled with thick growth.
(2) A private road leading from the farm buildings to the fields.

Fid   [= hefyd.] Also.
"Fe ddaw inte fid."
He will come also.

Fil   Brim. (Pron. fil).
"Llawn hyd y fil."
Full to the brim.
It is difficult to know whether it is regarded as an abstract or a concrete noun.

Fildor The timber above the frame of a door.

Finydd Mutation of *ymenydd*.
" Sta ge ddim fowr o finydd."
He has not much brains.

Fogfan Asthma.

Fol [= phiol.] N.f.s. A large bowl with a handle. (Pron. fòl).

Folant N.f.s. A valentine. A picture card sent on S. Valentine's Day.

Fowr-o-graff N. phrase. " Nothing much," nothing of any consequence. (Accent on grâff).
" Wês na ddim-o-grâff ar iol."
There is " nothing much " left.

Fraishc Adj. and Adv. Enceinte.
" Mae'n fraishc " is said derisively ; " Mae'n drom " either condolingly or without reflection.

FF

Ffado N.m.s. A farthing (Pron. ffàdo).
"Wês arna i ddim ffàdo i neb."
I don't owe any man a farthing.

Ffagal-yr-arth Aurora borealis; literally, the torch of the bear.

Ffalst Adj. Cunning.

Ffalstrwydd Abs. n. Cunning.

Ffamws Adj. Well, splendid, all right, &c.

Ffedoged N.f.s. Apron-ful.
"Ffedoged o ffâ."
An apron-ful of beans.

Ffeier Adv. Absolutely, altogether.
"Mae e wedi ffeilu 'n ffeier."
He has failed absolutely.

Ffein Adj. Palatable, nice, &c.
(1) "Dima ddiferyn o ddiod ffein."
Here is a nice drop of beer.
(2) "Dima gawl ffein."
Here is palatable broth.

Ffeirin N.m.s. A gift bought at a fair—a present.
"Ffeirin o ffair Wŷl Beder."
A present from the fair of the feast of S. Peter.
This fair is held at Little New Castle, and a *ffeirin* from it is regarded with special favour.

Ffelto-'l   To make headway; to "fight one's way";
·ffordd to succeed in life.

Ffenest
·grwen   A skin window. Oiled parchment was in use
formerly in lieu of glass panes. The windows
of the old style Pembrokeshire *clom* cottage
were very small, consisting of only one pane.
Poor people often used prepared skins instead
of glass. The term is now metaphorically used
for a man who is known to possess ideas, but
is not able to convey them clearly to others.

Ffens   In the phrase *Ar 'u ffēns 'u hunen*, best rendered by the English provincialism " On their
own hook."

Ffesant   N.c.s. Pheasant.

Ffeshwn   Abs. n. Fashion.

Ffetshin   N.m.s. Contretemps, any unforeseen accident or occurrence which causes delay or confusion.

Ffiedd   Adj. Vast, large, immense, whether of number or quantity.

"We na rwbeth ffiedd o ddinion wedi dŵad
i'r acshon."

There was a large number of people at the
auction.

Ffilet   N.f.s. A cheese band.

Ffinel   N.f.s. A fishing line.

Ffiol-gardod   N.f.s. A wooden bowl formerly used by poor
people for carrying the alms *(cardod)* received
at Christmas.

I

Ffiolo

V. Intran. Several persons laying in bed in such a way as to fit into one another, back to front, are said to *ffiolo*, i.e., they fit like bowls into one another. This is the method adopted when there are too many in bed, or when the weather is cold.

Ffiol-wallt

N.f.s. A wooden bowl cut so as to fit down over the head much like the old style bonnet, around the rims of which the hair was formerly cut. Down to within thirty-five years ago hair was invariably cut in round-head fashion in all the districts bordering on the Gwaun Valley. Indeed, it was regarded a sin to cut it otherwise, as were also all attempts at parting or dressing it. The author remembers well when cutting in the modern style came into vogue, the old puritans of the Gwaun looked upon the practice as an invention of the Devil, and denounced the younger generation in their religious meetings. Until recently, there was a fine specimen of an old *ffiol-wallt* at Vagwrgoch, in the parish of Morfil; what became of it no one seems to know.

Ffirdot

Abs. n. Vanity, that which is of no value. (Pron. ffir-dòt, accent on second syllable).
"Mae e'n hala 'i arian ar bob math o hen ffirdot."
He spends his money on all sorts of things that are of no value, i.e., on vanity.

Ffiret

N.f.s. A ferret.

Ffireta

V. Tran. and Intran. To ferret, to go a-ferreting.
(1) "Ffireta lligod."
Ferreting rats.
(2) "Myn'd i ffireta."
To go a-ferreting.

Ffirllinge Coll. n. Copper coin.

"Sta fi ddim arian gleishon, ond ma digon o ffirllinge da fi."

I have no silver, but I have plenty of coppers.

Ffirst Adj. Fierce, eager.

Fire that is too hot to bear is said to be *ffirst*, and so is a man who bids eagerly at a sale, as if actuated by a mere desire to out-bid others.

Ffishcilen N.f.s. A mussel (fish). Plur. *ffishcilod.*

Ffisto V. Trans. To fight one's way, to find way, to make way, to progress.

(1) "Hen blant glew yw nw, fe ffistan 'u ffordd."

They are striving children, they will fight their way.

(2) "Fe ffistodd 'i ffordd i Hwlffor' heb ofyn i neb."

He found his way to Haverfordwest without enquiring of anyone.

Ffiwglo V. Intran. To square up for a fight; to show fight.

Ffiwgren N.f.s. A figure, digit.

Ffiwgro V. Intran. To write figures.

Fflachifwr N.m.s. The torch-bearer of the *biddin bisgota* (q.v.). He made and manipulated the torch—the *pellen bisgota*. It was an art not easily acquired to manipulate the torch to advantage, so that both the salmon would be enticed and the *pentrifwr* enabled to see at the same time.

Fflam-
-widden
N.f.s. Erysipelas.
" Y feddiginiaeth ore at y fflamwydden yw pàst trwchus o *starch*."
The best remedy for erysipelas is a thick paste of starch.

Fflasged
N.m.s. (1) Work basket. (2) Clothes basket.

Fflato
Part. To become insipid, to cease to ferment. Said specially of beer that has begun to ferment, but which suddenly ceases and becomes " flat."

Ffletem
[= lletem.] N.f.s. A wedge.
" Hala fflètem i bòlyn."
To drive a wedge into a pole.

Fflipen
N.f.s. A slap, or a gentle knock.

Ffliw
In the phrase *ar y ffliw fowr*, to be very drunk; to be sickly drunk. The word is stronger than *sliw* (q.v.).

Ffliwch
N.m.s. (1) A cloud of dust. (2) A conflagration.

Fflowro
In the phrase *fflowro'r llawr*, to embellish or " flower " the floor. Kitchen floors are mostly made of a composition consisting of lime and fine sand or *pridd melin*, which sets very hard. Cleanly house-wives are particular about having this floor stained every Saturday with foxglove leaves, and much ingenuity is shown in the variety of the patterns displayed.

Fflwchtri
N.m.s. Whey-cheese, formerly used as an early meal. Obsolete.

Fflwah
Adj. Having grown feathers and developed strength; a term used in reference to young birds that are fit to leave the nest.

Ffon-wen N.f.s. A white walking-stick. A stick presented to a young man who has been jilted by his sweetheart. The stick is usually of ash, denuded of its bark, and is sent anonymously by any wag who is acquainted with the young man's love affairs. When a young fellow receives the *ffon-wen*, he becomes the object of much good-humoured banter.

> " Ma Twm Penfigyn wedi colli 'i gariad,
> Ma cur yn 'i galon â dwr ar 'i ligad ;
> Rhowch help iddo gered a halwch iddo ffònwen,
> Ceith nosweth o garu gida Shân Pantyronen."

Fforc N.f.s. A fork. Plur. *ffircs*.

" Cillith a ffircs."

Knives and forks.

Ffordd

-angla Church road; literally, funeral road. It was formerly considered imperative that this road should be strictly followed in all funeral processions. Sometimes the road led through fields, woods, or out-of-the-way places, but that did not matter, it was undeviatingly followed. " Messengers were sent," we are informed on good authority, " the previous day to owners of fields through which this old road or pathway led, with instructions to open the stone gaps and get the road cleared. It often happened that the old road led through a field of standing corn, but the people insisted on following it that way, and trampling the corn, in preference to going over a new road or a highway which possibly ran within a hundred yards. At the head of the procession a woman walked bearing a basketful of evergreens—box and bay sprigs— which she dropped on the road at intervals, reserving a few sprays for the grave.

Ffordd-bopl   N.f.s. A pitched road, like a Roman causeway.

**Ffordd-y
-Blemiah**   N.f.s. A branch of the British Ryknield
Street. So called by the farmers of the neigh-
bourhood of Fwel Ery.

Fforon   [= ffordd hon.] This way. (Accent on second
syllable).
Similar words are:—
Fforna, that way;
Fforco, that way yonder.
A variant of *fforon* is *fforyn*.

Fforso   V. Tran. and Intran. To over-exert:

Ffotlach   N.m.s. A thick-set, straddling little fellow,
broad as he is long.

Ffralog   Adj. Romping, happy-go-lucky.
" Wil ffril ffralog,
A'i gledde tair cinog,
Yn erlid y lligod
Drwy dwlle'r gwiningod:
Aith y lligod i'r ddôl,
Aith Wil ar 'i hol,
Aith y lligod i'r môr
A dina Wil yn boddi." —Old Saw.

Ffram   N.f.s. Frame, used in various compounds,
such as *ffrâm-drus*, *-bicture*, *-cart*, *-ffenest*, &c.

Ffras   N.f.s. A form of bidding to a marriage ceremony. (Pron. ffrâs).

Ffri   Adj. Single, un-married.
" Fechgyn ffri dewch yn hy',
Sawl sy'n dewish myn'd i garu,
D'wed i ddiscu ataf fi." —(Old ballad).

Ffrimpan N.f.s. Frying-pan. A variant is *ffreimpan*.

Ffrimplo V. Intran. To roast or toast almost to nothing; said of bacon, cheese, &c., that has been roasting or toasting so long that there is little of it left.
"Ma'r caws wedi ffrimplo bant i ddim."
The cheese has been toasted into nothing.

Ffrinsieth Abs. n. Friendship.

Ffrit Adj. Good-for-nothing.

Ffriten N.f.s. A good-for-nothing girl.

Ffrog-fach N.f.s. A small frock. This is the frock which, after a beautiful old custom obtaining here, is presented to the young mother at the birth of her first-born. It is a custom very religiously observed even at the present day. Some mothers get as many as forty or fifty *ffroge-bach* presented them on this happy occasion. Friends and relatives vie with one another in bringing the most pleasing or useful frock, and the collection of frocks, when completed, is on show so long as the child remains in long clothes—or, as the expression has it; "hyd nes bo'r plentyn wedi 'i dwcco" (till the child has been tucked). A list of the donors is carefully kept, so that the *puyth* may be repaid in due time.

Ffronc Adv. Puffed up, referring to a condition of the flesh.
"Mae 'i gwmed hi mor ffronc a hwch dew."
Lit.: Her face is as puffed up as a fat sow.

Ffrwcs N.m.s. Garbage.
"Pob math o hên ffrwcs."
All kinds of old garbage.

Ffrwcsach is also used in the same sense.
" Hên ffrwcsach o'r ardd."
Weed from the garden.

Ffrwcsach N.m.pl. Things, stuff (in a depreciatory sense).
" 'Stim moddion da gida nw yn y ty, dim ond crug o ffrwcsach."
They have no furniture of value in the house, but merely worthless stuff.

Ffrwcsan V. Intran. To walk about in the wet grass or on a dirty road till one has wet feet; to trudge about in the muck and get bespattered with dirt.

Ffrwd N.f.s. A waterfall. The words *rhaiadr, berw, scwd,* are never used here.

Ffrwyn-rydd Adj. Said of a horse which is over-sensitive to the reins, and whose head turns with the slightest pull thereof.

Ffust N.f.s. Flail. The terms in use for the several parts of a flail are : —
Ielffust—the handle, made of ash.
Trotffust—the swipple, made usually of white thorn.
Tricyn—the band, made of horse hide.
Pigych—the capping, also of horse hide.

Ffwdan N.m.s. Inconvenience.
Restricted to this meaning in the phrase *towli ffwdan.*
" I ni 'n towli ffwdan arnoch chi 'fid, ma'rna i ofon."
We are inconveniencing you, too, I am afraid.

Ffwndo V. Intran. To be very tired ; to be fagged out, especially after a long walk.

Ffwrchogeth   N f.s. The junction of the thighs.

Ffwrdo   V. Tran. To afford.
"Alla i ddim ffwrdo rhoi dim."
I cannot afford to give anything.

Ffwrna   Part. Baking, to put a batch of bread in the oven.

Ffwrwm   N.f.s. A form, a seat.
Pl. *ffwrmydd*, and *ffwrwme*.

Ffwstian   N.m.s. Fustian. The word is also used metaphorically for a horny-handed son of toil.

Ffwtin   N.m.s. A toll or a charge which a novice pays on being initiated into anything; also any money paid by a person for some kind of privilege. The English provincialism " footing " is an exact equivalent, even as *ffwtin* itself is the same word.

G

Gabled

N.m.s. A fighting place. This old word, which is probably from the Gaelic *gabhail*, is preserved in the phrase *gabled-y-gofid*, which means the place of contention or of trouble.

Gadawon

N.m.pl. Leavings.

"Gadawon y da"—hay or corn left in the manger.

Gadel

V. Tran. To consider, regard.

"Dyw Shemi ddim yn câl 'i adel yn eitha sownd."

James is not considered quite *compos mentis*.

Gafar

N.f.s. A small stack of corn consisting of four or six sheaves placed nearly upright, with two sheaves for *copsi* (q.v.) or crest. *Gafro* is the verb.

Gafel

V. Intran. To interfere with.

"Odi Twm Ty'rddol wedi bod yn afel a thi to?"

Has Tom, of Ty'rddol, been interfering with you again?"

Galafanto

V. Intran. To gad about, to run about in pursuit of pleasure and not to settle down at anything serious in life.

Galap

In the saying, "Tròt hwch a galap clacwy yw 'i gidag e o hyd," the equivolent of which in English would be:—

"Come day, go day,
God send Sunday."

Galos   N.m.s. Braces.
Plur. *galosis.*

Galler   [= gallu.] To be able to.

Gambo   N.m.s. A hay cart.

Gam-bwyll   V. Intran. To take time, to go leisurely or slowly.
"Gam-bwyll, fechgyn! "
Take time, lads!
"Dewch i ni gâl myn'd gam-bwyll bach."
Come, let us go slowly.

Gamil   N.m.s. Camomile. (Anthemis nobilis).

Gamster   N.m.s. An expert or adept; one who is a master of anything.
"Ma John Dafis yn gamster ar y Sol-ffa."
John Davies has mastered the Tonic Sol-fa.

Garetsh   N.f.pl. Carrots.
Sing. *garetshen.*

Garnesh -flawd   A flour bin. Every farmhouse was provided formerly with a large oaken *garnesh flawd.* It was usually kept in a warm, dry corner of the loft, above the fireplace.

Gaton   Adv. All-to-shivers, in a hundred pieces.

Gatre   [= gartref.] Home, native neighbourhood.

Geingo   V. Intran. To be convalescent.
"Ma William wedi bod yn sâl iawn am hir amserodd, ond mae e'n geingo nawr."
William has been ill for a long time, but he is convalescent now.

**Geire
-nifeiled**

Animal calls. The following are the chief :—

Hwi, in driving sheep.

Prwy, *prwy fach*, and *prwyen fach*, in calling cows.

Swc, a calf call.

Cw, in driving away a dog, or telling it to stand aside.

Hwtsh, in calling a horse.

Hwy-lâc, in driving away geese.

Biwcs, calling pigs.

Dic, calling fowls.

Bil, calling ducks.

Haw, driving horned cattle.

Pwlen fach, an affectionate cow call.

Crâ, in frightening crows.

How'r làn, in driving sheep away to the mountain.

Hwshw, driving fowls away.

Hesw, driving a pig away.

Bishto, calling a small dog whose name is not known.

Pws, calling a cat.

Hwsh-cit, driving a cat away.

Hès, urging a dog.

There is an un-spellable word in urging horses, which is familiar everywhere.

Geletsh

N.m.pl. Yellow iris, the flower so called.

Gelligion

Coll. n. Razor-fish.

Gewin-geni

N.m.s. An infant's nail, the nail of a babe at birth.

The " birth nails " of an infant are never pared with an instrument, but are instead bitten off by the mother. There is a belief (prevailing even to-day) that an infant whose *gewine geni* are pared with a knife or scissors will develop into a thief. The nails grow their length in a year, it is said, and thus the whole of the *gewine geni* are bitten off by the teeth, when the danger of applying an edged tool is over.

Giach N.m.s. A drop of moisture hanging at one's nose in cold weather. (Pron. gīach).

"Ma gīach wrth i drwyn e" signifies that a man is extremely cold. Metaphorically it signifies that a man is poor—too poor to own a handkerchief to wipe his nose.

Gialen [= gwialen.] N.f.s. A rod.

Gialen-fedw A term now used metonymically for correction. Mothers formerly kept a twig of birch in the house for the general benefit of the youngsters. According to bardic lore it was with a branch of the *bedwen* that the Druids lustrated their disciples with consecrated dew from their sacred vessels.

Gidol In the phrase "drwy gidol y dydd," all day long.

Giewyn N.m.s. (1) Nail. (2) A segment of an orange or of any other fruit which divides into portions.

Giffrwyth In the phrase "dim ar giffrwyth," nothing in the world, nothing whatever.

"'Stim ar giffrwyth yn tiddu ar y tewi ŵer 'ma."

Nothing in the world grows this cold weather.

Gillwn Verbal n. Unyoking, unharnessing.

The act of relieving the horses of their day's work.

"Amser gillwn" in the olden days was 2 o'clock from November to March, and 3 in the sowing season.

Gimbwl N.c. A silly and frolicsome person.
"Y gimbwl dwl"—said of anyone who indulges in horseplay.

Gimp N.m.s. Embroidery.

Gine [= gynneu.] Adv. A little while ago.

Gine-fach Adv. A little while ago. Pronounced in two ways. When the accent is on *gin*, the word means about half-an-hour or so ago; when on *fâch*, it means only a few minutes ago.

Ginta Adv. Undoubtedly, very likely, &c.
"Odi, ginta"—Yes, very likely.
"Mi ginta fydd galw mowr am fôch tewon leni."
I daresay there will be a demand for porkers this year.

Gipys N.m.s. The staggers—a disease of horses.

Girwr-da
-mowr A driver of cattle, referring to a man_whose occupation it was to drive cattle to England after fairs in the old days. The cattle were driven in large herds, and always shod before the journey began.

Gislad [= cystal.] Adv. As well as, as good as.

Giwgaw N.f.s. A Jew's harp.

Glanast
-rwydd Abs. n. Mischief, evil deed.
"Ma'r hen Dwm Pantygors yn gneyd pob glanastrwydd yn y byd."
Thomas, of Pantygors, is up to all sorts of mischief.

Glas Coll. n. Liberals. (Pron. glâs).
The colour of the party in this county is blue.

Glas   N.m.s. A mirror, a looking-glass.

Glasddu   V. Intran. To become blue-black, from exposure to the cold.
" Ma nwylo i wedi glasdduo gida'r oirfel."
My hands are blue-black with cold.

Glas-giewyn   A small bit of anything. Lit. *the blue of the nail*, meaning that part of the nail which is pared.
" Hen griadur cibydd yw Nanni Pantglas, roith hi ddim cwmint a glâs-giewyn dyn i neb."
Anne, of Pantglas, is an old miser; she will not give anything to anybody.

Glastwr   N.m.s. A drink consisting of equal parts of skimmed milk and water. So called probably from its colour, which is of a pale bluish tint, especially if the quantity of water exceeds that of the milk.

Glasyn   N.f.s. A female crab.

Gleifi   [= gloewi.] V. Intran. To clear, especially of beer clearing.

Gleifon   [= gloewon.] The clear of liquids, such as *gleifon sican, gleifon-dwr-calch*, &c.

Glewder-a
    -grym   Feats of skill and strength, practised by farm hands. These are : —
(a) GLEWDER.
    1. Troi dan y bicwarch.
    2. Sefyll ar 'i ben.
    3. Cered ar 'i ddwylo.
    4. Pligu bwa.
(b) GRYM.
    1. Whare'r 56.
    2. Bwrw'r bàr.
    3. Codi'r bicwarch.
    4. Codi pwyse.
    5. Cario'r lled mwya.

Gliborwch   Abs. n. Moisture, referring to a damp condition of the atmosphere more especially.

**Glibyn-neu
-sichyn**   A method of drawing lots. A flat stone—one side of which has been wetted—is tossed up, and the side falling uppermost, wet or dry, determines the lot.

Glichtirion   N.m.pl. Fragments.
"Fe gwmpodd y badell oddiar y fainc, a fe dorodd yn glichtirion."
The pan fell from the bench and broke in fragments.
"Fe dorodd yn glichtir " is also used.

Glin   Abs. n. A phonetic corruption of Calan, in the compound *Glin-gauaf* = Calan gauaf, the 12th of December.
Clame is the phonetic corruption of *Calan-Mai*, the 12th of May.

Gliwo   V. Intran. To yield substance of the consistency of fluid glue at the udder,—an indication that a cow is nearing the time of calving, or a mare of foaling.

Glofestra   N.m.s. Destruction, loss.
"Fe nath y llifogydd lofestra ofnadwy."
The floods wrought great havoc.

Gloifach   [= gloewach.] Comp. Adj. of *gleiw* [=gloew.]

Gloifi   [= gloewi.] V. Intran. To clear.

Gloin   N.m.s. Low-lying land in a sheltered place.

Gloishigion   Abs. n. A sickly feeling, a desire to vomit, but not actual vomiting.

Glo-ring   Coll. n. House or steam coal. (Accent on second element).

Glosced   N.m.p. Charred furze.
Sing. *gloscedyn.*

Large tracts of furze are set on fire in March,
and the charred stumps are used for firewood
by " y bobol bach " (the poor people) in the
winter. Farmers readily allow the poor to go
on their land to gather *glosced.*

Glowty   N.f.s. Cowshed or house.

**Glwchu-'r
  -arad**   Wetting the plough. The old custom of wetting or sprinkling the wooden plough with beer
formerly observed here at the Christmas
festivities.

**Godre'r
  -owyr**   N.m.s. The horizon.

Godro-'r-ser   N.m.s. A gelatinous matter believed to fall
from the stars. Literally it signifies the milk-
ings of the stars. *Vide* also *trip-y-sêr.*

In some parts of the county it is called
pwdre'r sêr. Under this head the following
note appeared in a recent issue of the " Western
Mail " : — " Country people sometimes find a
lump of jelly-like substance—called *pwdre sêr*—
on the ground, which they attribute to shooting
stars. When the star hits the earth it is supposed to turn into jelly. Quite recently a
detailed study of this substance has been made
by Professor Hughes, of Cambridge, and he
has established that *pwdre sêr* is a fungus. It
has nothing to do with shooting stars, and it
is extremely difficult, remarks the ' University
Correspondent,' to tell how the two became
related to each other even in popular fancy."

Gofer   N.m.s. A small stream of water running
along the roadside, and almost covered with
brushwood.

Goferidd   N.m.s. Low-lying, moory ground, with reference more especially to the haunt of the wild duck and other aquatic birds.

Gogian   Part. Shaking.
"Wedd e'n wherthin nes bod e'n gogian."
He laughed till he shook.

Gole   N.m.s. Light, in a psychical sense. The premonitory flash which is believed to precede small events, and the steady light which precedes events of greater importance, such as death, &c. "Coming events cast their shadows [in this case lights] before them." It does not matter what the event may be—whether it be the smashing of an old family teapot or the sounding of the war trumpet—it is believed that its *gole* goes before it.
"Mi weles 'i ole fe 'n myn'd."
I saw its light passing—an expression often heard when an article of crockery is smashed, or when any kind of accident occurs.

Gole   In the phrase "bwrw gole" = lightning.

Golim   V. Intran. To pour, to rain immoderately.
"Mae'n golim y glaw"; equivalent to the provincial phrase, "It is raining pouring."

Golwgedd   Indef. Pron. Much, many.
(1) "Wê golwgedd o ddinion wedi dwad ynghyd."
  Many people had come together.
(2) "Ma golwgedd o fwyar i gâl leni."
  There is a quantity of blackberry this year.

Gone   Adv. Prim-and-prop, precise, affectedly nice.

Gorffod   [= gorfod.] V. Intran. To be obliged, compelled, &c.

Gori   V. Intran. To influence unduly, to induce, &c.; literally, to brood.

"Ma rhen Ddeina wedi gori ar y rhoces, stim dadl ar hiny, a wedi câl perswad arni."

Old Dinah has unduly influenced the girl, no doubt, and has persuaded her.

Gorphidol   Abs. n. Entire length, from one end to the other; usually in an abstract sense.

"Sticwch, 'merch i, te tima lle biddwn ni trwy gorphidol y dydd."

Hurry up, my maid, or we shall be here all day.

Gorwai   V. Intran. To lie about. (Pron. gor-wài).

"Dyw rhen grwt o wâs sy gida ni leni werth dim, dyw e'n gneyd dim ar ilw'r byd ond gorwai o bwti'r lle."

The old fellow we have for a servant this year is no good; he does nothing but lie about the place.

Gosod   [= ymosod.] V. Intran. In the phrase *gosod arno* = to set upon him.

Gotta   N.f.s. A hare.

Gowith   Adj. Wrong, left, awkward. The word is used in many senses, such as (1) Of food that goes the wrong way in swallowing. (2) Of a child putting on a boot on the wrong foot. (3) Of a man that is left-handed and awkward. (Accent on with).

Graban   Coll. n. The seed of wild mustard.

**Graban-y
-moch**   Coll.n. Haw.

Grac

Adj. Wrathful.
" Wêdd e'n gràc ofnadwy."
He was very wrathful.

Grafet

N.f.s. Cravat.

Grain

N.m.s. A whit, small bit.
" Dim grain gwâth na newy'."
Not a whit worse than new.

Grainus

Adj. Tidy, orderly.
Used in the same sense as the Gwentian *dethe*.

Gramintion

Abs. n. An abundance, especially of every assortment.
" Gramintion o bethe."
A vast assortment of everything.

Gran

Abs. n. Condition. (Pron. grân).
" Ma grân yn iawn ar y gaseg."
The mare is in good condition.

Granshinor

N.m.s. (Accent on nôr). Any public-house which makes pretence at greater respectability than the ordinary beer-house is so called now, but the name originally belonged to a tavern in Fishguard.

Grapach

Abs. n. Numbness of the fingers, due to cold weather or frost.

Grapit

Adj. Economical.
" Menyw fach grapit iawn yw hi."
She is a very economical little woman

Grat

N.f.s. Grate. (Pron. gràt).

Greigi

N.m.s. A glutton, or better, one who likes the sensation of something going down his throat.

Gresh　　N.m.s.　Grease.　(Pron. grèsh).

(1) *Gresh clocs.*　Made of hog's lard and lampblack.

(2) *Gresh cart.*　Made of the same, with the addition of linseed oil.

Gretsh　　Onomatopœic. The sound of a thing breaking.
" Fe dorrodd gretsh fel garetshen."
It broke crack like a carrot.

Gribaldi　　Abs. n.　Ribaldry, and perhaps from that word.

Grifisgar　　Adj. A word applied to a far-sighted person who has the knack of always doing the right thing at the right time.

Grimion　　N.m.p.　Lit.: Strengths.

" Dima'r parced gore o farlish a weles i ariod a grimion 'n lliged."

Lit.: This is the finest field of barley that I have ever seen with the strengths of my eyes.

Grinad　　Part.　Wallowing.
" Own i'n grinad y ddeiar gida'r bŵen."
I was wallowing on the ground with pain.

Grinta　　In the phrase " Odi, mi grinta " = Yes, I dare say.

Grof　　N.m. (Coll.).　Fine sand, especially in a river-bed.

Grondo　　[= gwrandaw.]　V. Intran.　To listen.

Growns　　N.m.pl.　Tea grounds.

The leaves left in a teapot, and from which the juice has been extracted.

Grwgne   N.m.pl. Wrinkles. Sing. *grwgnyn*.
"Gwmed grwgnog."
A wrinkled face.

Grwn   Indef. Pron. All, altogether, whole, every
whit, &c.
"Rhaid i fi rosto'r rhowndin cig yn grwn."
I must roast the whole round of beef.

Grwnshal   Part. Grumbling.
"Ma grwnshal mowr fod y trethi mor uchel
leni."
There is much grumbling that taxes are so
high this year.

Gwacsu   Adj. Flabby.

Gwadolieth   Abs. n. Extraction, descent, lineage.
"O wadolieth uchel."
Of noble descent.

Gwad-y
-grwes   The shrub known in some localities as "love-
lies-bleeding."
Gwâd-y-grŵes = the Blood of the Cross.

Gwadden   [= gwadd.] N.f.s. A mole.

Gwaddni   V. Intran. To flee.
"Mae e wedi 'i gwaddni hi."
He has fled the country.

Gwagrin   V. Tran. To separate meal from the husk,
and more generally, to sift.

Gwair-cletsh   Mouldy hay.

Gwair-pwla   N.m.Coll. Mountain hay.
Gweiryn pwla = Sing.
Gweirydd pwla = Pl.

Gwailtog   In the phrase "bob copa walltog"; every one: literally, every hairy scalp.

Gwallt-to   Coll n. Hair that is combed over a bald part of the head, and appropriately enough called "thatch." (Accent on tô).

Gwan   N. com. Occurs in the phrase "Y gwàn bach "—the dear thing, the darling.

Gwanaf   V. Intran. To clear off, to hurry away.
"Mae e'n 'i gwanaf hi nerth 'i are."
He is hurrying off as fast as his shanks can carry him.

Gwanichdod   Abs. n. Lingering illness or weakness.

Gwanol   [= gwahanol.] Adj. Different.
"Gwânol shorte "—Different kinds.

Gwaredu   V. Tran. To do away with.
"Gorffod i ni waredu 'r hen fuwch fraith, wêdd i wedi erthilu ddwy waith."
We were obliged to do away with the speckled cow, she had brought forth her young out of time twice.

Gwarro   V. Intran. When one man in mowing or reaping with the scythe follows too closely upon the heels of the other, he is said to *gwarro*.

Gwartheg   N.pl. Milch cows. Restricted to this sense.

Gwas-derwy   N.m.s. The winder of a spinning wheel.

Gwast   N.m.s. A corset. (Pron. gwàst).

Gwas-y -neidir   N.m.s. The yellow bunting.

Gwas-y -shiriff   N.m.s. The bull-finch.

Gwawdd   [= gwahodd.]   V. Pret.   Invited.
A variant is *gwâdd*.

Gwcw-gw-gw   Onomatopœic.   Cock-a-doodle-doo !   (Accent on
last gw).

Gwdderbyn   [= gyferbyn.]   Prep.   Opposite.
Gidderbyn is the form used round Eglwyswrw.

Gwddereb   Prep.   Towards, in support of.
" Rhoi rhwbeth gwddereb a rhipârs."
To give something towards repairs.   This is
said of landlords who remit a part of the rent
as an allowance for repairs.

Gwedde   N.m.s.   The leading chains of the fore-horse
in a tandem, also the trace chains of the plow
harness.   Plur. *gweddeifon*.

Gweiad   N.m.s.   Weaving.
Gwanol shorte o weiad wedd i gâl slawer dy
yw rhein : —
(1) *Gweiad plain.*
(2)   ,,   *carsi.*
(3)   ,,   *camrhedinen.*
(4)   ,,   *shains dwye.*
(5)   ,,   *minco.*
(6)   ,,   *mochyn-deiar.*
(7)   ,,   *lligad-y-deryn.*
(8)   ,,   *ecs-ar-o.*
(9)   ,,   *crimsi.*

Gweiad-go   (10)   ,,   *trifrwd.*
-whith-a-go
-dde   Ribbed knitting.

Gweidir   [= gwydr.]   N.m.s.   Glass.

Gweiddu   V. Intran.   To approve of.
" Sana i'n gweiddu gida'r drefen newy ma o
drin llafur."

I do not approve of the new plan of harvesting; literally, " I do not shout with the new plan of handling corn." A peculiar expression, but one heard almost daily in one connection or other.

Gweinon N.f.s. Moors.
In the N.E. this is invariably the plural form of *gwaun.*

Gweiryn N.m.s. The nail fixed on the handle of a scythe near the junction of the blade, to prevent hay " clogging " at that point.

Gweithe Prop. n. The name by which Glamorganshire is known here.
" Mae e wedi myn'd bant i'r Gweithe " was formerly said of one who had bid adieu to his native land.

Gweitho V. Tran. To compose. In the following and similar phrases : —
" Gweitho pregeth "—To compose a sermon.
" Gweitho pishin o gân "—To write or compose poetry.

Gwelw -tiddiant N.m.s. Growing pains.

Gwely-codi N.m.s. A folding bed.
Gwely-cwpwrd is the old-fashioned cupboard bed.

Gwelleifon N.m.pl. Shears.
The classical form *gwelleifiau* is never used. *Gwelle* is also used.

Gwendid N.m.s. The privy parts of a male person.

Gwenin -meirch.duon N.f.pl. Hornets.

Gwenin
-meirch
-melin

N.f.pl. Wasps.

Gwenwnllyd   Adj. Grumbling, discontented.

Gwerbin   N.m.s. A hill, uphill.

Gwerid   N.m.s. Manure.
Gwerido. V. Tran. To manure.
" Gwerido'r wrglo."
Manuring the meadow.

Gwermwd   N.m.s. Wormwood.

Gwewl   N.f.s. A wry face, to make a face as though one were about to cry.
Tini gwewl is to pull a wry face.

Gwewlan   Part. Blubbering.

Gweyd   [= dywedyd.]   Part. Saying.
" Ma nw'n gweyd y bydd lecshon 'to cyn bo hir."
They say there will be another election before long.

Gweyd-'l
-ddiletswydd   Saying his prayers; literally, " Saying his duty."
" Myn'd-ar-ddiletswydd " is another expression for the same thing.
" Myn'd-at-ddiletswydd " is the expression for engaging in extempore prayer at a dissenting place of worship.

Gweyd-pwnc   The annual catechising of Sunday Schools on Whit-Monday. Originally a Church institution, now a monopoly (or practically so), of Dissenters.

Gwgdde   N.m.pl. Necks. The plur. of *gwddwg.*

Gwgwrnod Coll n. Oddments, an assortment of things like old shoes, nails, irons, cast-away tools, &c. Nearly obsolete.

Gwhwru [= gweryru.] V. Intran. To neigh.

Gwialchen [= mwyalchen.] N.f.s. Blackbird.

Gwibrol Adj. Of the sky.
In the phrase " Bob dy' gwibrol," lit. : " Every day of the sky." With this cf. Burns' line, " Every sky-lit day."
The meaning is: Every day without exception.

Gwichal [= gwichad.] Part. Squeaking.

Gwidman N.m.s. A widower.

Gwidd-corn N.m.s. Spider's web.

Gwidde-bach Coll. n. Willow catkins.

Gwiddni [= gwythi.] N.m.s. Muscle, sinew.

Gwilni N.m.s. Shyness, diffidence.
" Ma gormod o wilni arni i ddangos 'i gwmed."
She is too shy to show her face.

Gwillti Abs. n. Hurry
V. Intran. To hurry.
" Peidwch gwillti."
Don't hurry.
" Beth yw'r gwillti sy arnoch chi? "
What is your hurry?

Gwimona V. Intran. To gather sea-weed for manure. Cottagers on the coast use sea-weed almost exclusively for their gardens.

Gwingris N.m.s. A surplice. (Pron. gwing-ris).
"Gwingris y ffeirad."
The parson's surplice.

Gwiningen [= cwningen.] A rabbit.

Gwinos N.m.s. Dusk.
"Mynd i garu 'n ginar gida'r gwinos."
Going a-courting early at dusk.

**Gwithiene
-geni** N.f.pl. Varicose veins. Called also *gwithiene-gleishon*. In popular superstition they are believed to be caused in women by childbirth, hence the name.

Gwlacen The word occurs in the following old saw:—
"Dwgwl Fair a dwgwl Ddewi,
Daw'r whiaden fach i ddidwy;
Daw'r gŵlacen fach i odro—
Ni gewn limed gida hono."

Gwlai V. Intran. I suppose, I believe, surmise.
A contraction of *gwela i*. (One syll.).
"Fe neith Tomos Dafy acshon, gwlai, cyn rhoi fini'r lle."
Thomas Davies will make an auction, I suppose, before he gives up the farm.

Gwlana V. Intran. To go round the country-side begging wool.
Formerly it was the regular thing for poor people to go round the farms in the month of June for the purpose of soliciting a gift of a small quantity of wool.

Gwleia V. Intran. To talk.
This word is much more frequently used than *sharad*, *ymddiddan*, &c.

Gwlydd   N.m.s. Marsh wort (Samolus).

Old people now passing away believed that unless there was an abundance of *gwlydd* amcng the produce of the garden, the crop would not be blessed.

Gwm   N.m.s. A gown. (Pron. gŵm).

Gwm-bach   N.m.s. The old-fashioned Welsh gown. Called also *betgown*.

Gwmed   [= gwyneb.] N.m.s. The face.

Gwmolch   [= ymolchu.] V. Intran. To bathe in the sea or river.

Gwndwn   Adj. Lay; invariably used in conjunction with the noun *tir*.
" Tir gwndwn."
Lay land.

Gwnstegion   [= gostegion.] Banns of marriage.

Gwntrechu   [= gorthrechu.] V. Tran. To defeat, to overcome.

Gwrach-y
  -shimle   N.m.s. A bundle of furze tied together something after the fashion of a sheaf of corn, used for sweeping chimneys.

Gwreca   V. Tran. To gather wreckage. Many people around the coast of Pencaer made it their chief occupation to gather wreckage in the dark days of long ago. It is said that they sometimes lured vessels to their destruction by means of false lights.

Gwrichenu   V. Intran. The rushing about of cattle in summer when tormented by flies. Said to be a sign of approaching rain.

Gwrio   Part. Asserting or affirming.

Gwriahgon   N.m.s. Straw arranged in a stack ready to be carried out and distributed to cattle.

Gwrug   [= grug.] Coll. n. Heather.

Gwaneithu   [= gwasanaethu.] V. Intran. To be out in service, to be in someone's employ. The word is very rarely used in a transitive sense.

Gwt   N.m.s. Cat-gut. (Pron. gẁt.)

Gwyn   N.m.s. In the phrase "Trwy wẏn y dydd," All day long.
"Wdw i wedi bod wthi trwy wẏn y dydd, ond heb beni 'to."
Lit.: I have been at it throughout the white of day, but I have not yet finished.

Gwynt-i'r -gesel   Work away! At it, my lads! Literally it means "Wind to the arm-pits!" In these words foremen encourage farmhands to re-double their efforts. The expression is often heard at harvest-tide.

Gwyr -shigowt   N.m.pl. The companions of the *teilwr* (best man) at a wedding. *Shigowt* is very probably a corruption of *scout*, and the word points back to the old Welsh marriage customs.

Gyr-y-gwr -drwg   Vervain. Great store was set on this herb by the old Welsh, and the custom is hardly yet obsolete of gathering it in large quantities at a particular season of the year, and of applying its properties to the person in a semi-mystical manner. To inhale the steam of its leaves when boiled was said to prevent fevers, and to drink its docoction was a cure for "many ill humours."

H

Habanc N.m.s. A monster of a fellow.

Hadlip N.f.s. A seed-lip, used for holding corn at sowing. It was suspended from the shoulder by means of a strap. Made of straw.

Hadyn N.m.s. Equivalent to the English slang, *card, caution,* &c.

Hafedd Adv. Leisurely.
"Ma nw'n dŵad yn hafedd."
They are coming leisurely.

Hafog Abs. n. Abundance.
"Ma hafog o fwyar i gâl leni."
There is an abundance of blackberries this year.

Haffdrors N.m.s. Chest of drawers. (Pron. haff-dròrs).

Halen N.c.s. Hake (fish).

**Hala'r-ci-ar
-iol-y-gath** V. phrase. To vomit, especially vomiting after drinking or smoking.

Halen-per The salt which was formerly put in a pewter dish on a corpse immediately after it was laid out to prevent it from swelling. It was sometimes called *halen-y-fendith.* I am informed on credible authority that the custom is even now observed in some parts of the county.

Handl Adj. Nimble.
"Fe fu'n agos i mi foddi,
Oni bai fy mod yn handi;
Ac mi golles hat werth coron,
Wrth roi naid i lan o'r afon."
(Old ballad).

Hani and
Heni [= honi.] Pron. Prep. Of, from, or out of her.

Hannera An old custom, not yet obsolete, of putting sheep, and sometimes cattle, to graze on a neighbour's land on the half-profit system. This often happened when one man possessed more sheep than silver, and the other more acres than sheep.

Hannercall Adj. Half-cracked, silly. (Accent on nèr).

Hannercyn N.m.s. Manikin.
Fem. *hannercen*.

Hanner-dy The dinner hour, or rather, the respite from 12 till about 1.30.
"Gorwe hanner-dy'."
Resting at mid-day.
"Ciscu hanner-dy'."
Sleeping during the dinner hour.

Hans Part. n. Dealing.
"Dyw Shòrs a Shams yn gneyd un hàns a'u gily nawr."
George and James have no dealings with each other now.

Hansh N.m.s. A mouthful, a piece.
"Dewch i gâl hànsh o fara chaws."
Come and have a mouthful of bread and cheese.

Harin [= harn.] V. Tran. To endure, to bear, to tolerate.
"Alla i ddim 'i harin e."
I cannot tolerate him.

Hast N.m.s. Haste. (Pron. hàst).

Hat-beltoper N.f.s. A silk hat, top hat. (Accent on tòp).

Hat-gopa-dal N.f.s. The old Welsh chimney-pot hat, worn by women. (Accent on dàl).

Hatrish N.pl. Wild mustard.

Hawch [= awch.] N.m.s. Edge, keen-edge.

Hawchus Adj. Keen, eager, with reference specially to a good appetite.
"Bita'n hawchus."
Eating eagerly, or heartily.

Hechdwe [= echdoe.] Adv. Day before yesterday.
Similarly *hechnos* = *èchnos*.

Heddel N.f.s. A tribe, a clan, a set.

Hegad N.m.s. Echo.
Hego is a variant.

Heger [= egr.] Adj. Sharp, acid, tart.

Heiti Adj. Open, elevated, bright. Always used in reference to a house, or the site thereof.
"Ma ty heiti neis gida chi."
You have a nice bright house.
"Dima fan heiti i fildo ty arno."
Here is a nice elevated spot for a house.

Helem N.f.s. A round stack of corn. The word is never used of a square stack, or rick, nor of a stack of anything other than corn.

K

Heligen-our   N.f.s.   Yellow willow.

  „ **lwyd**   N.f.s.   Common willow.

  „ **widdin**   N.f.s.   Great round-leaved willow.

  „ **sawr**   N.f.s.   Sweet willow.

  „ **y-gors**   N.f.s.   Bog willow.

Hellwn   Coll. n. Strangers, in an opprobrious sense. Probably from *alien*.

Hemo   V. Tran. To beat, chastise.
"Ma eisne hèmo 'r hen grwt."
The lad ought to be beaten.

Hen-ddigon   Amply sufficient.
Hên is prefixed to many words in the dialect intensively; instances are: *hên-bryd*, *hên-amser*, *hên-wella*, meaning full-time, a long time, fully recovered, &c.

Heni   [= honynt.] P. Prep. Of them, &c.
"Ddaw neb o heni nw nol."
Not any of them will return.

Hen-stander   N.m.s. An old hand, an experienced man at anything.
"Mae e'n hen-stander wrth y gwaith."
He is an old hand at the work.

Hen-wheddel   Abs. n. A tradition, an old saw, a wise saying.
This is always the signification of the term *wheddel* when used in conjunction with the Adj. *hên*. As an instance of what is described as *hên-wheddel*, the following may be quoted :—
"Ma'r dydd yn mistyn—
Gam ceilig [ceiliog]

Dydd Nadolig,
Awr gifan
Hen ddy' Calan,
Dwy awr hir
Dwgwl Fair;
Dros ben cifri'
Dwgwl Ddewi.''

Henwil-bach   Second sight (not in an occult sense). Old people whose sight has failed sometimes have their sight restored for a brief while. This is regarded as an omen of approaching death.

"Ma diddie henwil-bach wedi dwad, fydd y diwedd ddim yn hir."

He has received second sight, the end will not be long.

Here   N.f.s. A hop, a one-legged jump.

Here-a-cham -a-naid   A hop, a step. and a jump. A pastime frequently indulged in by farm hands during the dinner hour, and in the evenings after work.

Hercan   Part. Limping.

Hergel   Abs. n. A bother, misunderstanding.
"Ma rhyw hen hergel rhwnti nw o hyd."
There is some old bother between them always. A variant is *hegl*.

Herlid-claps   V. Intran. To go a-gossiping.

Hes   V. Intran. To urge a dog to attack cattle, &c.

Het   N.m.s. A difficulty.
"Wê llif mowr yn yr afon ac own i'n meddwl bisech chi'n cāl hèt i groeshi."
There was a great flood in the river, and I thought you would have a difficulty in crossing.

Hetial   A word used to describe the peculiar noise made by a workman while striking with a heavy sledge. The noise is produced by the sudden emission of breath, and somewhat resembles a low grunt.

Hido   V. Intran. To care for or about, to be concerned.

"Dyw e'n hido dim am neb."
He cares nothing for anybody.
"Dyw e'n hido dim am y peth."
He is not at all concerned about the matter.

Hifen-y-gors   N.m.s. The creamy substance found on the face of bog water.

Hifforddi   V. Tran. To encourage.

"Wyt ti'n hifforddu'r rhoces yn 'i champe câs."

You are encouraging the girl in her bad habits.

The word is rarely used in the literary sense of imparting knowledge, or instructing.

Himpen   N.f.s. A wench.

"Bum yn caru Becca'r felin,
Lawer nosweth wrth dân eishin;
Ac mi gesim gida'r himpen
Lawer plated da o boten."

(Old ballad).

Hina   Untranslateable.

"Chês i ddim hina [poerad] ar 'i law e ariod."
I never received that [then a spit on the ground] at his hands.

Hinda   [= hindda.] N.m.s. Fair weather.

Hiol　　　N.f.s. A farmyard. The enclosure (excluding the garden) about a farm house and out-buildings. Syn. with *clôs*. (Pron. hì-ol).

Hirf　　　Adj. Long and slender.
"Yn y cribyn dèl ma cŵed hirfion."
In the deal plantation are long and slender trees.

Hirfa　　　N.m.s. Room for a fight.
"Wê 'r hen darwod yn gallu wmla 'i heitha hi; wê eitha hirfa gida nw lle wê nw wrthi."
The bulls were able to fight in deadly earnest; they had an excellent spot for the fray where they were at it.

Hirlaw　　　N.m.s. Rain driven by the wind.

Hitio　　　V. Intran. To happen.
"Fe hition yn dda iawn."
We happened very fortunate.

Hitrishal　　　V. Intran. To sneeze.
Variants are—
Trishial (Pencaer).
Trisho (Fishguard).
Hitrisho (Maenclochog).

Ho　　　N.f.s. A rest.
"Sticwch ati, mechgyn i, ni gewn hô fach hanner dy'."
Lay to, my lads, we shall have a rest at noon.

Hoblan　　　Part. Hawking. To hobble about at odd jobs, but to do nothing in particular.

Hoblwr　　　N.m.s. A man who drags boats up a river. The farmers of N. Pembrokeshire of former days were familiar with *hoblwyr* through frequenting Haverfordwest, where they procured lime.

Hobyn-llaw   N.m.s. A small hand mow.

Hocca   N.f.s. A short scythe to cut furze or brambles with.

Hod   In the phrase "yn 'i lawn hôd": in the full ear.

Hofran   [=hofian.] V. Intran. To hover.

Hogl-glewyn   Part. phrase. Sharpening its claws. Said of a cat clawing trees or other objects.

Hoglan   V. Intran. To go about begging alms.

Hoglin   The alms given to blacksmiths and lime-burners formerly at old New Year's Day. Both the custom and the word are now obsolete.

Hol   [= nol.] V. Trans. To fetch.
"Myn'd i hôl y gwartheg."
Going to fetch the cows.
The quantity of *o* becomes short with the addition of a syllable.
"Hòlwch y da"—Fetch the cattle.
"Hòlest ti'r fuwch?"—Did you fetch the cow?

Hole   Prep. Behind.
"Pwy sy'n dwad ar 'n hole ni?"
Who is coming behind us?

Holi-ag
    -wrthi   Questioning and so on. This is a typical idiom and one heard almost daily.
"Un bishi iawn yw Sheci Shams, mae e'n holi-a'g-wrthi byth a hefyd."
Lit.: John James is very fussy, he is for ever questioning and so on.

Holsten   V.t. Bring the beer!

Hôlsten! was the cry of mowers at the hay harvest when they wanted more beer. The mowers, sometimes a dozen in number (in the days of the scythe), would shout thus in unison, and it was considered to be the height of meanness to disregard the cry.

Hon   N.f.s. A hone. (Pron. hôn).

Hono   V. Tran. To set edge, to sharpen a keenedged tool. Almost restricted to the setting of a razor. (Pron. hôn-o).

Hors-gans N.f.s. Cheese-horse, a stand for holding cheese.

Hosbins   N.m.s. Stone steps for assisting a person to get on horse-back. A feature of every old farmyard. The word is probably a corruption of " horse-bench."

Houlin   N.m.s. Sunshine between showers.

How   N.m.s. A hoe.
               The verb is *howo*.

Howcyn   N.m.s. A small salmon. Nearly obsolete.

Howca   Part. Poaching salmon. The word is practically obsolete.

Howfati   [= how, âf ati!] Inter. At it! Heigho!
               " Howfati, fechgyn! "
               At it, boys!

Howg   N.m.s. A full-grown salmon. Nearly obsolete.

Howlt   Abs. n. Respect, thought, idea, and numerous other meanings.
" Wê fowr o howlt gen i arno."
I thought very little of him.

Hual   N.m.s. A shackle on both fore-legs, connecting the two together. The word *hual* is restricted in meaning to this one particular kind of shackle.

Hwch   Used metaphorically for bankruptcy in the expression : —
" Ma'r hwch wedi myn'd trw'r shòp " ; lit., The sow has gone through the shop, i.e., the shopkeeper has become bankrupt.

Hwda   N.m.s. The scum and refuse thrown up and left on river-banks by a flood.

Hwdel   N.m.s. A helpless mass.
" Cwmpo'n hwdel ar y llawr."
To fall on the ground a helpless mass.

Hwdog   Adv. Over-plentiful.
" Ma'r hwrddod mor hwdog 'leni, stim prishodd am deni nhw."
There is a glut of rams this year, and they command no price.
This perfectly idiomatic phrase is nowhere heard in Wales except in Dyfed, and it is worth noting on that account.

Hwdu-brogats   N.m.s. Frog-spawn. (One accent, on gâts).

Hwdwch   N.m.s. A bugbear.
" Yr hen hwdwch fel wyt ti! "
The old bugbear that you are!

Hwddi and Hwthi   [= gwythi.] N.m.s. Muscle.

Hwmmo   Part. Mouldy; a term applied to sheaves of corn that have been overheated in the stack, and which yield corn that is, consequently, of little value. The term is also applied to the corn itself.

Llafur wedi hwmmo is grain that has been over-heated or fermented.

Hwnco   [= hwn-acw.] That one yonder. The fem. is *honco*.

Often used as a mere expletive, in the same way as N.W. *bethma*.

Hwp   N.S. A push. (Pron. hẁp). *Hwpad* is also used.

Hwpo   V. Tran. To push.

Hwp-di-ap   Onomatopœic. Haphazard.

Hwre   Def. V. and Inter.
(1) Take this.
(2) Here!

Hwrndroi   [= chwyrn-droi.] V. Tran. To brandish, to wield.

" Wêdd e'n hwrndroi 'i ffon, ac yn bwgwth yn ofnadwy."

He brandished his staff and threatened terribly.

Hwrnell   N.m.s. A lump or swelling on the head, caused by a blow.

" Alla i ddim a gwishgo'n hat, ma hwrnell boinus ar 'mhen i."

I cannot wear my hat, I have a sore swelling on my head.

Hwrni   Coll. n. The fly in cows, cow-maggots.

Hwrnu   [= chwyrnu.] V. Intran. To snore, to grunt.

Hwro   V. Intran. Hurry up, go quickly, make speed.

Hwahi-bei   Inter. Lullaby!

Hwtro   V. Trans. To push goods, to press the sale of articles.

"Sana i'n leico gwraig y shop, mae'n hwtro 'i hen bethe ar ddyn; stim shwt beth a dwad o na heb bwrnu llwyth o ffrwcsach diwerth."

I do not like the shop woman, she pushes her goods upon one; it is impossible to come away without purchasing a load of worthless things.

Hyd-at   Conj. Unless, except.

"Ma Wil, 'n hen was ni, 'n gwsneithu yn Pantglas leni, ond fe leicse ddwad nol; welodd e ddim bara-a-llath-enwyn i freewast ma ariod, hyd at fod e'n 'i geisho fe."

William, our old servant, is in service at Pantglas this year, but he would like to come back. He never had bread and buttermilk for breakfast here, unless he asked for it.

This is the regular idiom, although a peculiar one. The classical *oddigerth* is never used.

I

Iach Adj. Light-hearted and frivolous.

" Ma Twm yn iâch 'i wala, dyw e'n hido dim be sy'n myn'd i ddŵad o bethe."

Tom is light-hearted enough, and cares not a jot what might happen.

Iar-gisht N.f.s. The common moth, the grey moth, the meal moth, and one or two other species of moth are so named.

Iar-wrug N.f.s. Grouse.

Iasu V. Intran. To become lukewarm, to begin to heat. Said of water or milk in a vessel on the fire that is passing through the intermediate degrees of temperature from cold to hot.

Iawn, yn Adv. All right.
" Shwt y'ch chi nawr, odych chi wedi gwella?"
" O, wdw i'n iawn nawr."
How are you now, have you come well?
Oh, I am all right now.

Iawnu [= ymunionu.] V. Intran. To straighten one's-self, to stretch out the limbs.

Ichened N.m.s. The soft flesh adhering to the breast-bone of a goose, somewhat resembling the liver of that bird.

Idnich N.m.s. A pigmy.

Iddew-hib [= -gwib.] N.m.s. A wandering Jew; used metaphorically of a man of unsettled abode or habits.

Iero N.m.s. Yarrow.
Another local name of this herb is *milddalen*.

Iet N.f.s. A gate.
Iet is a gate made by a carpenter, properly finished and hung; *clwyd* is a roughly made gate or hurdle, not hung but merely placed against or in a gapway.

Iet-dwrpeg N.f.s. Turnpike gate, i.e., the turnpike road toll-gate.

Ifidw N.m.s. The last or only thing a man has in his possession.
" Mae e wedi hala'r cifan ; ma'r ifidw dwetha we gida'g e wedi mynd nawr."
He has spent all his substance; the last thing in his possession is gone now.
Almost obsolete.

Iglan [= ydlan.] N.f.s. Haggard.

Ilfyn N.m.s. An atom, a small particle of anything.

Ilod-papur N.pl. The burnt remains of a printed paper, with the print still showing.

Imbed [= enbyd.] Adj. Dangerous, perilous.

Imobor
  -eglwn The bride's gift to the parish church on her bridal day. A custom no longer observed.

Imobor
  -ffeirad The forfeit of the first kiss after marriage formerly paid by the bride to the celebrating priest. The custom was in vogue within the memory of the oldest inhabitants.

Impitans　Abs. n. Impudence.
"Paid a rhoi di impitans i fi!"
Don't give me your impudence!

I'n　[= ydym, y'm.] We are.
" 'R i'n ni 'n iach i gyd."
We are all well.

Incil　N.m.s. Tape.

Inced　Teeth on edge.

Indo　[= ynddo.] P. Prep. In him, in it.
The fem. is indi.

Indodid　Adv. Without a doubt, in very deed.
Probably a corruption of "in double deed."
" Indodid fe ddaw "—He will come, no doubt.
" ' Is indîd,' a ' No indòdid '—
Dina Sisneg gwr beneddig."
(Old Saw).

Iol　[= ôl.] Prep. and Adv. After. (Pron. iôl).

Ion　[= eofn.] Adj. Bold, daring, forward.
(Pron. ïon).

Irifeddi　Adv. Excellent, wonderful.
" Mae wedi gneyd wthnos o dewi irifeddi."
It has made a week of excellent weather.

Irlath　N.m.s. The first milk a cow yields after calving.

Iscawn　[= ysgafn.] Adj. Light.

Iscawndid　Abs. n. Relief after a great trouble or anxiety.
" Iscawndid meddwl "—Mental relief.

Iscarllbwn Adv. Helplessly.
"Fe gwmpodd yn iscarlibwn."
He fell helplessly.

Iscrid N.m.s. Cold shivers.
"Wdw i'n cliwed iscrid arna i bob tamed."
I am shivering all over me.
Lit.: I hear cold shivers upon me every bit.

Iscus [= esgus.] Abs. n. (1) Excuse. (2) Pretence.
In the second sense it is used verbally in the following and similar expressions:—
"Mae e'n iscus caru tipyn ar Ann."
He is pretending to make love to Ann.

Iscwyd The sudden drying of the ground produced by sunshine and breeze after a shower of rain.
The word conveys a very poetical idea.
"Y cawr [the rain-god] yn iscwyd 'i hunan ar iol cawed, fel y gna ci wedi bod yn yr afon."

Isgawn Adj. Quick.
In the phrase "Isgawn 'i gliw" = Quick of hearing.

Isgawnu V. Intran. To brighten, to clear up (of the weather).
"Mae'n isgawnu nawr, fe ddaw'n hinda yn y fan."
It is clearing up now, it will cease to rain presently.

Isheldra Abs. n. Melancholia.

Ishelhad Abs. n. Indignity.
Salhad is also used in the same sense.

Ishws [= eisoes.] Adv. Already.

Isto

V. defec. Quoth.

"'Gwell blingo buwch na thrensho hwch,' isto Ifan Blancwm."

"It is better to flay a cow than to drench a a sow," quoth Evan, of Blaenycwm.

There is a superstition in N.E. Pembrokeshire that a sick sow brings bad luck. *Drensho* means to administer medicine to an animal.

Istyn

V. Tran. To hand to, to pass, to reach.

"Istynwch y figin i fi."

Reach me the bellows.

Istyn-clust -y-gath

A poacher's term for catching rabbits with a large net. The rabbits are put to death by having their necks stretched—hence the term.

Itta

[from *yd.*] V. Intran. To go about to beg corn. Cottagers with three or four acres of land would often go to farmers around to beg a peck or two of oats or barley for seed.

Ithlon

Adj. Poignant.

"Gofid ithlon."

Poignant grief.

The word is nearly obsolete.

Iws

N.m.s. Interest.

"Iws ar yr arian."

Interest on the money.

J

Jaciraca N.m.s. The water-boatman; the aquatic insect commonly so called. (Pron. jac-i-ràc-a).

Jac-pen-stol N.m.s. A lay preacher among the Dissenters.

Jac-pren N.m.s. A cart jack.

Jac-y -jwmper N.m.s. Grasshopper.

Jac-y -lantarn N.m.s. Ignis fatuus.

Janglo V. Intran. To have a wordy warfare, to dispute.

Jant N.f.s. A journey.

Jantan Part. Journeying.

Jar i Inter. Dear me! *Diàr i* (accent on âr) is a variant.

Jar-i-bo-i Inter. Gracious me! *Jàr-i-bòno-i!* is a variant.

Jawlo V. Tran. To curse or swear vehemently.

Jengyd [= dianc.] V. Intran. To escape. A variant is *jangyd.*

Jer N.f.s. A jolt. (Pron. jèr). A variant is *jerrad.*

Jero V. Intran. To jolt. (Pron. jèro.)

Jestis [= ustus.] Magistrate.

Jim-crow N.f.s. Soft-felt hat.

Jini-flewog N.f.s. A large, hairy caterpillar.

Jior and Jor [= dyor.] V. Trans. To stop.
" Jior y da i fynd dros y claw."
Stopping the cattle to go over the hedge.
" Jôr y ceffyl na, fachan! "
Stop that horse, lad!
(Jior has two syllables, accent on *ji*).

Jiwels N.f.pl. Ear-rings. Restricted to this meaning.
Sing. *jiwelsen*.

Jocan Part. Joking, teasing.

Jogi [= diogi.] Laziness.

Jogel Adj. Considerable.
" Fe starton am whêch bore heddy; ma nw wedi mynd bishyn jogel 'o ffordd erbyn hyn."
They started at six this morning; they have travelled a considerable distance by now.

Jom N.f.s. Jamb. used not only in reference to the jamb of a gate, but also to the hob of a fireplace.

Joni [= daioni.] Abs. n. Goodness, good.

Jo-o-ddibaco N.f.s. A quid of tobacco.

Jwmp Adj. Perpendicular.
" Dodwch y blwmen ar y wal na, gâl gwel a odi ddi 'n jwmp."
Put the plummet on that wall to see if it is perpendicular.

L

L

Labar   N.m.s. Labour, specially used of work well done.
"Dina bishyn o labar pert."
That is a bit of well-executed work.

Labgi   N.m.s. A gad-about person, an idle tale-bearer.

Labrer   N.m.s. A day labourer, that is, a man who is engaged from day to day, and who receives his wage at the end of each day's work.

Lach   Abs. n. Lash, the bite of the tongue.
"Sana i'n leico'r pregethwr, mae e a'i hen làch ar bawb a phopeth."
I don't like the preacher, he lashes everybody and everything.

Ladi-wen   N.f.s. The white-lady. An apparition seen by imaginative people in the old days of super-stition.

Lampwr   An old-fashioned lamp consisting of "a common saucer with a strip of well-dried rag, smeared with fatty substance, so placed in the saucer that about one-quarter inch projected over the edge, and a moderate-sized lump of hog's lard placed within the vessel."

Lamlac   N.m.s. Lamp-black. The word is also used for a shade of black.

Lansed   N.f.s. The upright flank of a plow.

Larwm N.m.s. An alarm clock.

Lasher N.m.s. The pole used in locking or tightening the rope over a load of timber.

Lasied N.f.s. Door-latch.
The word is nearly obsolete.

Lasin N.m.s. Boot-lace.

Laso V. Trans. To lace.
" Laso scidie "—To lace boots.
" Laso gwast "—To lace a corset.

Latsen N.f.s. A lath.

Lataho V. Tran. To shut a door and fasten it with a latch.
(Observe, the word means shutting as well as fastening).

Lawrans Abs. n. Laziness.
" Ma lawrans wedi cidio gafel yn Sheci."
Laziness has taken hold of John.
[Query: Does the word come from a proper name?]

Lechco [= welwch acw!] Inter. See there! Behold yonder!

Lechna-chi Inter. There now! Lo! Behold now! &c.
An exclamation heard daily.

Lefane Coll. n. Budget, a promiscuous collection.
" Ma gida Ann rhyw lefane o hanesion."
Ann has a budget of tales.

Leico V. Intran. To desire, wish, like.
" Leicech chi fyn'd? "
Would you like to go?

Les

A proclitic: a corruption, probably, of *lass*.
" Taw son, lès! "—Hush, maid!
" Dal dy dafod, lès, rhag dy gwily di! "
Hold thy tongue, lass, for shame's sake!

Leshans

N.f.s. A license.
" Codi leshans."
To take out a license.

Liban

[= lleithban.] N.m.s. The soft roe of fish.

Libin

N.m.s. Liquid food, used with *enllin* (q.v.).

Licsyn

A primitive tape or match. It was made of a splinter of wood, about the thickness of a slate pencil, and about ten inches long. The stick was soaked in boiling resin for a couple of hours. A large quantity was prepared in summer, and tied in bundles of fifty, ready for use in winter. Obsolete.

Lifret

N.f.s. A maiden in her teens.

Lingeredd

Adj. Careless.
" Hen griadur lingeredd, diwerth."
A careless, worthless old fellow (lit.: creature).

Lingryn

N.s. Ailment, lingering complaint.
" Ma rhyw hen lingryn arno o hyd."
He has some ailment or other always.

Limwnsen

N.f.s. A lemon.

Limwr

N.m.s. The limber, or projecting pieces at the tail-end of a cart.
Plur. *limwri.*

Linbwst, y

N.m.s. Lumbago.

Lip   N.f.s. A small seed-lip, made of straw, and used for the purpose of carrying corn to horses, feeding the winnowing machine, &c.

Lirw, ar   Adv. After the fashion of, in the shape of.
"Wês ffist gida chi ar werth, Tomos? Ma eishe arna i gâl un i hala i'r *Museum*."
Ateb: "Wn i ddim, wir, ma rhwbeth ar lirw i gâl ma."
Have you a flail, Thomas? I want one to send to the Museum.
Ans.: Indeed, I don't know; I think I have something in the form of one.

Listi   Adj. Lusty, strong.
Indifferently for masc. and fem.
Dyn, neu fenyw listi.
A lusty man, or woman.

Liwer   N.s. The pole used in tightening the chain that fastens a load of timber.

Loilec   N.m.s. Lilac tree.

Loshin   Coll. n. Lozenges, sweets.

Lowryn   N.m.s. An overcast sky.

Lowro   Part. Lowering, becoming cloudy or overcast.
"Mae'n lowro at y glaw."
It is lowering for rain.

Lowsed   N.f.s. A slit in a wall, for the purpose of letting in air and a little light into cowsheds, stables, &c.
Probably from *lancet*.

Lwans   N.m.s. (1) Permission. (2) Allowance, bounty.
"Stim lwans i bisgota ar dir Pontfân."
There is not permission to fish on the Pontfaen land.
"Cwart o ddiod y dydd yw'r lwans."
The allowance is a quart of beer a day.

Lwba   N.m.s. A lout.
"Cerdd o 'ma 'r lwba!"
Get away, you lout!

Lwc   Abs. n. Luck.

Lwcus   Adj. Lucky, fortunate.

Lweth   Adv. Again.
"Chlwes i byth wrtho lweth."
I never heard from him again.

Lwmpyn   N.m.s. A lump of anything.

Lwo   V. Intran. To concede, to allow.
"'Dyw'r *agent* ddim yn lwo i neb fyn'd i'r allt."
The agent does not allow anybody to enter the wood.

Lwp   N.m.s. Knob.
"Lwpe'r drôr."
The knobs of the drawer.
Nwb is also used.

Lwtsh   A certain quantity of any kind of liquid.
"Sana i wedi berwi lwtsh fowr o gawl heddy."
I have not made (or boiled) a large quantity of broth to-day.

Lwtshan   Part. Gurgling, referring to the sound produced by liquid shaken in a vessel.

Lwtshyn   Abs. n. A baggy condition of any article of wear.
"Ma penol 'i drowser e'n lwtshyn mowr."
The seat of his trousers is very baggy.

Ll

Llabrog Adj. and Adv. Scraggy.

"Ma'r hen ddafad wedi colli 'i glân jwst i gyd, a dina olwg labrog sy arni."

The ewe has lost nearly all its wool, and it looks scraggy.

Lladd -mochyn Killing a pig. An expression used metaphorically for any important event.

"Sano ni'n llâdd mochyn bob dydd."

Lit.: We are not killing a pig every day; meaning: We are not celebrating such an event as this every day, so let's be merry.

Llafur Coll. n. Chapters, verses, or Collects recited in a Sunday School, and which have been committed to memory during the week. This is still a feature of Sunday School work in North Pembrokeshire. A quarter-of-an-hour is allowed at the end of the lesson to *casclu llafur*.

Llafurio V. Intran. To sow corn, to have land under corn.

Llapre Adj. Ragged, torn.

Llapreio V. Tran. To tear, more especially in reference to the clothes one is wearing.

Llath-buwch -benwen The milk of a white-headed cow. This was considered a specific for rickets.

Llath-efrith N.m.s. Skimmed milk.

Llawndid Abs. n. An abundance.
" Ma llawndid o bopeth yn y tŷ."
There is an abundance of everything in the house.

Llawnu [= llyfnu.] V. Tran. To harrow.

Llawrbant N.m.s. A small pit in the floor of a " llawr-pridd-a-chalch."

Llawr-coch A floor made with the finest clay and ox-blood mixed well together. Builders of a generation or two ago made the floors of the parlours and best rooms on the ground floors with this mixture. It set as hard as cement, and took a fine polish. It was the pride of the housewife to exhibit her beautiful *llawr-côch*.

Lle N.m.s. A farm, a tenement.
" Hen lê trud yw Treyet."
Treyet is a dear farm.

Lleder-caled Leather that is hardened for the purpose of making suckers of pumps, screw washers, &c. The method of preparing the leather is to soak it for several weeks in the water that has lain a long while under a grindstone (mân-llif), or in other water where there is a store of iron filings.

Lled-o-fate " Un-llâth-ar-bwmtheg o hyd a ẅyth o led. Dina yw stàc [quantity allowed] un ffarm am un timor [season], a hanner-coron yw 'i werth e." (From an old MS.).

Lledrin N.m.s. Leatherette.

Lledu In the phrase *lledu bara menyn* = cutting bread and butter.

Lled-y-pen Adv. Wide-open.
" Ma'r ièt yn 'gored lêd-y-pen."
The gate is wide open.

Llefydd The word is used as the plural of *lle* = place.
Lleoedd is never used.

Lleidir-y
-ganwyll N.m.s. Candle-fly, called also daddy-long-
legs.
Jawl-y-gwêr is another name of the same
insect.

Lleitho V. Trans. To give milk to calves.
" Cer' nawr, merch i, i leitho'r lloi, mâ'r
cerins bach bron a llwgi."
Go now, my maid, to give milk to the calves,
the poor little things are almost parched.

Lleithreg N.f.s. Dairymaid.

Lleithder Abs. n. Diffidence, nervousness. The word
is applied to a person suffering from " stage
fright," or from nervousness whilst attempting
to address a meeting. It is also used of a man
who is over-emotional in extempore prayer.

Llenden In the expression " Wyt ti 'n mofyn gwel'd
Llenden? " which is sometimes asked a small
boy by an older one. If the answer is " Wdw,"
the big lad lifts the smaller one by the ears.

Llesg Adv. To be heavy on the legs, with special
reference to animals with young. It is never
used in the classical sense.

Llestri-jeini N.m.pl. China ware.

Lleu'r
-ffeirad Coll. n. Cleavers, or the seed of chickweed,
which cling to the clothes in a manner which is
supposed to be reminiscent of monks' lice.

Llidrew [= llwydrew.] Hoarfrost.

Llidrewi V. Intran. To cast hoarfrost.

Llifelwyd N.m.s. A plan, design, &c.
Usually heard in the phrase *Dim ar lifelwyd y cread*—Nothing in the plan of creation.
" 'Dyw e werth dim ar lifelwyd."
It is worth nothing that has been devised.

Llifento V. Tran. and Intran. To invent, to comprehend.
" Ma nw'n llifento pob math o fashins y dyddie hyn."
They invent all kinds of machinery nowadays.
" Alla i ddim llifento beth yw'r matar arno."
I cannot comprehend (or imagine) what is the matter with him.

Llifo V. Tran. To lick, to lap.

Lligad-perlin N.m.s. An artificial eye.

Lligad-y -geinog A miser, literally, the eye of the penny.

Lliged N.m.pl. The spots on the wings of butterflies are so called, and also believed by the ignorant to be the real eyes of the insect.

Lligio V. Intran. To wallow in the mire, as pigs do. The word is obsolescent.

Lligoden -ffernig N.f.s. A rat.

Lligotreg N.f.s. Mouse catcher ; a term applied to a cat that is good at catching mice.

Llimrig Adj. To be scantily dressed, shabby-genteel.

Llimrigyn }
Llimrigen } Nouns derived from the Adjective.

Llinango [= gollwng yn anghof.] V. Tran. To forget.
"Wdw i wedi llinango y dât."
I have forgotten the date.

Llise
-lleitheg N.m.pl. Sow-thistle. (Sonchus oleraceus).

Llise'r
-gerwnt N.m.pl. [The same as the next below, according to some, but it is not easy to say.]

Llise'r
-horwn Horehound.

Llisewyn
-melyn N.m.s. Weld (Reseda luteola).

Llise
-Wirddon N.m.pl. Parsnip.
My grandfather used to relate a pretty tale that S. Patrick, who stole the shamrock from Wales, was told by Mary to make amends by introducing to Wales the parsnip, which was called by the grateful inhabitants of Dyfed *llisyn Wirddon* by way of compliment to the conscientious saint.

Llisewyn-y
-fwdog N.m.s. Ground-ivy.

Llisgad N.m.s. A small load of anything.
A full load is always *llwyth*, the diminutive of which is *llisgad*.

Llisiwr N.m.s. (1) A herbalist. (2) A botanist.

Lliswaden [= llyswen.] N.f.s. Eel.
Lliswen
-rawn N.f.s. A fresh-water eel. A small eel often to be found in horse ponds, and which is believed by the superstitious to be developed from the hair of horses' tails. The notion is still prevalent in North Pembrokeshire that if *rhawn* be pulled out by the root and put in the

horse or machine pond it will grow into eels. There is a similar belief on the coast with regard to the barnacle, which is said to become a goose when cut off from the bottom of a vessel. Giraldus Cambrensis was familiar with this superstition, and evidently believed it, for he says: " When our first parent was made of mud, can we be surprised that a bird should be born of a tree? "

Llithie   The Book of Common Prayer.
" Darllen y llithie " means reading the prayers, and not the lessons. The expression is heard, of course, in the mouth of Nonconformists only. It is difficult to account for the wrong use of the word.

Lliwcho   V. Intran. To tell lie after lie, to pile up lies one on another. The same word is used for the drifting of snow.

Lliwrich   N.m.s. A very small quantity. Hardly ever used except of fire.
" Ma rhyw liwrich o dân yn y gràt."
There is a remnant of fire in the grate.

Lliwo-gwen   Part. Yawning; lit. : colouring a smile.

Llobed   N.f.s. The lapel of a coat.
Laped is a variant of the word.

Lloged   N.m.s. A guiding star; a directing power. That which a Socrates would call his " demon," and a Christian his " guardian angel."

Lloithir   N.m.s. A shackle. Different kinds are :—
Lloithir-dwbwl—Shackles on both pairs of legs of an animal.

Lloithir-gwddwg—A shackle on neck and one of the fore-legs.

Lloithir-crwes—A shackle from a fore to a hind leg crosswise.

Lloithir-cris-crwes—Two shackles placed crosswise.

Lloithrio   [= llyffeitheirio.] V. Tran. To fetter, to tie the legs of sheep, to prevent their trespassing.

Lloried   N.f.s. A batch, &c.
"Lloried o fara"—A batch of bread [in the oven.]
"Lloried o farlish"—A floor-ful of barley [on the barn floor.]

Llorio   V. Intran. To make a mark, to do a noted thing.
"Mae e wedi 'i llorio hi o'r diwedd."
He has made a mark at last.

Lluddedi   Part. Panting. Used only in reference to a dog which has been running and is breathing hard.

Llunie   N.m.pl. Wry faces.

Lluscad   N.m.s. A small load of anything conveyed in a cart with frame.

Llusg-ar -dafod   N.m.s. Impediment of speech of a general character, differing from *cecial, achial,* &c. (q.v.).

Llwanen   N.f.s. A sheet of sacking or coarse cloth used for carrying hay or corn.

Llwer-saith -nos-ole   The harvest moon; literally, the moon of the seven bright nights. (*Llwer* is pronounced llw-er).

Llwffian

V. Tran. To gobble.
"Mae e'n llwffian 'i fwyd fel ci."
He gobbles his food like a dog.

Llw-gole

A solemn oath among children. When a child's word is doubted, he makes a *llw-gole* by holding up and crossing both arms, in the form of a ×. Such is the sense of responsibility among the children of the peasantry, that this form of solemn oath is very rarely, if ever, violated or abused.

Celwy-gole is the word for an open and a daring lie.

Llwgwr

Abs. n. Havoc.
"Fe âth 'r hen hwch i'r parc tato a mi nath lwgwr na."
The sow broke into the potato field and wrought havoc there.

Llwgu

V. Intran. To be very thirsty.
"Wdw i'n llwgu 'n lân am ddiferyn o ddŵr."
I am thirsting for a drop of water.

Llwybir
    -llanc N.m.s. Galaxy, the milky-way.

Llwybir
    -tarw N.m.s. A short cut, an illegal path.

Llwybrach

N.m.pl. Small tracks made by sheep or other animals.

Llwydi

N.m.s. Laziness.
"Ma gormod o lwydi ar Lefi i illwn 'i fritshis fel dyn arall, ond ma'n rhaid iddo adel un galos ar fwtwn."
Levi is too lazy to attend to the call of Nature in the manner of another man, but he must leave one brace buttoned.

Llwyr-galon   Adj.   Down-hearted ; low-spirited.

Llwyr-'i-ben   Adj.   Haphazard, at random.
" Widde fe ddim lle wedd e'n mynd, ond mynd rwle lwyr-i-ben."
He knew not whither he went, but he went somewhere at random—lit. : by the path of his head.

Llwyr-'i-din   Adv.   Backwards.
" Cered llŵyr-i-din."
Walking backwards.

M

Ma   [= yma.] Adv. Here.

Ma   Onomatopœic. Sheep cry.

Madlath   [= madfall.] N.m.s. Lizard.

Magal
    -rhawn   N.m.s. A bird snare.
Made much like a sieve, as shown in the illustration. The hoop is of bramble, the cross cords of rushes, and the nooses are made with hair from a horse's tail.

Main-cefen   N.m.s. The spinal cord.

Maint   (1) Indef. Pron. (2) N.c.
" Faint o blant sy gida chi? "
How many children have you?
" 'R un faint o ddefed sy gida ni a chi."
We have the same number of sheep as you have.

Maintodd   A large number.
" Ma Josi bach wedi dala wni faintodd o ieir-bach-yr-haf."
Little Joseph has caught a large number of butterflies; literally : Little Joseph has caught, I know not what numbers of butterflies.

Maith   Adj. Wise, long-headed.
" Dyn maith yw Jòs."
Joseph is a wise man.

Maldod   Abs. n. Coaxing, " soft-soap."

Maldodi   V. Tran. and Intran. To coax, to flatter.
" Ma nw'n maldodi'r plant lawer gormod."
They coax the children a great deal too much.

Malddot   N.f.pl. Snails.
Sing. *malddoten*.
This form of the word is frequently heard
among the older people in the Gwaun Valley,
where the Demetian dialect is purest.
The form heard elsewhere is *molwad*.

Malwch   N.m.s. The fine dust which is generally floating in corn-mills.

Mammi   N.f.s. Mother, in an endearing sense.

Mancell   N.m.s. A small cot or hole made in a hedge
or old wall for ducks. Nearly obsolete.

Maneg   N.f.s. The timber used for keeping the *bise*
of the *cader* in position when that implement is
put by after harvest.

Mangen   N.m.s. Lichen, especially the grey species
of cellular cryptogamous growth which appears
on stones. (Pron. màn-gen).

Mangu   [= mamgu.] Grandmother.
**Man-gwan
ar-y-llwer**   A weak moment upon one; lit.: A weak
spot on the moon.

Manno   V. Intran. To be bruised.
" Pan bo tato a fale wedi manno, phara nw
ddim yn hir wedyn."
When potatoes and apples are bruised, they
will not last long afterwards.

Mansh   N.m.s. The mange.

M

Manshal   Part. Munching.

Mantellu   V. Tran. To tie up a baby in a shawl on one's back.

The generations of mothers gone by nursed all their children in this way, following their various occupations the while. I am referring here to the farming and lower classes.

Marce   N.m.pl. Marks.

" Bwti'r marce douddeg."

About twelve o'clock.

The word is rarely heard except in reference to time. Before the days of clocks people observed the position of the sun, and put marks down to indicate the time, hence the word *marce.*

Marlat   N.m.s. A drake.

Plur. *marlatod.*

Marshant   N.m.s. A merchant.

Marshantwr is also used.

Marshanto   V. Intran. To carry on the business of a merchant.

Marshanteth   Abs. n. Commerce, business on a large scale.

Maslach   Abs. n. Nonsense.

" Beth yw shwt faslach wyt ti'n weyd? "

What is that nonsense which you speak?

Maslaw   [= maes-o-law.] Adv. By-and-by.

" Fe ddewa i màslaw."

I will come by-and-by.

Masog   N.m.s. A local magnate; the man who is looked up to in a neighbourhood for counsel and advice.

Plur. *masogion*.
Nearly obsolete.

Mas-o'i-gof Adv. In a passion, in bad temper.
"Ma Deio mâs-o'i-gof heddy."
David is in a passion to-day.
Lit.: David is out of his memory to-day.

Matar N.s. Matter.
" Beth yw'r matar ar y ceffyl? "
What is the matter with the horse?

Meddalwy N.m.s. A soft or imperfectly developed egg.
(Accent on second syll.).

Meddylie In the phrase *Ma hen feddylie arno* = He is
low-spirited or melancholic.

Megen N.f.s. One who is prolific in giving birth.
The word is mostly applied to a woman depre-
ciatingly.

Mei [= mi a'i.]
" Mei gweles e heddy."
I saw him to-day.

Meiddu V. Trans. To mix.
" Meiddu cwlwm."
Mixing culm.
" Meiddu morter."
Mixing mortar.

Meindo V. Intran. To be sure, beware, &c.
" Meindwch ddwad fory."
Be sure to come to-morrow.

Mel-y-gwcw N.m.s. Cuckoo pint (Arum maculatum);
lit.: The cuckoo's honey.

Melyn-yr-yd Charlock (Brassica sinapistrum).
Also *hatrish* (q.v.).

Mente Def. v. Said he.

Other parts of the verb are:—*Mentwn*, *mentech*, and *menten*.

Menter Abs. n. A venture, daring.

Mentro V. Intran. To venture, to risk.

Mentrus Adj. and Adv. Daring, bold.

Mentyg [= benthyg.] A loan.

Variants are: *mencyd* and *mincyd*.

Menyn-llwmpe N.m.s. Butter made up in lumps of from four to seven pounds. The word refers rather to the quality of the butter than to the quantity or its shape. Butter of the second class was formerly made up and sold in lumps, the best being sold in pounds.

Menyn-wyl-Beder Lit. S. Peter's butter, or, the butter of S. Peter's festival.

Formerly, within the memory of the oldest people now living, poor people used to go about to solicit butter in lieu of alms on S. Peter's Day. They carried it in a kind of jug, which was called *Shwg-menyn-Peder* (the jug of Peter's butter). Old Benny'r Twcwr was wont to relate that his grandfather paid a tribute of menyn-wyl-Beder regularly on S. Peter's Day to the Vicar of the parish.

Menyn-y-felldith N.m.s. Witch's butter.

A fungus growing on old rafters in stables and cowsheds. There is a superstition that if it fall on an animal and cling to its back, the animal will shortly die. Farmers regard it with dread.

Meredd Adj. Lacking in moral courage; having no will power.

Mesur N.m.s. A hymn.
"Rhoi mesur mâs i ganu."
Lit.: Giving a metre out to sing.
Formerly (before the days of the hymn-book) hymns were given out in church and chapel in couplets. The singers relied on their memory, and it was not advisable to give out more than two lines at a time.

Menog Calm and soothing. The word is applied to a quiet dingle that is favourable to meditation.

Mharen [= myharan.] N.m.s. Mutton.

Mhel V. Intran. To interfere with, to meddle with.
"Peidwch mhêl a'g e."
Don't meddle with him.

Miaw Onomatopœic. Cat's cry.

Micorn N.m.s. The core of a horn.

Midrwyo V. Tran. To put a ring or a swivel in a pig's snout to prevent his burrowing or turning up the ground.

Midwidd N.f.s. A midwife.

Mierin N.m.pl. Castrated lambs.

Miewal Part. Mewing. The cry of a cat.

Milanes N.f.s. A daring one; one that has an evil penchant.
"Milanes yw'r hen gath ma am hufen."
This old cat is a terror for cream.

Milgast [=milast.] Greyhound bitoh.

Mimrudd N.m.s. The configuration of the mouth; sometimes used in the wider sense of *facial expression*, as e.g., in the saying, " Mae e 'run fimrudd a'i dad "—He has the face of his father.

Minno Adv. Anyhow, anywise.
A variant is *menno*.

Minoitach N.f.pl. Women-folk, in a depreciatory sense.

Minoitwr N.m.s. A flirt, a man who is fond of going a-courting on Saturday nights.

Mistyn V. Intran. To die, in reference to animals only.
" Ma'r llo wedi mistyn i."
The calf is dead.

Mishtir N.m.s. Landlord.
Meistr tir or *tirfeddianwr* is never used, but the simple *mishtir*, a term which is full of significance in the mouth of a N. Pembroke-shire farmer, who has hardly yet realized what it is to be free from the shackles of feudalistic ideas, for observe. *mishtir* has reference not so much to the land as to the human worm who subsists on that land.

Mitinga V. Intran. (1) To swear paternity. (2) To sue an action at petty sessions.

Mitsho V. Intran. To play truant.

Mith Adj. Fruitful.
" Tir mîth "—Fruitful land.
Obsolescent.

Miwl N.m.s. A mule.

Miwn-eil Adv. phrase. In a twinkle, in a moment.
"Dere miwn eil."
Come at once.

Miwsig N.m.s. A mouth-organ.
It is very curious that the word is hardly ever used in any other sense, and that most musical instruments other than the mouth-organ are designated by their proper name.

Miwt N.m.s. A hybrid between a donkey and a horse, the sire being a he-donkey, and the dam a mare.

Mocial Part. Mocking.

Mochyn-slip N.m.s. A young pig about six months old.

Moddion-ty Coll. n. Furniture. The words *dodrefn, celfi.* &c., are never used here.
There is not a singular. When one article is spoken of it is referred to by name.

Moddion N.m.s. Medicine. The word has a plural form, but a singular meaning. There is not a dialectic plural, but the periphrasis *dou short o foddion, tri short,* &c.—two kinds of medicine, three kinds, &c.. is used instead.

Mofi [= myfi.] Pron. I, me, myself.

Moidro V. Intran. (1) To be delirious in a fever. (2) To become confused through worry or anxiety.

Moilen N.f.s. A hornless cow.

Moilid

V. Trans. and Intran. (1) To upset a cart.
(2) To have a relapse after childbirth.
  (1) " Moilid y cart."
    To upset the cart.
  (2) " Y cart wedi moilid."
    The cart is upset.
In the sense of a relapse after childbirth,
the word is usually prefixed with *ail*.
" Mae wedi ail-moilid " (not *foilid*).
She has had a relapse.

**Melwoden
  -jangol**

N.f.s. A charm for warts.
A snail, of the fattest proportions, was
caught between forefinger and thumb (the rest
fingers must not touch it, or the charm would
not act), and rubbed on the warts, after which
it was placed on a bramble bush with the
thorns piercing its body. When the snail had
putrefied, the warts disappeared.

Montesh

Abs. n. (1) Advantage. (2) Any mechanical
power or advantage in raising or moving heavy
bodies.

Morca

N.m.s. A small lake in waste land or marshy
ground, which is full of slimy matter.

Morddol

N.f.s. A sheet of water seen at a distance
appearing like a meadow covered with daisies.
An illusion which is seen only at rare intervals,
during certain conditions of the atmosphere.

Moren

N.f.s. A servant girl.
This is the form used in and around Mathry.
Variants are : —
Morwn (Gwaun Valley).
Morwm (Maenclochog).
The Plural of the last is *morwini*.

**Morgan-y
  -mot**
A garden flower.

Mort Exclam. The call-word of masons when they require their attendant to bring them mortar.

Morwn-y -neidir N.f.s. The yellow-bunting.

Moshwn Abs. n. Pretence, dumb show, &c.
" Mae e'n gneyd moshwn pregethu, ond stim fowr o shàp arno."
He makes pretence at preaching, but is not much of a hand at it.

Mowr Indef. Pron. Many.
" Ma dinion mowr wedi passo ffor-yn i'r ffair heddy."
Many people have passed this way to the fair to-day.

Mowrder N.m.s. Pride.
Balchder is very rarely heard. *Brasder* and *mowrder* are used for the same idea.
" Mae e wedi whiddo fel lliffan gida 'i fowr- der."
He is swollen like a toad with pride.

Mwdbridd N.m.s. The excreta of worms, which resembles fine earth.

Mwdredd N.m.s. An accumulation of filth and stagnant liquid excretum.

Mwgo V. Tran. To delude, deceive.
" Mae e wedi mwgo canodd a'i hen weniaith."
He has deceived hundreds with his flattery.

Mwgrwch N.m.s. Dense, black cloud emitted from a chimney, laden with dust and charred stuff.

Mwngci N.m.s. (1) Neckband of a horse. (2) An apish fellow.

Mwngo   V. Intran. A term used in reference to horses rubbing or scratching one another's back.

Mwl   N.m.s. " Y gwellt mân a'r cola na eith trw'r rhaca fach wrth racanu'r llawr dwrnu. We'r mwl yn arfer câl 'i ridillo."

Mwlyn   N.m.s. " Crafion dâs o lafur wedi 'u clwmu yw mwlyn."

Mwllfwg   N.m.s. The smoke caused by burning wood with a red-hot iron. If the wood is green the smoke is particularly stifling, fully justifying the descriptive name *mwllfwg.*

Mwmmial   Part. Humming.
" Mwmmial canu wrtho 'i hunan."
Humming a tune to one's-self.

Mwni   [= mynydd.] N.m.s. (1) Mountain. (2) Arable land.
" Ma Jâms wedi myn'd i'r mwni i redig."
James has gone to the field to plough.
Mini is a variant, but is not often used in the secondary sense. Around the Gwaun Valley the tendency is to restrict *mwni* to arable land, or a field where work is going on; and *mini* to mountain.

Mwntach   N.pl. A number of obstacles meeting fortuitously at the same time.

Mwrddwr   N.m.s. A murderer.

Mwrnedd   Adj. Sultry.

Mwrnin-du   N.m.s. Mourning; lit., black mourning. The Nown *mwrnin* is rarely used here except in conjunction with the Adj. *du*, black.

Mwseed   N.m.s. A musket.

Mwsharwm N.f.pl. Mushroom (accent on rŵm).
Sing. *mwsharwmsen*.
In some districts bordering on the Gwaun the
word is masculine, in which case the Sing. is
mwsharwmsyn.

Mwth   Adj. Abstemious. Said of a person who eats
little, and that little in as short a time and
with as little ceremony as possible. (Pron.
mŵth).

Mwyaren-las Dewberry (Rubus coesius).

Mwydyn N.m.s. (1) Earthworm. (2) An inoffensive
person.
Pl. *mwydon*.

**Mwydyn
-grwn** N.m.s. The opening or first furrow of a
ridge.

**Mwydyn
-y-fladur** N.m.s. The rim of a scythe.

**Myn'd-ar
ddrwg** An expression denoting that an animal has
broken fence and gone trespassing.

**Myn'd-
bobo'n-gam** V. phrase. To stroll along slowly and
leisurely.

N

Na [= gwnaf.] V. Tran. I will make, take, do, &c.
"Fe na'n llŵ."
I will take my oath.

Nabiddswn [= adnabuaswn.] Plupf. Subj. of Irreg. V. *adnabod.*
"Mei nabiddswn e yn mhig y frân."
I would know him in the crow's bill.

Nachwaith Conj. Nor.
"Sarna i ddim eishe dillad newy leni, na scidie nachwaith."
I do not require new clothes this year, nor shoes.

Nad N.f.s. A habit, a trick. Always in reference to an animal, and in a bad sense.
"Ma'r gaseg wedi disgu nâd ddrwg."
The mare has [learnt] a bad habit.

Nadi [= nag ydyw.] Verb. Intran. and Adv. It is not; no.
Variants are *nagdi* and *nacti*, the latter is heard in the neighbourhood of Dinas.

Nafus Adj. and Adv. Bad, exceeding, very, &c. (in a bad sense).
"Tewi nafus"—Bad weather.
"Ma'r prishodd yn nafus leni."
Prices are exceedingly bad this year.

Naid-binsh   N.f.s. A standing jump.

Naid-irfa   N.f.s. A running jump.

Nan   Particle. Beg pardon! (Vide *e*).

Nashwn   Coll. n. Strangers, a promiscuous gathering of men of different nationality.
"Ma pob math o hên nashwn yn Wdig nawr."
All kinds of strange people are to be met with in Goodwick now.

Nawr-a-
-lweth   [= yn awr ac eilwaith.] Adv. phrase. Now-and-again.
Nawr-a-glıceth is a variant.

Nawr-fach   Adv. Just now.
Nawr-jwst is also frequently used.

Naws   Adv. Nothing.
"Chliwes i naws sòn am hiny."
I have heard nothing about it.

Ne   In the phrase *yn-wir-ne*, and never in any other connection. The Adv. *yn-wir* is rarely used except in conjunction with the particle *ne*, which is added enclitically. The accent on *yn-wir-ne* varies. In ordinary asseveration it is on the second syllable—*yn-wir-ne*; in strong assertion it is on the first—*yn-wir-ne*; in very solemn protestation it is on the last—*yn-wir-né*.
Query: Is *ne* = *nef*, heaven?

Neeloth   N.m.s. A pocket handkerchief; never used for a cravat or a covering for the neck, as the word would seem to imply. It is very often used in conjunction with *poced*.

Nedwy   [= nodwydd.] N.f.s. Needle.

Nedwy-gron N.f.s. A darning needle.

Neges Sometimes used peculiarly, as in the following:—" Ma rhaid i fi fyn'd i Bergwein i mofyn
neges dros Mrs. Ifans."
I must go to Fishguard on business for Mrs.
Evans.

Neges-gardis N.f.s. A message of a special character ; an
important errand. When a country woman goes
to market and has special business to transact,
or some special article to procure, she ties one
garter much tighter than the other, that the
consequent inconvenience may remind her of
the special errand.

**Neidir
-gantrwed** N.f.s. Centipede—the insect so called.

**Neidir-mish
-Mal** Metaphorically for " A snake in the grass."

Nel In the phrase " Ar nêl myn'd "—On the point
of going.

**Nerth-yn
-rhedeg** Hemorrhage at childbirth.

Nesim [= wneuthum.] V. Intran. I did.

Newid Abs. n. Cheapness.
Gof. : " Beth we prish yr aner? "
At. : " Pum punt."
Sylw. : " O, we newid arni."
Quest. : " What was the price of the heifer?"
Ans. : " Five pounds."
Remark : " Oh, there was cheapness upon it" ;
(i.e., it was cheap).

Newy-nawr Adv. phrase. Just now, a short while ago.
" Newy-nawr etho nhw."
They went just now.

Nhwynte [= nhwythaa.] Pron. Adv. They likewise.

Niawnyd [= ymunionu.] V. Intran. To lay to, to set about, &c.
" Niawnwch atti nawr, bois bach! "
Work away, now, my lads! "

Nidden N.f.s. Fog.
" Nidden lâs, menwent frâs."
Lit.: A blue fog, a rich churchyard.

Niddwr N.m.s. The night-jar.

Nife N.f.s. A peculiar kind of adze.

Niflaw N.m.s. Thick mist and small rain.

Nino'r [= yn enw'r.] In the phrases, *nino'r tad.
nino'r anwyl, nino'r dyn, &c.*
A variant is *neno'r.*

Nithion Coll. n. Rubbish winnowed out of corn, apart from the chaff proper.

No Adv. Anyhow, in any case, &c.
" Sana i'n dŵad, no."
I am not coming, anyhow.

Noblo V. Tran. To peel, a term applied to peeling turnips, and almost restricted to this usage.

Noclo Said of a shaft horse that leans too heavily on the lower joints of the hind legs while taking a load down hill.

Nod-goch N.m.s. Red ochre; used as a sheep mark.

Noflwr N.m.s. The wind bladder of a fish.

Northman N.m.s. A North Walian.
The term is never used except for a native of North Wales.
Plur. *Northmyn.*
Fem. *Northes.*

Notwr N.m.s. Music copyist.
Formerly, choirs were obliged to write or copy out their own music. The best local musician who had the neatest hand was usually assigned the task of copying, and came to be known as the *notwr* of the district. John Jâms, of Sychbant, was a celebrated *notwr* in the Gwaun district fifty years ago, and some of his MS. books, in the oblong, old-style shape, with brass nails and clasp, are still to be found.

Nwli N.m.s. A small trench, usually dug across a field for the purpose of irrigation. (Pron. nwl-i). Heard only around Fishguard.

Nwmor [= nemawr.] Adv. Hardly, scarcely.
" Weles i nwmor i un 'no."
I saw scarcely any one there.
A variant is *nimor.*

**Nwyfe
Nyth** [= nwyddau.] N.pl. Materials. goods.

·cwhwrw A mare's nest.
This refers to a practical joke played by lads at schools upon their younger schoolmates. At the nesting season a lad tells (with a serious face) a number of younger boys that he has found a *nyth cwhwrw.* The young " mischiefs," always on the alert for new discoveries and bold adventures, eagerly beg to be shown this wonder of nest-land. The cunning jester leads them miles away, through brake and bog, uphill and down dale, till at last, when the youngsters are quite out of wind, he arrives at the nest, which turns out to be nothing but a fresh heap of horse dung!

O

Obiti　　　　[= o ddeuti.]　Prep.　About, around.
A variant is *obuti*.
(Accent on bit and bwt).

Obo　　　　Inter.　An exclamatory particle.
" Obo'r oi ! "　Get away dog !
" Obo'r dyn wr ! "　What is the matter with
the man !

Odi　　　　[= ydyw.]　V. and Adv.　It is, yes.

Odyn-fwni　　N.f.s.　Field kiln.
The following interesting account of the old-
style kiln is taken almost *verbatim* from a letter
from the pen of Mr. Edward Evans, of Parselle,
which appeared in the " Pembroke County
Guardian," under date of January 1st, 1898 :
" The *odyn furni* was a primitive but efficient
invention for drying corn in ancient times,
before coal and culm came into use. As my
parents can remember it in use, I am in position to give a description of it. The kiln consisted of a large and long gutter, or flue, about
10 yards long, more or less. At the entrance
was the fireplace. and at the far end was a
square space like a room, over which was a
framing of timber. similar to a flat pitched
roof of a house, with an inclination of, say,
about 30 degrees. On this framing was put
thatch (wheat straw) called *cloig*, being fixed
close and tidy. It required an expert to do
this part of the work properly. On the thatched

N

flooring was spread a hair cloth, called *brethyn rhawn*, which was a large sheet, made specially for the work, and of home manufacture. On this sheet was spread the corn. Then beginning on one side, and as the process of drying went on, the corn was turned gradually towards the other side, and fresh corn put in its place. When the grain at the farthest side was sufficiently dry it was drawn down on a sheet spread on the ground to receive it, and conveyed thence in sacks. A matter of supreme importance was the fire. It was necessary to have a bright, flaming and smokeless fire, maintaining a current or steady blast towards the drying floor, which only an experienced kilnsman could manage. The fire material preferred was the straw of the corn itself, otherwise heath, furze and fern were used. A dry, breezy day, with frosty air if possible, was selected for the drying. The slight flavour of smoke on the meal was considered a relish by the old people, much as some like the flavour of smoked ham nowadays."

The *odyn* enters as an element into many field names right throughout the Welsh part of the county. We have:—wrglo'r odyn, parc-yr-odyn, allt-yr-odyn, weun-yr-odyn, &c.

Oferdda   V. Intran. To waste one's life and substance wantonly ; to live riotously.

Ofer-garu   N.m.s. Pansy, the flower so-called.

Ofiad   [= nofio.] V. Intran. To swim. A variant is *oifad*.

Ofnasol   Adv. Wonderfully, awfully. " Mae'n wer ofnasol." It is wonderfully cold.

Ofon [= heb fod yn.] In the phrase *ofon hir* = before long.
"Fe ddewan gatre ofon hir."
They will come home before long.

Offt N.f.s. A tilled field.

Oga [= ogof.] N.f.s. Cave.

Ogol N.f.s. Wheel-track, rut.
Plur. *ogle.*

Ogwan-y
  -moch Coll. n. Haws, the berries of the hawthorn

Ong [= o fy.] P. Prep. Of my.
"Fe ethim miwn i'r jinshop gida cwpwl ong hen ffrindie."
I went into the gin-shop with a few of my old friends.

Oifed [= aeddfed.] Adj. Ripe.

Oil Abs. n. Element, condition.
"Ma Jòs yn 'i oil dim ond iddo gâl tipyn o ganu."
Joseph is in his own native element when he gets a bit of singing.

Oil-o-bai N.m.s. A mercurial ointment used in destroying lice on pigs.

Oin [= oeddynt.] They were.

Ola-gwt Adv. Last of all.
"Yr ola-gwt i gau y ièt."
The last one must close the gate.
(Accent on gwt).

Olier N.f.s. A small room at the side of a larger room, with a sloping roof. *Vide* plan under *torad-ty.*

Oma [= oddiyma.] Prep. Hence, from here.

Ombeidis Adj. and Adv. Exceeding, exceedingly, awful, and awfully, &c.
"Wdw i'n grig ombeidis."
I am exceedingly hoarse.

Ombeis [= onibae.] Adv. Were it not, but for that, &c.

On [= o'r.] P. Prep. Used in the phrase *on gore* = all right.

Ona [= oddiyna.] Prep. Thence.

Ono [= oddiyno.] Thence, from that place.

Onte [= onid e.] Adv. Is it not? Otherwise, &c.
The word is used also as a veiled threat.
"Paid ti a myn'd, onte——."
Don't you go, or ——.

Opstrobilo Inter. Now then for it! Hey presto!
(Gair mowr John Ifan, y sâr).

Optop Adv. Face to face, unexpectedly, although not one of these words conveys the exact shade of meaning.
"Fe gwrddon yn optop."
We met unexpectedly, and right face to face. (Accent on first syll.).

Ordors Orders, commands. The word is thoroughly domiciled.

Orenshen N.f.s. An orange.

Organ-grib N.m.s. A plaything consisting of a dressing-comb and a sheet of thin paper. The comb is placed inside the sheet of paper and both are put against the mouth, when, by means of sound emissions, curious musical notes are produced.

Orgaml   N.m.s. Marjoram (Origanum vulgare).

Os   [= er ys.] Adv. Since, while, ago, &c.
"Ma William wedi dŵad gatre os wthnos."
William came home a week ago.

Oson   [= hosan.] N.f.s. Stocking.
Plur. *sane.*
Sane byron—Socks.

Oson   N.f.s. Metaphorically for a miser's purse, or riches.
"Hen oson y cibydd."
The miser's purse.

Ots   In the phrase *Stim ots* = It doesn't matter.
It also means different from, unusual, &c.
"Rhwbeth yn ots na'i gily'."
Something different from usual.

Our   [= aur.] (1) N. Gold. (2) Adj. Beautiful.
It has this meaning in the expression:
"'Mhlentyn our i" = My beautiful child;
literally, My golden child.

Our-y-gors   N.m.s. Marsh Marigold (Caltha palustris).

Owyr   [= awyr.] N.f.s. The sky, the air.

Owyr   Inter. Dear me! Gracious me! Goodness! &c.
Owyr-bach! owyr-fargol! owyr-anwyl! and
owyr-ole! are words similarly used.

℗

Padell-bres N.f.s. A large brass pan used for brewing purposes, or for boiling milk in, making cheese, etc.

Pango V. Intran. To faint.

Paimo V. Tran. To press down.
Used in this sense in the following and similar expressions : —
" Paimwch y blawd yn y garnesh yn dda a'r corlog, fe neith gadw'n well."

Paish-a-hwp N.f.s. Crinoline.

Paledig Part. Tiring.
" Gwaith paledig iawn yw rhwmo gwenith, mae e mor drwm."
It is very tiring work to bind wheat, because it is so heavy.

Palfen N.f.s. The paw of a cat or dog.
Plur. *palfen*.

Pale Part. To become insipid ; said of beer or other beverage.
The term is stronger than *fflato* (q.v.).

Palo Part. Tired out, wearied.
" Wdw i wedi pàlo 'n lân."
I am absolutely tired out.

Pam

N.m.s. A garden bed.
" Dima bâm ffein o winiwns."
Here is a fine bed of onions.
Pâmed is also used in the same sense.

Pancofen

N.f.s. A pancake.
Pl. *pancwg, pancogi,* and *pancogod.*

**Pancogi
-panas**

N.pl. Parsnip pancakes.
This was considered a delicacy by the old
people. It was made from sliced parsnip beaten
into a pulp, and kneaded with wheaten flour and
fresh butter.

Pantell

A quantity of furze trodden down into a
bundle ready to be carted home.
" Peder whin-fforched neith bantell, deugen
pantell neith lwyth."
Four forkfuls (of furze) will make a *pantell,*
forty *pantells* will make a load.

Papre

N.m.pl. Papers, more especially newspapers.

Papur-hala

N.m.s. Notepaper, oftener called *papur-
scrifeny* in most localities.

Papur-twtsh

N.m.s. Paper steeped in salt-petre. which
ignites slowly.
Papur-twtsh-a-fflinten—Touch-paper and flint.
Farm labourers formerly carried these for the
purpose of obtaining a light for their pipes.

Par

N.m.s. A bolt. (Pron. pâr).

Par

N.m.s. Used in the combination *par o
ddillad,* a suit of clothes.
" Ma eishe pâr o ddillad newy arna i."
I want a new suit of clothes.

Parlwr

N.m.s. Parlour.

Paro   [= para.] V. Intran. To continue, to last, to persevere.

Paro   V. Trans. To bolt.
"Paro'r drws dros y nos."
Bolting the door overnight.

Parrog   N.m.s. A sort of esplanade, or walk by the sea.

Parte   N.m.pl. Parts.
"Yn y parte hyn."
In these parts.

Partoians   Abs. n. Preparation.
The word is a funny hybrid, the second element evidently being the English *ance*.

Pas   Abs. n. Sale, in the phrase *dim pàs ar bethe* = no sale.

Pasnetah   N.m.s. A parsonage, a clergyman's residence.

Pasnod   N.c.pl. People who live on the fat of the land.
"Y mân grâch a'r pasnod breishon
Yn y pridd yn fwyd i gindron."
— (Old ballad).

Paso   Said of a horse that throws its legs evenly and regularly, and trots smoothly. (Pron. pàso).

Passo   V. Tran and Intran. (1) To pass an examination. (2) To pass by.

Pastbord   N.m.s. Cardboard.

Paste   N.f.s. Pastry.
Plur. *pasteiod.*

" Dwgwl Istwyll, cestyll y gwile,
Pob hen wrachen yn whilo'i chedache
Am damed bach o grwstyn paste."
(Old Twelfth Day Song).

Patins   N.f.pl. Pattens, formerly used by women who were particular about keeping their feet dry and their shoes clean.
Sing. *patinsen.*

Pecilled   N.m.s. A peckful.

Peco   V. Intran. To beat with the finger while reckoning.
" Ellir dim rhifo trwp o ddefed yn gowir heb bèco."
One cannot reckon a flock of sheep correctly without beating with the finger.

Pechod-win   A small fault. a pardonable or venial sin. (Accent on win).

Pedlin   Adj. Strolling.
" Cario shop bedlin."
To go about as a pedlar.
" Hen ddyn bach a shop bedlin gidag e."
A poor old man of a pedlar.

Pedrwbwl   Num. Adj. Quadruple.

Peil   Indef. Pron. Many.
" Peile o ddinion."
Many people.
There is a plural *peile.*

Peilo   V. Tran. To throw.
" Peilo cerig "—To throw stones.

Peiment   N.m.s. A paved way or floor.

Peimo V. Trans. To pave a floor.
"Llawr wedi 'i beimo a cherig poplis."
A floor that is paved with pebble-stones.

Peis N.m.s. Cheese-press.
Occasionally the forms *pois* and *pwys* are
heard in the N.W., from Letterston towards
Mathry and the coast.

Peito V. Tran. To excel, surpass.
"Ma Willie Vagwrgoch wedi peito Dafi Blân-
pant yn seiffro."
Willie of Vagwrgoch has excelled David of
Blanpant in arithmetic.

Peitur N.m.s. Pewter.
"Y March Prês a'r Gaseg Beitur"—names
of two small farms in the Parish of Morfil. The
latter is no longer in existence, the land having
been added to that of the former, and the
building demolished.

Peilderodd Abs. u. A long distance.
"Mae e wedi cered bellderodd o ffordd."
He has walked a long distance.

Pellen
-bisgota N.f.s. The torch used at salmon poaching.
Made of old sacking sewed into a big ball with
wire thread. The sacking had been previously
treated with coal-tar, and the ball, when completed, was soaked in paraffin oil. A fresh
application of paraffin was put whenever necessary. The ball was attached to the end of a
long pole, and borne by the *fflachifwr* at the
head of the *biddin*. On a dark night, when the
atmosphere was dry, its light could be seen at
a distance of five or six miles, and the whole
countryside knew that the dreadful *biddin* was
bent on its depredations.

Pen N.m.s. The mouth.
Geneu is never used here for the mouth.

Pen Used prepositionally in the phrase *ar ben ffair* = in or at a fair.

Pen In such phrases as :—
Pen dyn—an excellent man ;
Pen boi—a jolly fellow ;
Pen hen gibydd—a real old miser ;
Pen cantwr—a fine singer ; &c.

Pen-blwydd N.m.s. Birthday.
" Mae e'n câl i ben-blwydd heddy."
To-day is the anniversary of his birthday.

Pencifaredd Abs. n. A small bit of work, a " stitch."
" Stim o hano wedi gneyd pencifaredd heddy."
He has not done a " stitch " of work to-day.

Pendo N.f.pl. Straw thatch.
Pendoien, the singular, means a sheaf of thatch.

Penddaru To become listless or drowsy whilst listening to uninteresting talk.

Penddof Adj. Said of a colt which, when broken in, takes kindly to the reins.

Peneth N.f.s. A penknife.

Penfarch N.m.s. An aqueduct, a canal.

Pengalchu V. Tran. and Intran. To lime wash the outside roof of a house.

Pengogo V. Intran. To argue in a somewhat bickering spirit.
Usually said of an old couple sitting on either side of the fire talking or arguing for the purpose of aggravating one another.

Pengored   Adj. A term applied to one who cannot keep a secret.

Penhen   Adj. Precocious, wise beyond one's years. (Accent on hên).

Penisha   N.m.s. Parlour.

The word *parlwr* is heard only among the better class, never among the ordinary people.

Penloian   Part. A term applied to a person who, with head leaning on hand, sits down and indulges in day dreams.

Penllinyn   N.m.s. A long account or yarn rehearsed from beginning to end.

" Dina gôf sy gida Ifan Mwrw ; mae e'n gallu adrodd hanesion am hên bethe yn un penllinyn, ma'n show i chi glwed e."

Evan Murrow has a wonderful memory, he can give long accounts of old things in a manner that is charming to listen to.

Pennad   N.m.s. A mouthful. Used synecdochically for a meal.

" Sana i wedi câl pennad y dydd heddy."
I have not had a meal to-day.

Penog   N.m.s. The head of the family.

" Penog y ty."
The goodman of the house.

Penrewi   V. Intran. To be benumbed with cold.

Pensel-nadd   N.f.s. A home-made slate pencil. The lads of Ysgol Felin-Bictwn obtained stone for the purpose from a quarry near Llanychllwydog Church.

Penshingrug   N.m.s. A winnowing mound, the elevated spot where winnowing was anciently done.

Pensithu   Part. Standing about till one is cold.

Penstiff   Adj. Headstrong, self-willed.

Penswrdanu   V. Tran. To make the head giddy, to confuse one.
"Ma 'i hen frawl hi 'n ddigon i benswrdanu dyn."
Her old talk [or babble] is enough to turn a man's head.

Pentigili   Adv. All the way.
"Fe geres i 'Bergwein bentigili."
I walked all the way to Fishguard.

Pentrifwr   N.m.s. The captain of the organised gang of salmon poachers, which called itself the *biddin bisgota*. He always carried and manipulated the *trifer*—the specially constructed pronged hook with which the fish were caught.

Penu   [= dybenu.] V. Tran. and Intran. To finish, complete.

Penwalldod   Abs. n. Dementation.

Penwast   N.f.s. An improvised bridle. A bridle made of rope, for the purpose of leading a young colt, or a horse to a fair.

Penwendid   Abs. n. Imbecility.

Penwent   N.m.s. The batch of corn taken annually to the mill to be ground for bread.
"Mae'n rhaid i ni fyn'd i grasu a melina penwent drost yr hâf."
We must take the necessary quantity of corn to the kiln and mill to last over the summer.

Penwngar   Adj. (1) Opinionated. (2) Headstrong.

Pen-y-glust   N.m.s. The drum of the ear.
"Ma'r sŵn mowr ma 'n ddigon i dinu pene cluste dyn lawr."
This great noise is enough to shatter the drums of one's ears.

Perfe   N.m.pl. Works, i.e., the mechanical parts of a clock, watch, &c.
"Perfe'r clòc " = the works of a clock.

Perfeddiwn   Coll. n. Entrails.

Permeisho   V. Tran. and Intran. To promise.

Persen   N.f.s. A pear.

Perswad   Abs. n. Persuasion.
"Mi gesim berswâd arno i fyn'd."
I persuaded him to go ; lit. : I had persuasion upon him to go.

Perswado   V. Tran. To persuade. The word is thoroughly domiciled.

Pert   Adj. Pretty.

Perticiler   Adj. Important.
"Seni 'n berticiler i olchi'r crise •'r wthnos hon."
It is not important to wash the shirts this week.

Petan-cord   N.m.s.   Patent   cord,   the   best   corduroy. (Accent on cord).

Petrishen   N.f.s. A partridge.
Plur. *petrish* and *petrishod*.

Pethe-melus Coll. n. Lozenges, sweets, confection.

Pethifed N.m.s. Intoxicating drink.
Rarely used of any other drink.

Piana N.f.s. Pianoforte.
" Y biana hono."
This pianoforte.

Pibir
-cochion Coll. n. Chilly—the pod of Guinea-pepper.

Pibirment N.m.s. Peppermint.

Pibo V. Intran. To have diarrhœa, referring to animals only.

Pibonwinin N.m.s. An icicle.
Plur. *pinbonw.*

Pibren N.f.s. A peppermint drop, sweet.
Plur. *pibrod.*

Pibrwyn N.f.pl. Dwarf rushes.
The singular is *pibrwynen.*

Pibyn N.m.s. Diarrhœa, referring to animals only.

Pica A. j. Sarcastic, sharp, curt.
" Ma tafod pica iawn da hi."
She has a very sarcastic tongue.
" Dyn pica "—A curt man.

Picas N.f.s. A pickaxe.

Picil N.m.s. The brine made by the salting of meat.

Picleryn N.m.s. A fellow who is made the butt-end of every joke.

Piclo   V. Trans. To pickle.
" Piclo dail coohion."
Pickling red cabbage.

Picwarch   N.f.s. A pitchfork.
The implement used in haymaking, &c.

**Picwarch
-Sais**   N.f.s. A steel fork, in contradistinction to
picwarch-Gimro, a home-maae fork or pick,
generally made of iron.
Literally, an Englishman's fork.

Pidere   N.f.pl. Beads.
In the phrase " Ma gormod o bidere wrth i
stori e." Lit.: " He has too many beads to
his tale," said of a man who is inordinately
long at extempore prayer. An old man living
in he Gwaun Valley was noted for long, tedious
extempore prayers. The wags of the chapel
gallery used to lay themselves out for a snooze
when he was called upon i ddwad at waith,
remarking that they had ample time,—" Ma
pidere ——— yn ddigon hir i fyn'd i'r Nefôdd
a nol, ni gewn afel ar y ddou pen os collwn ni'r
canol."
" Shishal pidere " is the phrase for
soliloquizing.

Pidinc   An onomatopœic word.
" Pidoli, pidoli, pidinc,
Pidoli'r asen fach." &c.
                    (Old Nursery Rhyme).

Piff   Inter. and Adv. (1) Good-for-nothing. (2)
Suddenly.
" Fe ddiffododd y ganwyll piff."
The candle went out suddenly.

Pigad   N.m.s. A small bit, a particle.
Pigadyn—the diminutive of the above, means
the tiniest bit or particle.

Pigeidad A small bit of anything.
Plur. *pigeide.*

Pigena V. Intran. Beginning to rain, raining a few
scattered drops.
"Odi 'n bwrw? "
"Na di, ond mae'n pigena peth."
Is it raining?
No, but there are a few scattered drops.

Piglwyd Adj. Pallid.
"Golwg digon piglwyd sy arno."
He looks pallid enough.

Pigodyn N.m.s. A pimple.
Plur. *pigode.*

Pigwn N.m.s. A species of dog-fish.

Pigwrn [= migwrn.] N.m.s. The ankle.

Pig-y-grechi N.m.s. Herb-Robert (Geranium robertianum).
"Pig-y-grechi yw'r llisewin gore 'n y byd at
nifel yn pisho gwâd."
Herb-Robert is the best herb in the world for
an animal that has the bloody issue.

Pilffrin N.m.s. A small, weedy child, especially one
with a weak appetite.
Fem. *pilffren.*

Pilw N.m.s. Pillow.

Pilyn N.m.s. An article of clothing.

Pin-bach N.m.s. An ordinary pin.

Pin-clopa A larger pin, with a boss.

Pin-drainen   A pin made of a white thorn spike.
Formerly used by poor people who could not
afford the luxury of bought pins. The spikes
were denuded of their bark and then hardened
in an oven.

Pin-mwrnin   A small black pin, used in pinning mourning
to hats.

Pincas   N.m.s.   A pincushion.

Pinco   V. Intran.   To tidy.
" Ma eishe pinco tipyn arna i cyn myn'd i'r
cwrdd."
I want to tidy myself a little before going to
the meeting.

Pinshad   N.m.s.   A pinch, a small quantity of anything.

Pinshin   N.m.s.   A pension.
" Mae e'n tinu pinshin nawr."
He draws a pension now.

Pinshwrn   N.m.pl.   Pincers.

Pinwyn   N.m.s.   Bed.
" O'r pinwyn i'r pentan "—From bed to the
fireside.
The bed in a small cottage is on a level with
the pinions of the roof, hence the word.

Pipin-show   N.f s.   A side-show ; lit. : a peeping show,
but the term has a much wider signification :
it means any covered side-show, but does not
include merry-go-rounds.
To enter a *pipin-show* was regarded as a
serious fault in a chapel communicant in by-
gone days, and the delinquent was invariably
excommunicated.

Pircs Coll. n. Fatted pigs about one year old, or a little more. The term is never used for a younger pig, or for one above 18 months old.

Piscodyn
-heuog N.m.s. Salmon.

Pisgod-cifrin N.m.coll. Salmon caught by the *biddin bisgota* (q.v.), i.e., by the organised band of poachers.

Pisho N.m.s. Urine.
V. Intran. To make urine, to pass water from the system.

Pisho'r
-gwely N.m.pl. The dandelion flower.

Pishwel N.m.s. A pool of liquid manure or dung.

Pishyn N.m.s. A piece, a recitation.
(1) " Gweyd pishyn "—To recite a passage.
(2) " Pishyn o frethyn "—A piece of cloth.

Pishyn N.m.s. A piece, bit. in reference to coin.
Pishyn-tair = a three-penny bit.
   ,,   *gròt* = a four-penny bit.
   ,,   *coron* = a five-shilling piece.
It is never used with *swllt, hanner sofren,* and *sofren.*

Plago V. Trans. To tease, vex.
" John! paid a plàgo 'r rhoces fach."
John! do not tease the little girl.

Plam N.m.s. A carpenter's plane. (Pron. plâm).

Plamo V. Tran. To plane (in carpentry).

Planc N.m.s. Bakestone.
" Bara planc."
Bakestone bread.

Plance N.m.s. The boarded platform of a thresh-floor.

Plani V. Intran. To arrange, to design, to plan.
" Rown i wedi plàni myn'd i Hwlffor fory."
I had arranged to go to Haverfordwest to-morrow.

Plant-Becca Coll. n. The Rebecca rioters; now used of any gang of rowdies.

Plante N.com.pl. Children, in an endearing sense: the equivalent of the classical *plantos*.

Plat N.m.s. A plate. (Pron. plàt).

Platin-escid N.m.s. The tip-plate of a boot.

Platshen N.f.s. A big squirt of tobacco or other spittle.

Pledins A hot argument.
" Fe âth yn bledins rhwnto ni 'll dou."
A hot argument ensued between us both.

Pleisen N.f.s. Any kind of flat-fish, not restricted to plaice.

Plentyn -shawns N.m.s. An illegitimate child; lit.: a chance chiid.

Pleso V. Trans. To please. (Pron. plèso).

Plet N.m.s. A leisure moment. (Pron. plèt).

Plet N.m.s. A chat.
" Ma Dafy wedi cwrdd a William Philib yn rhwle, a ma'r ddou yn câl plèt, te fise ma smityn."
David has met William Phillips somewhere, and the two are having a chat, or he wolld be here this long while.

Plet N.m.s. A bale, in conjunction with *gwair*, *plèt o wair*, a bale of hay.

Plicen N.f.s. A milch cow in fond language.

Plim Adj. To be full to the brim.
"Ma'r llestri llâth yn blìm."
The milk vessels are full to the brim.

Plow-brist N.m.s. A breast plough. The instrument used in paring ground for the purpose of making *bieting*, or of obtaining *mate*.

Plowman N.m.s. Foreman or head servant on a farm.

Plwmp Adv. Abrupt, in reference to speech.
"Fe wedodd plwmp."
He spoke abruptly.

Plyf-y-wein N.m.pl. Cotton grass (Eriophorum polystachion).

Pobi-neithor The custom of bringing gifts of foodstuffs to a young woman on the eve of her wedding which formerly obtained here. With these gifts the *cace-neithor* would be made, hence probably the name *pobi-neithor*.

Poced N.f.s. Pocket.

Poddwll N.m.s. A superfluity of melted wax or tallow in a lighted candle, which, accumulating around the wick, puts the light out.

Poindod Abs. n. A difficulty.
"Os cewn i gwmint o boindod i gâl cwlwm leni a geson i lline, ma'n well i ni fod hebddo."
If we experience the same difficulty in getting culm this year as we did last year, we had better be without it.

Polga   N.m.s. A fence at the junction of two hedges, much after the form of two hurdles placed crosswise, as shown in the illustration.

Polyn   N.m.s. A pole, a piece of timber. Plur. *polion.*

Pompren   [= pontbren.] N.f.s. A footbridge.

Pop   N.m.s. Lemonade.
Shinshir-pòp—Gingerade.

Poplis   N.m.pl. Pebble-stones, cobbles.
Sing. *poplisen.*
Another form is *popls.*
" Llwyth o boplis o Barrog Tidrath."
A load of pebble-stones from the Parrog, Newport.

Porfa-Edryn   The grass of St. Edryn's Churchyard.
There is a legend that it was a certain cure for hydrophobia in man and beast.

Pos   N.m.s. (1) A difficult task. (2) A riddle.
(1) " Mae'n dipyn o bôs i ddisgu'r ffidil."
It is a difficult task to master the violin.
(2) " Dima bôs i chi : —
    ' Mi weles i na welo phawb
      Y cŵd a'r blawd yn cered,
      A'r hen frân ddu ar ben ty 'n toi
      A'r wilan yn troi y defed.'
Beth wêdd e ? "
Here are a few other interesting *posis* : —
" Beth sy'n cisgu ar y dowlad a'i ddoupen yn ngheuad ? "
Ateb : Wŷ.
" Beth sy'n cisgu ar y dowlad a'i fys yn 'i ligad ? "

Ateb: Eirw.
" Milgi main wherw
Ar ganol parc garw,
Fe ladd ac fe fling,
Chiffarthith e ddim—Beth yw e? "

Ateb: Bladur.
" Llwydyn bach, llwydyn bach,
Ble wyt ti'n rhedeg?
'Ma rhaid i fi redeg,
Nawr ganed fy nhad—Beth yw e? "

Ateb: Mŵg.
" Beth sy'n myn'd trw'r claw ac yn gadel 'i
berfe ar iol? "

Ateb: Nedwy ac ede.

[There are hundreds of similar riddles, which
would make an interesting collection.]

Postol   N.m.s. A buttress.
These were rudely constructed ones, made of
stone and earth, built against a bulging wall to
prevent it from falling.
Plur. *postolion*.

Post-yr-houl   N.m.s. Sunbeam.
Plur. *pyst-yr-houl*.
            " Pyst yr houlos,
            Glaw yn agos."   —(Old Saw).

**Poten-pen
-genad**   A harvest term, defined thus by an old farm-
hand :—" Taro gida'r claw pan na bo tô agor
wedi 'i neyd."

Potrel   [= potel.] N.f.s. A bottle.

Potsh   N.m.s. A meal consisting of mashed potatoes
and buttermilk.

Poun   [= paun.] Com. n. Peacock.

Powdwr   Adv. Extremely, absolutely.
" Yn bowdwr feddw "—Helplessly drunk.
" Yn bowdwr ddwl "—Extremely foolish.

Powl   N.m.s. A long pole, especially that apper-
taining to a machine.

Powlo   V. Trans. To cut hair, to poll.

Powltis   N.m.s. Poultice.

Powlto   V. Tran. To refine flour at the mill.

Powri   [= poeri.] V. Intran. To spit.

Powryn   N.m.s. Spittle.

Powsen   N.f.s. A louse. A euphemistic word.

Powso   V. Intran. To look in the head of a child
for lice.

Prawn   [= prydnawn.] N.m.s. Afternoon.
This phonetic corruption of the word *prydnawn* is only heard in the greeting *prawn dâ
'chi!*—Good afternoon to you!

Pregeth   Used peculiarly in the following and similar
expressions : —
" Mae'n bregeth i weyd "—It is wonderful to
relate.
" Mae'n bregeth i wel'd "—It is marvellous
to behold.
" Mae'n bregeth meddwl "—It is astonishing
to think.
" Mae'n bregeth i'r byd i glŵed "—It is
remarkably strange to hear.

Preint   N.m.s. Print.
" Preint brâs "—Large type.
" Preint mân "—Small type.

Pren-gochel N.m.s. The mountain ash.

The *pren-gochel* or *cerdinen* was held in high esteem as a sort of guardian angel by the generation now passing away. Benny'r Twccwr remembered the time when he dared not go a journey in the dark without first arming himself with a sprig of the *pren-gochel*. A V-shaped twig was cut and put in a pocket on the left side, and was believed to have virtue in warding off ghosts, white ladies, &c.

Somewhere near every *clom* cottage—generally on a hedge opposite the door—stands a solitary mountain ash, the descendant of many an ancestor which thrived on the same spot, weather-beaten and lumbered by a host of dead limbs, but at one time a venerable guardian of the destinies of the old-world cottage.

When a lad at school, I used to put some of the berries of the *pren-gochel* in my pockets, believing that a double portion of luck would fall to my lot at *whare bwtwne*. Each berry, I thought, would win a button. It is not strange if the mountain ash berry quickly disappeared from the trees.

Pren-hollt N.m.s. A long wooden wedge used for splitting timber.

Pren-twshc N.m.s. A stick for holding thread or yarn in spinning.

Pren-y -pererin N.m.s. Wayfaring-tree (Viburnum lantana).

Pren-yr-ach N.m.s. Mistletoe.
The word is nearly obsolete, but sixty years ago it was in common use.

Pres N.m.s. A wardrobe with shelves. The lower part usually has drawers. (Pron. près).

Prica

N.m.s. A long stick with a hook at one end and pointed at the other used as a pin in thatching.

Pridie

N.m.pl. Meals.

The following is a list of foods in vogue half-a-century ago : —

Cawl—Broth. The N. Pembrokeshire broth contains a little of everything that grows in the garden, in addition to the inevitable *lwmpyn o gig mochyn* (piece of bacon).

Cawl erfin—Turnip broth.

  ,, *côch scwarnog*—Hare soup.

  ,, *llâth*—Very thin oatmeal porridge.

  ,, *maidd*—Whey and bread.

Bwdram—Thin flummery, sweetened with treacle.

Uwd-a-llâth—Thick flummery, allowed to cool into a jelly, served with milk.

Sopas—Oatmeal and buttermilk.

Potsh—Mashed potatoes and fresh buttermilk.

Poten-reis—Rice pudding.

Rheis-a-llâth—Rice and milk.

Twmplen—Dumpling—apple, gooseberry, or other fruit.

Troli—A ball of oatmeal dough mixed with lard and boiled in broth.

Tea drinking was rarely indulged in till comparatively recent. There were only three meals, viz., *brecwast*, *cino*, and *swper*. Breakfast was at 8, dinner at 1, and supper at 6.

Breakfast in the olden days consisted of *cawl-ail-dwmad* (broth re-heated) and bread and cheese, or of hot milk and bread and cheese. The old farmer rarely consumed his own butter, he sold it instead, and usually counted upon this produce for one-third of the rent. The evening meal consisted usually of *scadan sych a budram* (dried herring and flummery), or of *cawl llâth* with barley bread and cheese.

Prifedyn   [= pryfyn.] N.m.s. Insect.

Prifyn-clust   Ear-wig. Used metaphorically for a man who whispers vain words into a young woman's ears to poison her mind.

Prifyn-tan   N.m.s. Glow-worm, also called *Canwyll-y-dinion-bach*—the fairies' candle.

Pring   [= prin.] Adj. and Adv. Scarce, scarcely.

Pringder   [= prinder.] Abs. n. Scarcity.

Priodas-geffile   Literally a *horse-wedding*, referring to the old-time fashionable Welsh wedding among the well-to-do classes.

Prion   [= purion.] Adv. Purely, very well.

Priscili   N.m.s. A dense brushwood; land overgrown with thick shrubs. Several place-names have been taken from the common noun.

Purin   Abs. n. A whit.
"Dim purin gwâth na newy'."
Not a whit worse than new.

Pwdel   N.m.s. Fluid mud.

Pwdryn   N.m.s. A lazy fellow.
Fem. *pwdren*.

Pwdwr   Adj. Lazy.

Pwer   Indef. Pron. Many. (Pron. pŵer).
"Faint yw rhif pwer? Ma rhif pwer yn imddibinu ar y sawl sy'n iwso'r gair. Pam bo dyn sy'n byw yn y wlad yn gweyd 'pwer,' ma

hiny 'n goligu haner cant neu rwbeth tebyg;
pam bo dyn sy'n byw 'n y dre 'n iwso'r gair,
ma hiny 'n goligu cant a mwy; a pam bo dyn
sy'n byw miwn tre fowr fowr yn iwso'r gair, ma
hiny 'n goligu mil a mwy. Ma mowredd y
siniad yn imddibinu ar amgiffred a phrofiad y
dyn. Faint, 'nte, yw ' pwer ' Duw? Mwy nas
gellith neb 'i rifo. Nid yw twod mân holl
foroedd y byd ond megis dwrned o farlish i'r
Bod Mowr."

(Twmi Shams's sermon on the text, " Bringing many sons unto glory "; Heb. ii. 10).

Pwfflal Part. Puffing.

Pwgddu Adj. Dark, " pitch " dark.
" Nosweth bwgddu."
A dark night.

Pwl N.m.s. A spell of sickness.
" Mi gesim bwl tost."
I had a hard spell of sickness.

Pwl Adj. Dim, faint, weak.
(1) " Ma ngolwg i'n bwl iawn."
My eyesight is very weak.
(2) " Ma'r glàs ma'n bwl iawn."
This mirror reflects faintly.

Pwllffagan V. Intran. To labour under difficulties, to
work at a disadvantage.
" Ma'r gwaith mor ano [anhawdd], ond ma
rhaid pwlffagan a hi."
The work is so difficult, but one must toil at
it.

Pwllffyn N.m.s. A fat fellow.

Pwll-du N.m.s. The place of torment; nethermost
hell. In classical Welsh afagddu. One accent,
on du).

Pwllif N.m.s. A sawing-pit.

A *pwllif* was an invariable adjunct to every farmhouse in the olden days, when every farmer cut and prepared his own timber. (Pron. pw-llif, accent on second syll.).

Pwll-lludw Ash pit, usually found in old farmhouses at a side of the *pentan*, a yard or two from the fire. It was customary to clean it out once a week.

Lludu is a variant of *lludw*, generally heard in the most northerly parts of the county.

Pwll-melyn N.m.s. Yellow ochre pit. There are several in these districts. The walls of farmhouses are washed with the ochre obtained hereabouts.

Pwllyn N.m.s. A small pool on the roadside.

Pwmpiwn N.f.pl. Pompion.
Sing. *pwmpiwnsen.*

Pwnco V. Intran. To debate, argue.
" Pwnco a'u gily'."
Arguing with one another.

Pwno V. Tran. To flog.

Pwno-'i-wres Exercising the arms by throwing them out and whipping them around the shoulders violently, as is done by farm hands in cold weather.
Literally it means, beating his heat.

Pwnter N.m.s. A pointer (dog).

Pwrn Part. Bought.
In the phrases :—
" Diod bwrn "—Bought beer.
" Brethyn pwrn "—Bought cloth.
" Bara pwrn "—Bought bread ; &c.

Pwrnu   Adv. At that time.

The word is derived from the Adv. phrase *y pryd hyny.*

" Pan ddaw dy' Sadwrn dwetha'r byd, pwrnu daw'r ffwl ato 'i hunan.''

When the last Saturday of the world arrives, then will the fool come to himself.

Pwrnu   [= prynu.] V. Tran. To buy.

Pwrs   N.m.s. The sheath of the testicles in man or animal.

Pwrs-y-mwg   N.m.s. The blind toad-stool; a species of fungus.

When ripe the substance inside the skin becomes granular, and, on the fungus being tapped or kicked, goes off in a cloud of dust or *mwg.* There is a belief that if this dust gets into the eyes, blindness will follow. Children attack the fungus as they would an adder, with a long stick. The fungus is hit hard so that it emits the dreaded *mwg,* when a hasty retreat is made to a safe distance, till the cloud has dispersed.

Pwslo   V. Intran. To puzzle, to muse.
" Own i'n pwslan a fi 'n hunan.''
I mused with myself.

Pwt   N.m.s. A nudge, a poke.
" Mi roisim bwt iddo.''
I nudged him.

Pwt-y-ginen   N.m.s. The person who causes a dispute or a row.

Pwtsh N.m.s. The pocket worn by mowers and reapers on their back to carry the *cresten* or the *rhip* (q.v.) in.

Pwynto V. Intran. To point to, to indicate.
" Pwynto 'i fys arna i."
Pointing his finger towards me.

Pwyntred N.m.s. Shoemaker's thread, with bristle attached ready for use.

Pwythyn N.m... The length of thread attached to a needle, usually about half a yard long.

R

Rab   N.m.s. Rough, stony soil; sub-soil.

Rabian   N.m.s. A desolate place.
" Dina hen rabian o le yw Cil-y-cwm ! "
What a desolate place is Cil-y-cwm!
Query : Is it from the Prop. n. " Arabia " ?

Rabscaliwn   N.m.s. A rascal.

Rali   Abs. n. Merriment.
" We rali fowr yn Llwynbedw neithwr."
There was great merriment in Llwynbedw last night.

Ran-finicha   Adv. Almost.
" Ma'r pòst yn galw ma ran-finicha bob dy'."
The postman calls here almost daily.

Ranjan   Part. Roaming about.
" Ranjan o bwti i idrych am rhyw jòb i neyd."
Roaming about looking for a job.

Ratalio   V. Trans. To iron with the *talian* iron the fringe of the old-fashioned Welsh cap.

Rath   N.m.s. An ancient earthwork or mound. The word is almost obsolete. (Pron. râth).

Redimadesi   Prop. n. A corruption of the English words, " Reading-made-easy," which was the title of a reading book in use in the old-time school. (Accent on *es*).

Reiets N.m.s. Commotion, great noise.

"Arglwydd mowr, beth yw'r reiets ma wyt Ti'n gadw? "—Allan o weddi Twm Dafi Bach ar storom o drwste.

Ribaldy Coll. n. A promiscuous gathering of rowdies.

Ribela V. Intran. To set about to detect a witch.

When ill-luck attended a man or beast formerly, it was believed to be due to the wicked glance of the black witch. To discover the author of the mischief the names of all the local witches were written on separate slips of paper, which were folded up and placed in a bottle containing *lleishw*—urine that had been standing in a vessel for a number of days. The contents were shaken together, and then emptied. The slip of paper which came out first indicated the witch who was the author of the mischief. The aggrieved party went in quest of the same, armed with knives and other instruments for the purpose of extracting a confession or inflicting punishment. If the wretched woman confessed her crime, she was let off on the payment of a fine; if not, her body was bared and blood drawn. The supposed witches were, as a rule, friendless, living generally in a secluded cottage in some woodland nook, where the avengers had every opportunity to wreak their vengeance. Many tales of untold suffering lie buried in the sylvan wolds of North Pembrokeshire.

A passage in "Henry VI." is reminiscent of *ribela* : —

"—— I'll have a bout with the
Devil or Devil's dam: I'll conjure thee:
Blood will I draw on thee: thou art a witch."

Rislan Part. Rustling, as of a silk dress.

P

Robin-girwr   N.m.s. The gadder, or major gad-fly.
It is known in some parts of the county as *robin-y-jawl-gwyllt*. The attack of this insect makes cattle run madly. Its bite is often attended with swelling and local inflammation.

Roll-gifan   Adv. phrase. All around, everywhere.
" Wdw i wedi whilo 'roll-gifan am y ddafad."
I have searched everywhere for the ewe.

Rorors   N.m.s. Delirium tremens.

Run-faner   Adv. In the same way or manner.
" Wyt ti 'n sharad 'run-faner a'r hen Shams Tomos."
You speak exactly in the manner of James Thomas.
The word *faner* is thoroughly domesticated.

R-un-un   Indef. Pron. The same one.
" 'R-un-un yw e a fuo ma o'r blân."
He is the same one that was here before.
(Accent on last syll.).

RH

Rhacanu V. Tran. To sift chaff. A process which can be understood only by being seen. The chaff on a threshing floor or in a barn is sifted by passing it through a rake. The rake is held before and the stuff manipulated dexterously with the foot.

Rhachwel N.m.s. A bulge, or, more strictly, that which is out of line.

Rhadlon Adj. Quiet, easily managed.
Used only of a horse which is perfectly docile, never of any other animal.
" Caseg radlon yw hi."
She is a quiet mare.

Rhafen N.f.s. Corn stalk left on the field after binding. A stray ear of corn.
Plur. *rhafene.*

Rhagen-las N.f.s. A kind of whetstone held in high esteem for setting keen-edged tools.

Rhagwt N.m.s. The herb ragwort (Senecio jacobæa).

Rhailsen N.f.s. A rail.

Rhain [= y rhai hyn.] Dem. Pron. These.
A variant is *rhein.*
Rheina = those.
Rheiny = those (referred to).
Rheinco = those yonder.

Rhasen   N.f.s. The plate or shoe under the sole of a clog.

Rhaser   N.f.s. A razor.

Rhaspell   N.f.s. A rasp.

Rhaspo   V. Trans. To fasten a gate by means of a clicket.

Rhastal   N.f.s. Manger, rack.
Strictly speaking, the *rhastal* is the rack above the *mansher* or manger. The former holds hay, the latter the chaff or oats.

Rhawlarch   N.f.s. A wooden shovel for taking bread out of the oven.

Rhebes   N.f.s. A long rigmarole.

Rhec   N.f.s. A rack placed under the roof for the purpose of curing bacon, or for any other useful purpose.

Rhech   N.f.s. Wind broken.

Rhechgi   N.m.s. A stinkard.

Rhechu   V. Intran. To break wind.

Rhedig   [= aredig.] V. Tran. and Intran. To plough.

Rhedyn-Crist   N.f.pl. Harts-tongue ferns, but according to others the great fern (Osmunda regalis).

Rhedyn-cadno   N.f.pl. Male fern.

Rheffyn-penbys   N.m.s. A straw rope made by twisting with finger and thumb. Metaphorically used for a long story or rigmarole.

Rheffyn-tro   N.m.s. A kind of band for binding sheaves. Another kind in use was the *rheffyn-gwydd*, but only experienced and ingenious binders could twist it.

Rheinog   N.m.s. Reynard, a fox.

Rhen -Gribbin   Prop. n. The Old Nick.

Rhes   N.m.pl. Live cinders. Sing. *rhesyn*.

Rhesin   Coll. n. Resins.

Rhespe   N.pl. Extravagant sayings. No Singular. " Hen respe dwl." Silly, extravagant sayings.

Rhest   N.c. The rest, the remainder. The word is thoroughly naturalised.

Rhesu   V. Tran. To stir red-hot cinders. The cinders in both cases are those of *tân twarch-a-matte*, and not of *tân-culwm*.

Rhew -bargod   N.m.s. Icicle; often heard instead of *pibonw*.

Rhewlin   N.m.s. A tiny rivulet, a mere thread of a stream. A form of the word sometimes heard is *rhiwelyn*.

Rhialtwch   Abs. n. Uproariousness. Never used in the literary sense of splendour.

Rhic   N.m.s. Hiccup.

Rhico   V. Trans. To tear.

Strictly limited in usage to the tearing of clothes, the leaves of a book; it never means *hacking* or *hewing* in the classical sense.

Rhico   V. Intran. To boast, brag, vaunt.

" Mae'n rhico fod gida 'g e well bustechu na neb yn y gimdogeth.''

He boasts that he has better bullocks than anybody in the neighbourhood.

Rhichwel   N.m.s. The ridge of a mountain; more strictly, perhaps, the line of the horizon.

Rhidio   Part. Serving, strictly in reference to rams at the serving season.

Rhidwedd   Abs. n. Scent, trail.

Rhidwel   N.m.s. A mill pond.

The word is restricted to a pond formed in the bed of a river by means of a dam. The word probably referred originally to the dam itself, but is never understood so now. *Rhidwel* never means a pond constructed apart from a river; *pwll* is then used.

Rhifel-yn
-yr-owyr   Literally, war in the sky. This refers to a strange mirage seen near Fishguard immediately before the outbreak of the Crimean War, and which the old people speak of as a warning sent by God of the dreadful times to follow.

Rhigam   N.m.s. Organy, the herb so called.

Rhigian   Part. Teasing.
" Rhigian 'u gily'.''
Teasing each other.

Rhigol   N.f.s. A wheel track.

Rhingyll N.m.s. A tall, lanky man.

Rhiniog [= eminiog.] N.m.s. Door-post.

Rhinti [= rhyngddynt.] P. Prep. Between them.
" Myn'd i gifringu rhinti nw."
Going to arbitrate between them.
Observe that *nw* is redundant.
A variant is *rhunti*.

Rhipo V. Tran. To strip a roof.
" Ma'r mashwned wrthi 'n fishi, yn rhipo'r scubor."
The masons are busily engaged, stripping the roof of the barn.
The word is restricted to this meaning here

Rhip -sand-o-fan N.f.s. A wooden riff or rip used for sharpening scythes. This specimen was covered with a thin layer of grease, upon which was placed another of crushed sandstone. It was cleaned before a fresh application of grease and sand, and in this respect differed from the *cresten*.

Rhitbost N.m.s. A stone or post put up in a field for cattle to rub on.

Rhithiant Abs. n. Semblance, the shadow of a thing.
" 'Dyw e ddim rhithiant gwell na chyn iddo gâl i gospi."
He is not a shade better than he was before he was punished.

Rhith N.m.s. A nick-name given to the inhabitants of a district.
" Wê rhith yn cal i roi slawer dy ar bobl pob cwmdogeth."
A nick-name was attached in olden times to the peoples of every neighbourhood.

" Dima rai o'r rhithodd mwya enwog:—
Brain Llanchâr.
Bwbachod y Bwncath.
Bwchod y Dinas.
Cilion Casnewy'.
Cwn Trelettert.
Dwrgwn y Nifern.
Gwibed Casmâl.
Gwilanod Pencâr.
Meirch Mathry.
Moch Cwmgwein.
Mwydon Maenclochog.
Shilgots Drewyddel.
Scadan 'Bergwein (Fishguard).
Twrchod y Twffton (Fishguard).

Rhiw   N.m.s. Rue.
Tê *rhiw*, a decoction of rue, much used formerly as a food beverage.

Rhiwmitis   N.m.s. Rheumatism.

Rhiw-tredin   The downward path to ruin; the descent to failure and despair; the road to bankruptcy.

Rho   [= rhy.] Adv. Too, over, &o.

Rhocesen   N.f.s. A girl. Diminutive of *rhoces*, used in a depreciatory sense. It has a plural *rhocesach*. *Crwtsach* (masc.) is also used in the same way.

Rhoch   Abs. n. The death-throttle; the gurgling sound heard in the throat of a dying person. (Pron. rhòch).

Rhod-fach   N.f.s. A hand spinning-wheel.

Rhodd-Mair   N.m.s. Hedge hyssop (Lycopodium Selago). The old people of a generation ago used to gather this herb with great care, and they regarded it with almost superstitious awe, since it was never allowed to be touched by iron. It was said to possess many virtues.

Rhoflo Part. Sprawling.
" Mi bwres e nes bod e'n rhoflo."
I hit him till he was sprawling; lit.: till he was shovelling.

Rhoflon N.pl. That which is scraped with the shovel. Muck or dross scraped together in the farmyard.

Rhog [= rhag.] In the phrase "rhog ofon."

Rhoi'n-sownd V. phrase. To put in the charge of the police.
" Fe fidda i'n shwr o'ch rhoi chi 'n sownd os ewch chi mlân a'ch campe rhagor."
I shall be certain to put you in the charge of the police if you carry on your game much further.

Rhoiaim [= rhoddais.] Other forms to be noted are :—
Rhoiest, rhows, rhoison, rhoisoch. A full table could be given only in a grammar of the dialect.
Rhoies is an interesting form.

Rhonc Adj. Rank, luxuriant, applied to vegetation.

Rhonc Adj. Brimming, applied to a sow.

Rhonden
   -felen A term applied to the last woman to get up on May morning—*bore clame* [=boreu calan Mai.] "On this morning it was the custom of the members of the family and servants to rise as early as they possibly could—in fact, it was a race out of bed, and the last in the race was termed *Rhonden felen* [it appears the masculine gender was never used], and was taunted all day with the words:
" Rhonden felen
Lap yr hufen."

Rhondyn   N.m.s. A big, lazy fellow.
" Hen wr rhondyn,
A hen wraig ronden,
'N cwsgu 'n y gwely
Ar asgwrn 'u cefen.
Cwthwm tro a ddelo heibo,
I whithu'r ty a'i fagle drosto.''
(Old Saw).

Rhost   Part. Toasted, roasted, baked.
" Caws rhòst ''—Toasted cheese.
" Tato rhòst '' —Roasted potatoes.

Rhoswn   N.m.s. The resinous substance that oozes out
and adheres to the bark of pine trees.

Rhou   N.f.s. The chain used in fastening a load of
timber.

Rhowler   N.m.s. Roller, that is, the heavy roller used
for farming purposes.

Rhowndo   V. Trans. To traverse, to pace to and fro so
as to inspect every inch of ground.
" Mi ddarum i rowndo rhen finy bob modfedd
o hano.''
I have walked over the old mountain every
inch of it.

Rhuddlawr   N.m.s. Ground that is bare of grass, where
children play or animals tread.

Rhuddo   V. Tran. and Intran. To singe, to discolour
cloth with a hot iron, to be browned. The word
is never used of singeing hair.

Rhwbeth
  -dierth   Adv. phrase. Considerably, very materially,
etc.
" Ma'r menyn wedi cwmpo rwbeth-dierth.''
The price of butter is down considerably.

Rhwbeth
-neu-gily   N. phrase. Something or other.
"Ma eishe mynd i Hwlffor arna i, ond ma rhwbeth-neu-gily 'n rhwstro i o hyd."
I want to go to Haverfordwest, but something or other hinders me continually.

Rhwden   N.f.s. Ox collar, used in the olden days.
"Rhwden a iwc."
A collar and yoke.

Rhwden   [= taroden.] N.f.s. The ringworm.

Rhwff   Adj. An epithet applied to a person who is somewhat "boisterous" but kind-hearted. It does not mean *rough* in the English sense of the word.

Rhwff   Adj. Level with, up to, filled up.
"Mae'n rhwff a phen y wàl."
It is level with the top of the wall.

Rhwffo   V. Trans. To rough-shoe horses when there is hard frost.

Rhwff-raff   Adj. and Adv. Rough-and-ready; harum-scarum.

Rhwffyn   N.m.s. A jolly fellow, always in a kind sense.
"Eitha hen rwffyn yw e."
He is a downright jolly fellow.
No doubt the word is from *ruffian*, but it has a diametrically opposite meaning.

Rhwgwn   N.m.s. A groove.
Plur. *rhwgwne* and *rhwgne*.

Rhwng
-dou-ole   Lit., between two lights, i.e., daylight and candle-light; dusk.

Rhwmo V. Intran. To bind corn. Restricted to this sense.

Rhwnt [= rhwng.] Prep. Between.

Rhwntoch [= rhyngoch.] Between you.

Rhwntu In expressions relating to time.
" Pum minud rhwntu a naw."
Five minutes to nine.

Rhwp Adv. Instantly.
" Fe jengodd rhwp rhwng 'n dwylo ni."
He escaped instantly between our hands.

Rhwtad N.m.s. A sore caused by a rubbing off of the skin.

Rhwto V. Tran. To rub.

Rhwyog Adj. Liberal, free.
" Mae e'n rhy rwyog, phâr 'i arian e byth, tai nw fel y grôf."
He is too liberal, his money will never last, even though it were like the sand.

Rhydd Adj. Libertine.

Rhyw-bridodd Adv. phrase. Late, far advanced as to time.
" Ddaw Shemi ddim gatre nes bod hi ryw-bridodd o'r nôs."
James will not return till late at night.

S

Sacamwren [= sycamorwydden.] N.f.s. Sycamore-tree.

Saco V. Tran. To thrust, push, putting.
"Sào dy fys i ligad e."
Thrust thy finger into his eye.
"Saco corcyn i'r botrel."
Putting a cork into the bottle.

Sach [= serch.] Conj. Notwithstanding, in spite of.

Sach-ni [= serch hyny.] Prep. Albeit, nevertheless. (Accent on *ni*).

Safion-i Inter. Save us!

Saff Adv. Sure.
"Sana i'n sâff pwy yw e."
I am not sure who he is.

Salgar Adj. Fond of malingering.
The term is applied to a person who is bedridden through fear of work rather than on account of any real illness. The following lines are said to have been an epitaph on an old stone in Nevern Churchyard:—
"Yma gorwe Deio salgar,
Lawr yn ishel yn y ddeiar;
Os carith e'r bedd fel carodd e'r gwely,
Fe fydd y dwetha yn atgifodi."

Salgi N.m.s. A dirty, lazy fellow.

Salwedd   Adj. Sickly, frail.
"Golwg daran salwedd sy' ar Ann."
Ann has a rather sickly appearance.

Salwino   Part. Becoming overcast, said of the sky when rain is near.

Sana   V. Intran. I am not, do not. The only parts used are :—

	SING.			PLUR.	
1st,	Sana		1st.	Sanon	
2nd.	Sanat			Senon	
3rd.	masc.	Sano Seno	2nd.	Sanoch Senoch	
3rd.	fem.	Sani Seni	3rd.	Sanin Senin	

Sane -garddwn   N.f.pl. Legs of stockings, worn by women formerly on their arms and down over their wrists in very cold weather, when out filling carts or otherwise engaged in farming pursuits. The present generation of women know nothing of the hardships endured by their sisters of generations gone by.

Sane-our   The golden sheen due to the reflection of the sun on sea at sunset.
"Ma'r houl yn gwishco 'i sane-our heno to, ma rhagor o dewy teg indi."
Lit.: The sun is wearing his golden stockings this evening again. There is more fair weather in it.

Sane'r-gwcw   N.f.pl. Wild violets.

Sardinad   N.f.s. Quietus.
"Mi roia i sardinad iddo nawr."
I will give him his quietus now.

Sarn   N.m.s. Bedding for cattle.
Usually of worthless straw or dried bracken.

Sarnu   V. Tran. (1) To spill, such as water or any other liquid. (2) To lose or waste.
" Sarnu dŵr "—Spilling water.
" Sarnu gwair "—Wasting hay.

Sawlgwaith   Indef. Pron. Many times.
" Wdw i wedi gweyd wrthoch chi sawlgwaith."
I have told you several times.
(Accent on *sawl*).

Sawl-un   Indef. Pron. Several.
" Ma sawl-un wedi myn'd i'r acshon."
There are several gone to the sale.

Scablo   V. Tran. To lop branches of trees.

Scadan   N.m.pl. Occasional stalks of corn left uncut.
A verb *scadana* is used also.
" Hen fladur ddrwg i scadana yw hon."
This scythe is a bad one, it leaves an occasional stalk uncut.

Scadly   Adj. (1) Strong, muscular. (2) Boisterous.
(1) " Dyn scadly yw Caleb mowr."
Big Caleb is a muscular man.
(2) " Mae'n dewi scadly."
It is boisterous weather.

Scaing   N.f.s. A skein.
" Scaing o ddafe."
A skein of thread.

Scant   Adj. Scarce.
" Ma'r driwod yn scant,
Hedfasant i bant ;
Ond deuant yn ol
Drw' lwybre'r hen ddôl."
(Cân y Dryw Bach).

Scapo V. Tran. To skip, to omit.
"Scàpo dalen."
To skip over a leaf.

Scarfyn N.m.s. A long-pointed peak of rock.

Scarjo V. Intran. To become rough, applied to the condition of the skin in cold or frosty weather.

Scathri V. Intran. Drying, clearing up of weather, wind rising and drying the ground after a *scwithen* (q.v.).
"Mae'n scathri 'n ardderchog nawr 'to; fe ddaw i rwmo ar unwaith."
Lit.: It is drying magnificently now again; it will come to bind at once;—i.e., we shall soon be able to resume binding.

Scathru V. Tran. To rub off the skin by falling, or by coming into violent contact with an object. Stronger than *rhwto*, which signifies rubbing off the skin by friction.

Scefen [= ysgyfaint.] The lungs. But it is doubtful whether the word is to be regarded as singular or plural, since the expression *dwy scefen* is often used.

Scegan Part. Yelling.

Sceibyn N.m.s. A sneak.

Sceiddig Adj. Lithe, active, robust.

Sceimer N.m.s. A plotter, a person who hatches plots or mischievous schemes.

Sceimo V. Tran. and Intran. To scheme.
A variant is *scemo*.

Soeipan   V. Intran. To crawl or creep stealthily.

Seeni   [= nid oes genyf fi.] V. Intran. I have not.

Sceran   N.f.s. A wicked little girl.

Scergwd   N.m.s. Carcase. Used interchangeably with *scerbwd*.

Scib   N.m.s. A small, oblong wicker basket. (Pron. scîb).

Sciba   N.m.s. A small herring boat.

Scibarin   N.m.s. A boatman.
The Fishguard herring fishermen are often so called. (Accent on last syll.)

Scifino   V. Intran. To have strangles.

Scifyn   [= ysgyfeinwst.] N.m.s. Strangles.

Scildanu   V. Tran. and Intran. To scald, to be scalded.
" Scildanu llâth."
To scald milk.
" Ma Riwth wedi scildanu."
Ruth is scalded.

Scilfyn   N.m.s. A small bit of anything, but more especially of anything edible.

Scilla   Abs. n. Heartburn.
Scella is a variant.

Scimbren   N.m.s. A beam placed across a shed to hold the ends together.

Scimun -yr-angen   N.m.s. A term of extreme reproach and contempt. It would appear that the term originally signified a person that, for heinous sin, was

R

deprived of the rite of extreme unction, and who was looked upon with horror by his neighbours. With the decay of Catholicism the original signification was lost, but the word has survived.

Scipyn   N.m.s. A small clothes basket.

Scirled   N.m.s. A heap, mass.
" Ma'r llif wedi cario scirled o hen rwbetah lawr i ochor y bont."
The flood has carried a heap of rubbish down to the bridge.

Scirlwm   Adj. Exposed, said of land that is high and much exposed to the weather.

Scirnu   [= ysgyrnygu.] V. Intran. To snarl.

Scirt-las   N.f.s. A woman's riding habit.

Sciwiff   Adv. On a twist, all akimbo. (Accent on *wiff*).

**Sclamwryn
-y-fall**   N.m.s. An accursed man; frequently used also of a thing.

Sclent   Adj. Slant, diagonal.

Scob   N.m.s. A small stinging fish, with a prominent fin.

Scoldan   Adj. Scalded, parboiled.
" Llâth scoldan."
Parboiled milk.

Scolden   N.f.s. A virago.

Scrabinio   V. Trans. To scratch.
" Ma'r gâth wedi scrabinio Jân fach."
The cat has scratched little Jane.

Serachen N.f.s. Corncrake.

Serad N.f.s. Horse rattle, a sort of ratchet made of wood for the purpose of frightening horses. Called in some parts of Glamorganshire *telyn ayffyla.* (Pron. scrâd).

Serechgi N.m.s. One given to crying or shouting.

Scrimen N.f.s. A thin layer.
"Scrimen dene o fenyn ar fara."
A thin layer of butter on bread.

Serineo Part. Shrinking (of cloth).

Serinahlyd Adj. Stinty, near.

Serinsho V. Tran. To stint one's-self, always used with the Ref. Pron. *hunan.*
"Scrinsho 'i hunan"—To stint himself.

Serongol N.m.s. A large, ugly, disproportionate house.

Serwbo V. Tran. To clean by rubbing or scrubbing.
"Scrwbo tato newy."
Cleaning new potatoes.

Serwff N.m.s. Dregs. Rarely used except in connection with tobacco; *scrwff dibaco*—the dregs of a pipe.

Scubelli N.f.pl. Brooms, besoms. The different kinds in use in Pembrokeshire were:—
Scubell-wrug—made of heather.
    ,,   *fwswm*—made of moss.
    ,,   *fanal*—made of butcher's broom.
The first was used for sweeping the kitchen, the second for the parlour and bedrooms, and the third for cleaning out ovens. Brushes in

the modern sense of the term were not in use
here till towards the last quarter of the nine-
teenth century. A regular feature of the Fishguard market formerly was the *scubellwr* (broom
maker), who occupied a conspicuous corner of
the market with his ware. The price of the
scubell wrug was one shilling to fifteen pence,
and of the *scubell fwswm* fifteen pence to one-
and-six. This was not a bad price, inasmuch
as an expert *scubellwr* could make three brooms
per day. The right kind of moss for the parlour
broom was, however, difficult to get except in
the summer months, and it was often necessary
to go long distances from home to procure it.

Sculyn   N.m.s. A sneak.
Fem. *sculen.*

Scuthan   N.f.s. A term of reproach applied to a thin,
disagreeable woman. It is remarkable that the
term is never applied to a fat woman, however
sour or ill-tempered she may be.

Scwarnog   [= ysgyfarnog.] N.f.s. Hare.
"Hen scwarnog" is used metaphorically for
a show sermon. i.e., a sermon which preachers
deliver again and again about the country.

Scwarog   Adj. Firm-set.
"Hen ddyn bach scwarog."
A firm-set little man.

Sewaru   V. Tran. and Intran. To scatter manure over
land, to spread.
"Scwaru pridd a chalch."
Spreading earth and lime.
"Myn'd mâs i scwaru."
To go out to throw (compost).

Scwils Coll. n. Fragments, bits.
"Fe dorrodd y botrel yn scwils."
The bottle broke into fragments.

Scwithen N.f.s. A sudden, short shower of rain in the
harvest season, which does little harm beyond
hindering work for a few hours.

Scwlin N.m.s. Schoolmaster—a term of contempt.
Nothing but contempt was felt for the schoolmaster of the old style who delighted in im-
posing the odious task upon the children of
trying to forget their mother tongue.

Scwlo V. Intran. To speak disdainfully. (Pron.
scŵlo).

Scwryn N.m.s. Diarrhœa.

Sefyll V. Intran. To become with foal, calf, &c.
This is the word invariably used to denote
that a mare, a cow, a sow, &c., has become
with young.

Sefyllach Part. Loitering and gadding about.

Sefyllan Part. Loitering.

Sefyll-n-gily V. phrase. To oppose each other.

Seiffro N. and V. Intran. (1) Arithmetic. (2) To
perform arithmetical operations.

Seino V. Tran. and Intran. To sign.
"Seino 'i enw."
Signing his name.
"I chi wedi seino?"
Have you signed [a document]?

Seis N.m.s. Size.
Seisin is also used.

Seithini Part. Sighing.
Restricted to the sighing or sobbing of a child
after crying.

Ser N.m.s. Sir.

Seriws Adv. Really.
" Odi seriws, 'te."
Yes really, then.

Sersog Adj. Starry.

Sertenol Adj. Settled ; of fixed habits.

Seso V. Intran. Barking and teasing. Said of a
dog that barks at and worries anything, without actually biting it.
" Be sy ar yr hen gi wr, yn seso ar y gath
fan na! "
What's the matter with the dog, annoying
the cat so!

Sespin N.m.s. Shoe-horn, shoe-lift.

Set-Wiliam N.m.s. Sweet-William—the flower so called.

Set-y-ffenest N.f.s. Window-sill.

Sezn N.f.s. Season.
Restricted to the period in which entire
horses go about.

Siber Adj. Well-behaved, more especially in reference to behaviour at table.

Siberwi V. Tran. To scald or cleanse a vessel with
boiling water.

Sichbon
Adj. Austere and distant.
" Hen griadur sichbon yw e."
He is an austere, distant old creature.
(Accent on sich).

Sichgolu
V. Intran. To dry, to clear (of sky).

Sichu
V. Tran. To heal, to dry up (a wound).
" Eli Treffynon sy'n gwella bob clwyfon,
Eli Tregwynt a'u sichyth nw'n gynt."

Sidan
[= sydyn.] Adv. Suddenly.
" Fe fu farw 'n sidan bach."
He died very suddenly.

Sifil
Adv. Seriously, earnestly.
" I'ch chi 'n gweyd yn sifil nawr, te jocan
i'ch chi? "
Are you speaking seriously now, or are you
joking?

Sifrisol
Adj. and Adv. Useful, handy.
Probably a corruption of *serviceable*.
" Peth sy' wedi dwad yn sifrisol iawn yw'r
machines ma at bob gwaith."
Machines have become very serviceable for
all kinds of work.

Siffred
V. Trans. To endure, to bear.
" Alla i ddim 'i siffred e rhagor."
I cannot endure him any longer

Silwgar
Adj. Observant.

Simach
N.s. Notice, attention.
" 'Dyw nhw 'n gneyd dim un simach o'r dyn."
They take no notice whatever of the man.

Simans
N.m.s. Summons, writ.
Simanso is the verb.

Simpil   Adj. (1) Lean. (2) Mean.
"Ma'r aner yn simpil ofnadwy."
The heifer is awfully lean.
"Hen dro simpil nâth e a fi."
He played me a mean trick.

Sisneg   [= Saesoneg.] N. and Adj. English.

Sithlyd   Adj. Chilly.
"Mae'n sithlyd ofnadwy heddy."
It is awfully chilly to-day.

Siw-na-miw   N. phrase. Not a word, not a sound.
"Chliwd na siw-na-miw am dano byth wedin."
Not a word about him was heard ever after.

Siwto   V. Intran. To suit, to accommodate.

Slabar   N.m.s. The mess made by a small child on itself in eating food.

Slabog   Adj. Dirty, in reference to the weather.
Slabrog is a variant.

Slabredd   Abs. n. Dirtiness, strictly in reference to the state of roads after rain.

Slabyn   N.m.s. Spalpeen, and probably a corruption of the Irish word.

Slac   Adj. Slow, slack.
"Ffair slàc."
A slow fair.

Slac   N.m.s. Slaked lime.
The word is often used alone, and also in conjunction with *calch—calch slàc*.

Slaco Part. Abating, in reference to the elements, pain, &c.
"Ma'r gwynt yn slàco."
The wind is abating.
"Ma'r bŵen wedi slàco peth."
The pain has eased a little.

Slafdod Abs. n. Slavish work, toilsome work.
"Mae e'n gorffod gneyd pob slafdod."
He is obliged to do all kinds of slavish work.

Slafio V. Tran. and Intran. To do slavish work, to abuse the body.
"Ma gweishon Panteg yn càl i slafio 'n ofnadwy."
The servants of Panteg are obliged to do slavish work.
"Wdw i wedi slafio."
I have abused my body.

Slang N.m.s. A long narrow field.

Slapen N.f.s. A slap administered with a rod.

Slaten N.f.s. A writing slate.

Slawer-dy Adv. Long ago. A phonetic corruption of er ys llawer dydd. (Accent on dy).

Sleibwt N.m.s. A sly fellow.

Sleidro V. Intran. To sleigh, to skid along ice.

Sleidryn N.m.s. A place to sleigh on, a slide, especially that which is made by lads on a road.

Sleishyn N.m.s. A slice.
"Melus idoedd càl ryw sleishyn
O gig mochyn gida'r daten,
Ond yn awr rhaid byw heb iddo,
Y mae'r mochyn wedi mado."
(Old ballad).

Slic
Adv. Easily digested, digestible.
" Ma bwdram yn fwy slic na chawl."
Bwdram (q.v.) is more digestible than broth.

Slimyn
N.m.s. A tall, slim man.

Slip
N.m.s. A gap.
" Codi slip yn y claw."
Repairing a gap in the hedge.

Slip
In the phrase, *fe áth yn slip arna i*, equivalent
to the English expression, " The cat is out of
the bag."

Slipo
V. Intran. To run, to go hurriedly.
" Slip lawr i'r shop i mofyn tamed o facco
i fi."
Run down to the shop to fetch me some
tobacco.

Slipyn
N.m.s. A fairly good sized anything.
" Slipyn o grwt."
A biggish boy.
" Slipyn o fochyn."
A good sized pig.

Slithion
Coll. n. An accumulation of stones and
rubbish at the foot of a hill.

Slithrig
Adj. and Adv. Slippery.

Slithro
V. Intran. To slip, stumble, to slide along
and fall.

Sliw
N.m.s. A boose, drunkenness.
" Ma Dai ar y sliw fowr. '
David is very drunk.

Slobryn   N.m.s. A sloppy fellow.
Fem. *slobren*.

Slorwm   N.f.s. Slow-worm or blindworm.

Slwta   Adj. Dirty.
(1) " Hen dro digon slwta nath hi a fi."
    She served me a dirty trick.
(2) " Tewy slwta."
    Dirty weather.

Smoco   V. Intran. To smoke (tobacco).

Smwglin   N.m.s. A shebeen.
" Cadw smwglin " is the expression for keeping a beerhouse without a license.

Smwt   N.m.s. Smoke black, the discoloration caused by smoke.

Snob   N.m.s. Snivel, mucus.

Snotyn   N.m.s. A small bit, but rarely applied to anything except a candle that has burnt down to the socket of the candlestick.

Snwffial   Part. Snuffing.

Snwffo   V. Intran. To sniff, as a dog does in following a trail.

Soceded   N.f.s. A pipeful.
" Soceded o ddibacco."
A pipeful of tobacco.

Sofol   [= sofl.] N.m.pl. Stubble.
Sing. *soflyn*.

Sofren   N.f.s. A sovereign.
A variant *sofryn* (masc.) is also frequently heard.

Sog　　　N.m.s., (1) Coma. (2) Semi-consciousness. (3) Lethargy produced by illness. (Pron. sòg).

Soga　　　N.f.s. A lazy slut.

Solsyn　　　N.m.s. One who hates society and loves to roam about by himself.

Sopas　　　N.m.s. A meal consisting of uncooked oat-meal and buttermilk.
" 'Stim byd at sopas i fagu cèst."
Sopas beats all foods for the development of a paunch.

Soven　　　N.f.s. A truss of straw larger than an *isgub*, but smaller than a *bwrn* (q.v.).

Sowdlwr　　　N.m.s. A dog that bites animals on the heels.
" Sowdlwr da yw'r ci hwn."
This dog is a good " heeler."

Sownd　　　Adv. Undoubtedly, supposedly, by-all-means, in-all-reason, and a variety of shades of meaning.
" Ni gewn dewy teg nawr, sownd i chi, ar iol yr holl law mowr ma."
We shall have fine weather now, undoubtedly, after all this heavy rain.

Spadd　　　Part. That which has been castrated.
" Wyn spâdd "—Lambs that have been castrated.
" Moch spûdd "—Pigs that have been castrated.
" Ebolion spâdd "—Colts that have been castrated.

Spaddu　　　[= dyspaddu.] V. Tran. To castrate.

Spafin　　　N.m.s. The spavin : a disease affecting horses.

Spag   N.m.s. A spar, spike, especially the top of an old withered tree.

Spagyn   N.m.s. A spar.

Spanish   N.m.s. Liquorice.
"Wdw i'n myn'd i'r shop i mofyn dimewarth o spanish."
I am going to the shop to buy a ha'porth [halfpenny-worth] of liquorice.

Sparbil   N. m.s. A whipper-snapper.

Spario   V. Tran. To spare.
"Gellwch chi spario llwyth o wellt i fi?"
Can you spare me a load of straw?

Sparion   N.m.pl. Leavings.
"Sparion y dâ"—The leavings of the cattle.

Specteli   N.f.pl. Spectacles.
The Sing. *spectel* is also used.

Spiff   Adj. Worthless; "a thing of nothing."
"Spiff o beth"—A worthless thing.

Spilbwr   N.m.s. An animal that trespasses upon another man's lands.
Spilbo is a variant.
Plur. *spilbwn*.

Spogen   N.f.s. The spoke of a wheel.

Spong   Adj. In the phrase "newy spong" = brand new.

Sponce   N.f.pl. Fits-and-starts.
Sing. *sponc.* which is rarely used.

Sposib [= oes hosibl?] V. Intran. Is it possible?

Spoto V. Intran. To cast a few drops, to rain a little.

"Mae'n dachre spòto peth."

It is beginning to rain.

Sprilyn -bacwn N.m.s. The bat.

The bat often lodges in the old-fashioned chimney, where bacon is dried—hence the name.

Sprilyn N.m.s. A sly, lanky fellow.

The feminine *sprilen* is often applied to a thin, prowling beast.

Spwnsh N.m.s. Sponge.

Spwtyn N.m.s. A small or short anything.

"Spwtŷn o bregeth."

A short sermon.

"Spwtŷn o bib."

A short pipe.

"Spwtŷn o ddyn."

A small man.

Spwylo V. Tran. and Intran. (1) To spoil. (2) To be spoilt.

Sta Prep. With.

"Pwy sta nw?"

Whom have they with them?

Stablad Part. Stamping with the feet, treading back-and-fore quickly on the same spot.

Stac Abs. n. An amount of work assigned to one to do.

"Wdw i wedi pennu'n stàc i."

I have finished my portion of work.

Stajman   An eloquent preacher among the Dissenters. One who is considered fit to appear on " stâj y Gimanfa Fowr "—the annual preaching services of the association of a particular denomination.

Stamp   N.s. Mettle.
" Ma'r eitha stamp indo."
He has splendid mettle in him.

Stander   N.m.s. The catch-pin of a cart.

Standin   N.m.s. A booth or stall at a fair.

Stando   V. Intran. To reflect, to grasp the situation.
" Ddaru mi ddim stando 'n iawn nes wedd hi 'n rhy ddweddar."
I had not grasped the situation till it was too late.

Stansh   Adj. Very prim and distant. Best expressed by the English provincialism " stand offish."

Stapal   N.f.s. A staple.

Start   N.f.s. Fright.
" Fe gas stàrt ofnadwy."
He had a dreadful fright.

Stees   N.m.s. Anything which is slimy, such as a smashed egg, a crushed snail, &c.

Steifer   N.m.s. A piece of timber, evidently from *stave.*
" Ma rhewun wedi dwgid y cŵed bob steifer."
Somebody has stolen the timber every scrap of it.

Steil   Abs. n. Surname.
" Beth yw'ch steil chi? "
What is your last, or surname?

Stenyn   N.m.s. A herring.
Also used metaphorically for a thin, puny fellow.

Sticil   N.f.s. A stile.

Stico   V. Intran. To stick, work away, lay to.

Stiff   Adj. Sore.
" Wdw i'n stiff bob tamed o hana i."
I am sore all over me.

Stiffeia   V. Intran. I dare say, I dare assert, presume.
" Mi stiffeia i yr eith e."
I dare say he will go.

Stiffeithtra   Abs. n. Obstinacy, stubbornness.

Stiffni   Abs. n. Soreness, especially after hard work or long riding.
Stiffrurydd is also used.

Stilo   V. Tran. To iron clothes.
" Stilo'r dillad cledrwyth."
Ironing the starched clothes.

Stillen   N.f.s. In the phrase *ar y stillen*, a euphemism for lying a corpse.

Stim   [= nid oes dim.] It is not, there is not.

Sim-byw -na-bod   Literally, there is neither living nor existing —the regular expression for persistence, restlessness, &c.
" Stim byw na bod gida'r hen rocyn eishe 'i fod e'n câl myn'd i'r môr."
There is no peace with the fellow, but he must needs go to sea.

Stimog   N.f.s. (1) Stomach. (2) Appetite.
" Ma pwen fowr yn yng stimog i."
I have great pain in my stomach.
" Sta fi ddim blewyn o stimog at fwyd."
I have not the least appetite.

Stimogus   Part. Having a good appetite.

Stitshan   Part. Loitering.
" Ma Willie 'n ddweddar yn dwad o'r iscol o
hyd ; mae e'n stitshan ar iol y plant erill."
Willie is always late coming home from school ;
he loiters behind the rest of the children.

Stiwpid   Adj. Stubborn. Never meaning the same as
the English word *stupid*.

Stoc   N.f.s. A brace (carpenter's tool).

Stoco   V. Tran. and Intran. To uproot, to dig up
furze, thorns, &c.
The term is now almost restricted to the
cleaning of furzy land for the purpose of tillage.

Stol-gader   N.f.s. An arm-chair.
Plur. *stole-cadeire.*

Ston-agolch   N.f.s. The big cask or wooden vessel which
holds pig's wash. (Accent on *ag*).

Stond   N.f.s. A large cask or vessel to hold water
or other liquid.

Stonyn   N.m.s. Chalk stone used for marking floors
when they are washed.

Storws   N.m.s. A granary over another building.
The word is never used of a separate building,
and very rarely for any storehouse except that
in which grain is kept.

S

Stowne N.m.pl. Fits and starts.

"Ellir dim imddibini ar Shanco, ma gormod o stowne arno."

Jenkin cannot be relied upon, he has too many fits and starts.

Stownllyd Adj. from *stowne*.

Straine V. Intran. To distrain.

Straino V. Tran. To sprain.

Stre N.f.s. An altercation, a wordy warfare.

Strebe N.m.pl. Profane sayings.
No singular.

Stred N.f.s. Rate, or perhaps more strictly the rate collector's table or book of dues.

Tinu'r strêd is the expression for making out a table of rate dues. *Codi'r strêd* is collecting the rate. *Y-strêd-fowr* and *y-strêd-hir* are the principal rates; *y-strêd-fach* is a supplementary rate.

Streic Adj. Level.

"Llwyth bach, dim mwy na streic y gisht."

A small load, not more than level with the body of the cart.

Streics N.pl. Streaks.
No singular.
"Careg wen a streics indi."
A white stone with streaks in it.

Streiner N.m.s. A small meshed strainer.

Stribyn N.m.s. (1) A long piece. (2) A long account.

Stric   N.f.s. A hasty sharpening of a tool.
"Rhoi stric fach i'r fladur."
Giving the scythe a hasty sharpening.

Strilyn   N.m.s. A fellow who has never performed one useful or fruitful act in his life.

Stripin   N.m.s. A good distance: in colloquial English "a tidy step."
"Ma stripin maith o Llanchâr i Bontfân."
There is a good distance between Llanychaer and Pontfaen.

Stripins   N.pl. The second milking of a cow. After cows have been milked, they are re-milked for the purpose of getting the last drop or after-milk from the udder.

Stripo   V. Tran. To second milk the cows. Vide *stripins*.

Strityn   N.m.s. One who fawns.

Striw   N.m.s. The art of coaxing.
"Ath Tomos Drewilan i dreio ei striw,
Dath adre yn gallach a'i galon yn friw."
—(Old amatory song).

Sroio   To wind its course sinuously, said of a stream.
"Fel cornant fach yn stroio
Dan sishal rhwng y brwyn," &c.
—(Amatory song).

Stropen   N.f.s. (1) A stirrup (of a saddle). (2) A strap.
Plur. *stropeni*.

Strowl   N.m.s. A vagrant, a stroller.

Strowlin N.m.s. A vagrant, a tramp.

" Dyn te Gwyddel yw'r hen strowlin na? "

Is that old tramp a man or an Irishman?

The query of old Betty Harries, of Taibach, Cwmgwaun, whenever an English-speaking member of the strolling community knocked at her door. She could not conceive of a Welshman being a *strowlin*, any more than she could of a *Gwyddel* being a man. She was a disciple of Giraldus Cambrensis, who remarks that " there are no beggars among the Welsh people "!

Stwcan N.f.s. A shock of corn, consisting in N.E. Pembrokeshire of five sheaves standing on end, with two reversed for cope.

Stwcano is the verb.

Stwetha Adv. of time. Recently, lately, a while ago.

" Fe fuodd 'ma stwetha."

He was here recently.

Stwffwl N.m.s. Sacking or other material put in a *lowsed* (q.v.) to stop draughts.

Stwffwlog Adj. Sinewy, wiry.

Stwmp A quandary, a puzzle.

" Chi'n haloch i miwn stwmp."

You put me in a quandary.

Stwro V. Trans. To reprimand.

" Ma eishe i chi stwro'r plant ma, Sal, ma nhw'n ddrwg ombeidis."

You ought to reprimand these children, Sarah, they are very naughty.

Stwytho V. Tran. To rub oil or liniment into some part of the body.

Suddig-y -cerrig N.m.s. Stonewort (Sedum acre,.

Suddo V. Tran. To melt.
"Suddo bloneg."
Melting lard.

Sudd-yr-heli Nothing absolutely.
"Châs hi ddim cwmint a sudd-yr-heli gida'r hen bobol pan briododd hi."
Her parents gave her absolutely nothing on her marriage.
Sudd-yr-heli means, literally, the juice-of-brine.

Surgas Adj. Musty-sour.
"Biwyn surgas."
A musty-sour kernel (of a nut).

Swabin N.m.s. Mashed potato and butter.
"Swabin a llath-menyn."
Mashed potato and buttermilk.

Swai N.f.s. (1) A row. (2) A fuss.
"We na swai ofnadwy yn y tafarn neithwr."
There was a great row at the public-house last evening.
"Dina swai sy gida nw am y babi."
What a fuss they make about the baby.

Swaiog Adj. Noisy.
"Hen ddyn swaiog."
A noisy old man.

Swalbyn N.m.s. Anything of a considerable size in relation to its own class.
Fem. *swalben.*
Swalpyn and *swalpen* are variants.

Swedsen N.f.s. The large red turnip.
Swedjen is a variant.

Swaipad N.f.s. A cut with a stick or whip which only grazes the object.

Swilad   N.f.s. A hurried wash.

Swilion   N.m.pl. Washings, rinsings out of a vessel.
"Swilion y llestri te."
The tea slops, or rinsings out of the cups.

Swilo   V. Tran. To rinse, to wash over.
"Swilwch y ddish na."
Wash that teacup.

Swish   Onomatopœic. The sound produced by the
falling of a large object into a pool of water.

Swlci   Adj. Sulky.

Swllt-coch N.m.s. The King's shilling. Men who were
eligible for military service and who did not
wish to enlist lived in constant fear of the
King's shilling. During the times of the
Crimean War, when the country needed men,
any stranger of military bearing was looked
upon with suspicion, and the peasantry gave
him a wide berth, lest the dreaded *swllt-côch*
should find its way into their *bliw* of beer, or
into their pocket, which meant that they were
from that moment to regard themselves as
" King's men " and destined for " bloodstained
battlefields in distant lands."

Swmp   Abs. n. (1) A guess. (2) Thickness.
" Wês da chi ryw swmp faint sy na? "
Have you any guess how many there are?
"Swmp bwti dri bys."
About the thickness of three fingers.

Swmpo   V. Tran.   To feel or touch over a thing.
"Swmpwch glun y ceffyl, gal gweld a wês
whiddu indi."
Feel the leg of the horse to see if there is a
swelling in it.

Swn-o'r-mor Literally, a sound from the sea; referring to the superstitious belief that the sound of the sea may be heard by holding a large sea shell to the ear.

Swp Adv. Suddenly.
"Fe bangodd swp."
He fainted suddenly.

Swpaffaster N.m.s. Superphosphate, a patent manure.

Swrffedi V. Tran. and Intran. To be cold and stiff after long exposure to the weather.
(1) "Ma'r tewy 'n ddigon i swrffedi dyn."
The weather is cold enough to freeze one.
(2) "Wdw i wedi swrffedi 'n lân."
I am very cold and stiff.

Swrth Adj. Sullen, abrupt of speech.

SH

Sha   [= tua.] Prep. Towards, in the direction of.

Shabwlso   V. Tran. To mangle.
"Fe shabwlsodd 'i fraich yn y mashin dwrnu.''
He had his arm mangled in the threshing machine.

Shafins   N.m.pl. Shavings, i.e., those produced by a carpenter at work.
Sing. *shafinsyn.*

Shaff   N.f.s. The shaft of a cart. (Pron. shàff).

Shaffy-y-seld   N.f.s. The shelf of the old-fashioned Welsh dresser.

Shangdifang   N.m.s. A litter; a place badly disarranged. Farm buildings that have been allowed to fall into disrepair and disorder are usually so described.

Shal   N.f.s. A jail, prison. (Pron. shâl).

Shan   N.f.s. A hare, in familiar language. (Pron. shân).

Shanco   In the saying "Màn a'r màn a Shanco"; "It's all one whichever way you take it": "Six of one, half-a-dozen of the other," and a variety of other meanings.

Shandler   N.f.s. A candlestick.

Shapse   N.m.s. Predicament, shape, condition, position, and a variety of other meanings.
"Beth yw'r shapse ma sy arnat ti?"
What is this predicament which you are in?

Shar   Abs. n. Share, portion.

Sharadus   Adj. Talkative and amiable. The word means more than to be merely talkative; there is also amiableness.

Shars   N.f.s. A charge, admonition. (Pron. shàrs).

Sharso   V. Trans. To charge, to admonish.

Sharso   V. Tran. and Intran. To charge, to enjoin upon.

Shawns   N.m.s. Chance.
"Ar dro shawns."
On a chance time.

Sheced   N.f.s. A drubbing.
"Mi rows eitha sheced iddo."
He gave him a good drubbing; literally, a good jacket.

Sheced -fraith -Joseph   A kind of wall flower.

Shecel   N.f.s. Piston, spindle.
"Shecel y mashin."
The piston or spindle of the machine.

Specplam   N.m.s. A small plane, a carpenter's tool. Probably from *check plane*.

Shedrem   N.f.s. The passage in a cow-shed between the two rows of stalls.

Shedrem Abs. n. Exactly the same, the very image of. Expressed best by the English provincialism, "exactly the same spit as."

"Ma Mari fach yr un shedrem a'i mham."

Little Mary is the very image of her mother.

Shedrem formerly meant the position of the reaper with respect to the *grwn* (ridge). The foreman took up his position *ar gefen y grwn* (on the back of the ridge), and all who occupied a similar position were said to be *ar yr un shedrem* (in the same position). Those who were next to the back of the ridges, or on or near the trench, were also said to be working similar *shedremi*. Hence, with the growth of the word, *shedrem* came to mean similarity in respect to persons.

Shengel Adj. Single.

Shengyd [= sangu.] V. Intran. To tread upon.

Sheinin N.m.s. Boot polish.

Sheino V. Tran. and Intran. To polish boots.

"Alla i ddim sheino'r scidie, 's'ma ddim sheinin i gâl."

I cannot polish the boots, there is no polish here.

Sherew Adj. Rude, vulgar.

"Hen fenyw sherew."

A rude old woman.

(Accent on *ew*).

Sherfo V. Intran. Reeling to and fro, swerving.

Sherp Adj. Acerb, sharp, in reference to cheese, or to small beer. (2) Quick-witted.

"Cosyn sherp "—Acerb, or hot cheese.

"Rhocyn sherp "—A quick-witted lad.

Shibaders   Adj. Ragged, all-in-tatters.
"Mae e wedi rhico llawes 'i gòt yn shibaders."
He has torn the sleeves of his coat in tatters.
(Accent on *dêrs*).

Shibedu   V. Tran. To gibbet.

Shibigw   [= yswigw.] N.f.s. Titmouse.

Shibolden   N.f.s. A small candle made of hog's lard, with a strip of rag for a wick. It is a ready-at-hand contrivance when the supply of ordinary candles has given out.

Shiffto   V. Intran. To shift, to make the best of it under adverse circumstances.
The noun *shifft* is also used.

Shifftwn   N.m.pl. The gipsy.
In no part of the country are these wanderers held in such repugnance as in N. Pembrokeshire.

Shigen   [= chwisigen.] N.f.s. Bladder.

Shigen   N.f.s. Quagmire.

Shiglyn   N.m.s. A tottering old man.

Shigwdo   V. Tran. To shake roughly, to take hold of by the neck and shake.
"Ma'r hen gi wedi shigwdo'r gath yn ofnadwy."
The old dog has taken the cat by the neck and shaken it very roughly.

Shigwti   N.f.s. Wag-tail.

Shigwti-felen   Yellow wag-tail.

Shigwti-lwyd   Grey wag-tail.

  „   -ddwr   Water wag-tail.

Shinglers   Coll. n. Beads and "bobtails." Said of female attire which is covered with beadwork and curious embroidery.

"Mae'n shinglêrs i gyd o'i phen i'w thrâd"—said of a woman who has so much gaudy and embroidered bead-work on her dress that the sound of her passing is like that of a small band of fairy bells. (Accent on *lêrs*).

Shingrug   N.m.s. Chaff-heap.

This word furnishes another instance of a common noun becoming a proper name. There are several cottages and many fields in Pembrokeshire bearing the name "Shingrug."

Shilots   N.m.pl. Shallot.

The singular is *shilotsyn* (masc.) and *shilotsen* (fem.), which are used indifferently.

Shilblin   N.m.s. Chilblains.

Shilfoch   N.f.s. That part of the mouth which is between the jaw-teeth and the cheeks.

Shilgota   V. Tran. Catching minnow.

Shilgots   N.m.pl. Minnow.
Sing. *shilgotsyn*.

Shilsyn   [= silyn.] N.m.s. A small bit of chaff, and secondarily a small bit of anything.

Shimlebis   N.f.s. Chimney-piece.

shimle   [= simdde.] N.f.s. Chimney.

Shinachu V. Tran. To attempt to graze, or to chew grass feebly, to nibble.

Shinco V. Tran. and Intran. To sink.
"Shinco winsh"—Sinking a well.
"Ma'r helem wedi shinco."
The stack of corn has sunk.

Shinshir
  -pop N.m.s. Gingerade.

Shipris N.m.s. A crop of barley and oats mixed.
The seed is sown in the proportion of two parts of barley to one of oats.
"Sharad shipris"—A mixture of English and Welsh.

Shishwrn N.m.s. Scissors.

Shiwrin Abs. Insurance.
"Odi'r ty yn y shiwrin gida chi?"
Have you insured the house?

Shiwyn N.f.s. A horned sheep.
Plur. *shiwod*.

Shobo V. Tran. To crush.
"Peidwch shòbo 'ng hat i."
Don't crush my hat.

Shol N.f.s. A shawl. (Pron. shòl).

Shol-war N.f.s. A small shawl worn over the shoulders.

Sholyn N.m.s. A small load of anything, such as hay, furze, &c.
Shwlyn and *showlyn* are variants.

Shon-a-Shan A mechanical contrivance for indicating weather changes, too familiar to need describing here.

Shoncen N.f.s. Mild home-brewed beer.

Shoncen N.f.s. A woman of ill repute.

Shonco V. Intran. To be a little flushed with drink; to take just enough liquor to quicken the pace.

Shocyn Surprise, never as the equivalent of *shock*, from which it is evidently derived.
"Fe gâs shocyn mowr."
He had a great surprise.

Short N.c.s. Sort.
"Mae e'n eitha short."
He is a very good sort.

Show N.f.s. (1) A show. (2) Any wonder. (Pron. as *cow* in English, only substituting *sh* for *c*).
(1) "Show fowr y criaduried gwyllton."
The large menagerie (referring to some particular one, such as Wombwell's).
(2) "Mae'n show i'r byd i weld y taie newy sy'n cal 'u bildo yn Bergwein."
It is a wonder to behold the new houses that are being built in Fishguard.

Shwfflo V. Intran. To muddle along, to get along somehow, by hook or by crook.

Shwg N.f.s. A jug. (Pron. shwg).

Shwgir N.m.coll. Sugar.
Variants are *shwgwr* and *shiwgwr*.

Shwgwdo V. Trans. To shake roughly, as of a dog catching a rat and giving a squeeze and a toss.

Shwl-mwl Utter confusion.
"Ma'r cifan wedi mynd shwl-mwl na."
Everything is in utter confusion there.

Shwr Adj. Sure.
Comp *shwrach* and *siwrach.*
Sup. *shwra* and *siwra.*

Shwrlog Adj. Surly.

Shwrls The fetlock of a horse.

Shwrne N.f.s. (1) Journey. (2) Turn, time.
(1) " Fe ganodd y ceilog,
    Fe dorrodd ŷ wawr ;
Mae'n bryd i ni ddeffro,
    Ein shwrne sydd fawr.
Mae milwyr y Brenhin
    Yn mhell yn y blân,
A minneu 'u dilinaf
    Drwy'r dŵr a thrwy'r tân."
                                    (Old hymn).
(2) " Cerwch chi 'r shwrne hon, a fe âf fi 'r
shwrne nesa."

You go this time, and I will go the next
(time).

Shwt [= sut.] Adv. How.

Shwtrws N.pl. Shatters.

T

Tablen   N.f.s. Home-brewed beer of medium strength. *Vide whiblen.*

Taccu   [= tad-cu.] Grandfather.
This is one out of a large number of similar instances of assimilation furnished by the dialect.

Tace   N.f.s. Boot-nails.
Sing. *tacen.*
The various kinds of boot-nails made at the local smithy were:
    (1) *Tace-man*—Small nails with round heads.
    (2) *Tace-milgi*—With elongated heads.
    (3) *Tace-penfas*—Flat-headed nails.
    (4) *Tace-tair-ergyn*—Nails with pyramid heads.
With these *asgurn scidenyn* were made, a method of putting the nails in the shape of the back-bone of a herring.

Tacle   Coll. n. A term of reproach or contempt in speaking of people.
    " Yr hen dacle melltigedig."
    The cursed old things.

Tacs   N.m.pl. Fellows, in a contemptible sense.

Tachiffra-i   Inter. If I never move!

Tafod-yr -ebol   N.m.s. The fleshy tissue which attaches to a colt's forehead when it is cast. The old-time farmer carefully removed it and nailed it to the stable door, to ensure that good luck would attend the colt.

Tangins N.m.pl. Bent or hooked hazel rods used in thatching straw cottages and ricks for the purpose of securing the rope. There were two kinds, the bent rod, and the hooked rod.

Tangleth N.f.s. A bother, in the colloquial sense of the word.
"Mae e miwn rhyw hen dangleth neu gily o hyd."
He is in some old bother or other continually.
There is a verb *tanglo*.

Tango V. Intran. To go to a wood to cut branches for fencing.

Tai [= petai.] V. Intran. If it should be.

Taie [= tai.] N.m.pl. Houses.
The plur. *tai* is only rarely used.

Taith An expletive, usually used in conjunction with *anwyl*.
"Y taith anwyl!"
Good gracious!

Talbren N.m.s. A meting rod, a perch long.
It invariably figured among the sundries of an old farm house.

Talddail N.m.s. A heap of decayed leaves. (Tail + dail?)

Talian N.m.s. A heater for smoothing frills; italian-iron.
In much use formerly for the purpose of smoothing the frills of the old style Welsh bonnet.

T

Talio

Adv. Diligently, busily.

" Ma bobol y gwmdogeth yn rhwmo talio heddy."

The people of the neighbourhood are binding corn busily to-day.

(Pron. tal-i-o, accent on o).

Talmen

Abs. n. Disbursements, expenditure, with special reference to rates and taxes.

Plur. *talmentodd*.

Taluedd

Adj. The word combines two or three ideas, and in the mouth of a Dyfedwr is most expressive. It means a handsome, kind, and industrious woman: it is never used of the male sex. It means much more than the classical *teuluaidd*.

" Merch dalùedd yw Ann y Wern."

Ann, of Wern, is a handsome, kind, and industrious lass.

Tameitach

N.m.pl. Small bits.

Tamellog

Adj. Fragmentary.

Tan-coch

N.m.s. The place of torment, but it is doubtful whether hell or purgatory was originally intended, because another word, *pwll-du*, is generally used for the worst kind of retribution.

Tan-eishyn

N.m.s. Husk fire.

In the olden days eishyn (oat husks chiefly) was used by poor people for fire material. It was fetched in sackfuls from the local mill and kept on the hearth near the fire. During the long winter evenings the older gossips would beseat themselves around the fire and indulge in small talk to their hearts' content. The good wife of the house would punctuate her remarks at regular intervals with the throwing of a handful of *eishyn* upon the glowing embers. Quaint picture!

Tanfa   N.f.s. A row of hay or corn.

Tanfaio   V. Tran. To gather hay or corn into rows or ridges several yards apart.

Tanierdy   N.m.s. Tanyard.

Tanwent   N.m.pl. Firewood.
Sing. *tanwentyn*.
" Baich o danwent "—A burden of firewood.
" Llwyth o danwent "—A load of firewood.

Tapyn   N.m.s. Sole of boot.

Taraf   N.m.s. A great hurry.
" Ma gormod o daraf arna i nawr i aros i sharad a chi."
I am in too great a hurry now to stop to talk to you.

**Tarddiant
-anwyd**   N.m.s. The breaking out of a cold on the face.

Tarddu   [= tarfu.] V. Tran. To scare, to frighten.
" Tarddu brain."
Scaring crows.

Taredd   Adj. An event that is pregnant with possibilities.
" Rhifel dàredd wê rhifel fowr Crimea."
The Crimean War was an event pregnant with possibilities.
The word is nearly obsolete.

Tasc   N.m.s. Home lesson given to school children.
Plur. *tascis*.

Tascen-fach
-y-dwr N.f.s. The water-flea.

An insect that appears on the surface of water morning and evening and moves about with short jerks or springs.

Tasci V. Intran. (1) To take fright, to startle, to bolt. (2) To squirt, splash.

(1) " Ceffyl drwg i dasci."

A horse that is apt to bolt.

(2) " Paid bwrw cerig i'r afon, ma'r dwr yn tasci arna i."

Don't throw stones into the river, the water squirts about me.

Tascion Coll. n. Squirtings.

" Tascion y ffordd."

The squirts of the road, i.e., the mud squirts caused by a vehicle.

Tascion-menyn = drops of liquid which spurt from butter when it is beaten by the hand.

Tato N.f.pl. Potatoes.

Sing. *taten*.

Tatsho V. Intran. To partake of.

" Nawr fechgyn, ma'r bwyd o'ch blân chi, tatshwch nawr."

Now lads, the food is in front of you, partake of it.

Tatsho V. Intran. To bicker.

" Dim ond tatsho a'u gily' ma nw byth a befyd."

They are for ever bickering with one another.

Tawch N.m.s. Smell; it is never used here as the equivalent of *vapour*.

" Tawch cryf yn codi o'r bedd."

A strong smell from the grave.

Tawte

That it is so.
" Mae'n debyg gen i tawte."
I am of the opinion that it is so.

Tebigon

Abs. n. Comparisons.
Following is a list of some of the more frequent comparisons : —
Mor felined a'r olden.
Mor wyned a'r eira.
Mor wyned a'r carlwm.
Mor wyned a dant y ci.
Mor wyned a'r galchen (said of a pale sickly person).
Mor ddued a'r frân.
Mor ddued a'r parddu.
Mor ddued a michin.
Mor lased a'r geninen.
Mor goch a chrib y ceilog.
Mor llwyted a lletwad.
Mor dewyll a'r fagddu.
Mor hagar a phechod.
Mor shonced a'r dryw.
Mor iscawn a'r plifyn.
Mor gonc a'r pinc.
Mor falched a'r bioden.
Mor falched a phoun.
Mor union a sâth.
Mor wanned a mŵg.
Mor istwyth a'r faneg.
Mor llon a'r bridill.
Mor wired a llîth.
Mor shwred a'r farn.
Mor gyflym a'r wànol.
Mor ddrewllyd a'r gingron.
Mor dwt a nŷth y dryw.
Mor bigog a'r eithinen.
Mor wanned a phabwrin.
Mor amled a drudwns.
Mor ffalsted a'r cadno.

Mor listi a'r eboles.

Mor benwan a'r loten. (Query: Is loten
Lot's wife?)

Mor iached a'r girchen.

Mor feddw a thincer.

Mor hên a bedd daccû.

Mor faned a mês (with special reference to
small potatoes, when the crop is poor).

Mor ddiwerth a rhêch mochyn gròt.

Mor llawned a'r wŷ.

Mor dewed a'r wâdd.

Mor dene a scithan.

Mor dwp a phòst iet.

Mor froued a garetshen.

Mor sich a thŵll-tin y gwynt.

Mor laned a ffinon Ddewi.

Mor arwed a chawse Llantwd.

Mor drodnoth a Gwyddel.

Mor siched a'r corcyn.

Mor ddishtaw a'r bedd.

Mor ddiddal a cheilog-y-gwynt.

Mor sherped a'r cwlltwr.

Mor llawen a'r gôg.

Mor dorled a broga.

Mor wancus a winci.

Mor stiffed a phocer.

Mor hallt a'r heli.

Mor wherw a'r bustil.

Mor wherw a'r wermwd.

Mor heger a barcud.

Mor âno a châl bwch i odyn.

Mor sich a chraswellt odyn.

Mor ddi-baro a ffagal o redyn.

Mor iached a dwr ffinon Deilo.

[There is a legend that the water of S. Teilo's
Well, Llandilo. is a certain cure for all pul-
monary complaints.]

Mor iached a chawl dinad mish Mowrth.

Mor dwllog a rhidyll mwl.

Mor sifil a'r jwj.

Mor bur a bara Ffaro.

[This was not the Egyptian Pharaoh, but Farrow, the flour merchant and baker, of Haverfordwest, whose fame for *bara gwyn* (white bread) had spread far and near.]

Mor ddeir a molwaden.

Mor nŵeth a dafad wedi 'i chneifo.

Mor ddiniwed a mwydyn.

Mor wyllt a'r cacwn.

Mor llifin a chareg y drws.

Teibo   N.m.s. A plow regulator.

Teilwr
  -Llenden   N.m.s. The goldfinch.

Teilwr   N.m.s. The best man at a wedding party.

Teirus   Adj. Tiresome, fidgetty.

Teirwch   [= taerni.] Abs. n. Importunity.

Teit   Adj. Close-fisted, miserly.

Tel   N.m.s. Five bushels and five pecks.

     " Pum winshin a phum pecad

     Yw têl da i ginwyshiad.''

Five bushels and five pecks make a *têl*, with good measure.

Tempri   V. Trans. To season, a term applied to the seasoning of various utensils before using them.

Y dull o dempri gwahanol lestri :—

(1) Ffreimpan—cladder hi yn y pridd am dridie.

(2) Cidl—berwer dŵr hallt indo am saith awr.

(3) Casc-menyn—sodder yn y ffynon am dridie.

(4) Ffiole, &c.—berwer mewn dŵr gyda bara am dair awr.

Tent   N.m.s. A weight, tightness, a leaning.
"Stim tent ar y polion.
The supports have no weight upon them.
Referring to the supports (poles) placed against a rick of hay or corn to prevent its leaning over-much.

Termad   N.m.s. A reprimand.
"Fe gâs dermad yn iawn am 'i ddrigioni."
He had a severe reprimanding for his mischief.

Terment   Funeral ale. Immediately after a person's death, it was the custom formerly to brew a large quantity of strong ale for the due observance of the Wake and the funeral ceremonies. The word looks like a corruption of *interment*. According to a contributor to the "Pembroke County Guardian": "The ale was served by two men on the funeral day,—one carrying the hot ale and the other the cold ale. The people formed a semi-circle, and those who carried the ale commenced helping them at one end followed around. Many in the company who were fond of *cwrw da* came on at the commencement, and having had one drink backed out, only to reappear again at the other end of the ring. Thus they did over and over again, till they had had several helpings, so that it was nothing extraordinary to see a number of drunken men at a funeral before starting from the house to the graveyard. While the men were carrying round the *terment* outside the house, two women, with white towels pinned on their left arm, would at the same time be engaged in distributing white and red wine to the special guests who were assembled inside."

Termo   V. Intran. To reprimand.
This is the form used in N.E. Pembrokeshire, in the N.W. it is *termu*.

" Peidwch a termo'r crwt fel 'na am ddim yn y byd."

Lit.: Don't reprimand the lad so for nothing in the world.

Teser N.m.s. Dancing heat. On a hot summer's day the air seems to be " alive " with vibratory movement—this is *teser*.

Tethe-caws N.f.pl. The small lumps seen on home-made cheese, produced by the holes in the vat when the new cheese is under pressure.

Tethe-difii N.f.pl. The small back teats of a cow, in which there is no milk.

Tewy [= tywydd.] N.m.s. Weather.

Tewy Rage, temper.
" We tewy ofnadwy ar Dafi am fod y scwlin wedi pwnw'r crwt."
David was in an awful rage because the schoolmaster had beaten the lad.

Tewy
-cifartal N.m.s. Mixed weather.

Tieyn N.m.s. The ticking of a bed.

Tidie N.m.s. The iron collar of the fore-horse of a team; now used generally of any iron horse-collar.

Tiddiant Abs.n. Growth.
Twddiant is a variant.

Tiddu V. Intran. To grow.
Twddu is a variant.

Tifwyth N.m.s. Rank vegetation, especially that which grows in wet soil.

Tingu

V. Intran. To swear, to make a solemn oath.

The following expressions, indicating different forms of oaths, are some of them of historic interest :—

Ar 'ngair i—On my word.

Ar f'incws i—On my life (?).

Ar f'end i—On my soul.

Men Wirif lán—By the Holy Virgin.

Wir Dduw—By the truth of God.

Men Duw—By God.

Men asen i—By my rib.

Ar 'nghred i—By my faith.

Men asgwrn—By the bone (i.e., the relic of a saint, perhaps).

Men llien i—By my chrisom (?).

[To swear by one's chrisom was an ancient form of oath.]

Men jain i

Men diain i (?).

Men Barna—By S. Bernard.

[There is a celebrated well, named after S. Bernard, in the parish of Henry's Moat.]

Men Dewi wyn—By the holy S. David.

[This is often rubbed down to *Dewin*.]

Ar gar'-fryna [= ar garreg Frynach]—By the stone (cross) of S. Brynach.

[There were many other similar expressions in use not so long ago, but the compiler cannot recall them.]

Tilsen

N.f.s. A teal.

Tilt

N.m.s. A tent.

Strictly limited to the beer tent which, once upon a time, was a regular feature of country fairs.

Tinfachu

Part. Grasping tightly.

Said of a miser who grasps his money-bag firmly.

Tindroi

V. Intran. Fussing about doing nothing: much ado about nothing.

Tini

V. Tran. To cultivate, to form.
Strictly limited to this sense in the phrase " tini 'nabiddieth," to cultivate acquaintance.

Tini-ato

In the phrase " Ma'r dydd yn tini ato "— the day is shortening; literaly, " the day is pulling towards himself."

Tinu

V. Tran. To wean.
" Tinu plentyn sugno."
To wean a sucking child.

Tinu

V. Tran. To dig, to uproot.
(1) " Tinu tato "—Digging potatoes.
(2) " Tinu erfin "—Picking or uprooting turnips.

Tinu

Part. n. Rivalry among suitors for a young woman's hand.

Mr. Daniel E. Jones, in his " Hanes Plwyfi Llangeler a Phenboyr," has a note on this custom, which I quote here, taking the liberty at the same time of substituting the Gwaun dialect for that of Llangeler: " Yn y neithor, ar iol talu a châl cwpaned o de, elsid yn gwmnie miwn gwanol starelli ac yn y tai nesa i ifed diod, treto'r rhocesi a chace pan ddele'r gwahoddwr a llond 'i ffedog heibo, a halid nosweth ddifyr a llawen. Wê *tinu* mowr ar y merched ar yr achlisuron hyn. Ar iol i ferch ifanc ishte lawr gida rhyw fachgen dewishol, bidde rhwun arall yn hala 'i mofyn hi, ac yn 'i *thinu* miwn modd deniadol ato. Tebyg yr anfonsid i'w mofyn yn ol wedin neu fe fuse rhwun arall yn shŵr o'i *thinu*, a fel 'na o un cariad at y llall, a châl cace gida pob un o heni nw i roi yn 'i phacyn, fidde'r ferch 'n

> gneyd nes bidde 'i 'n amser myn'd gatre. Wê
> ddi 'n câl 'i histiried yn glôd i ferch fod pŵer
> o *dinu* arni miwn ffair neu neithor."

Tinu-ar-i
-oedran V. phrase. Getting up in years.

Tinu'r
-bwmbwr This expression has several metaphorical
applications. Literally it means removing a
cover from the eyes, and it was originally
applied to the re-opening of windows that had
been built up when the window tax was in
force. Blind windows were termed *bwmbwr-y-*
brenhin.

Tinu-dros
-y-ffordd A euphemism for committing fornication.

Tir-bei-howlt N.m.s. Land held for one year. A farmer
who has too much land for his own use, or who
is "gone back in the world," is obliged to let
his spare land, and he usually does so by
auction about Michaelmas. This is called *tir-*
bei-howlt.

Tish-baw Inter. Tut, nonsense!

Tistio V. Intran. To swear or affirm solemnly. It
is stronger than *gwrio* (q.v.) and *heiru*. It is
never used in the classical sense of testifying.

Titen N.f.s. The nipple of a woman's breast.
"Rhoi titen"—to give suck, to give the
breast.

Tiwn-un
-anal Lit. A tune-of-one-breath, i.e., a tune which
was to be sung in one breathing. Tune, in
the Pembrokeshire dialect, applies primarily to
the words, and not to the music. There were
several of these tunes in vogue a quarter-of-a-
century ago, but the author can remember only
one, which is given here. The first four or five

301

verses could easily be sung during one breathing, even by one who was not practised in breath control, but the verses went on increasing in length, so that only one who had learnt the art of economising his breath and who could articulate rapidly stood the least possible chance of completing the last verse in one respiration.

TIWN Y PREN.

First Verse.

O'r bryn fe ddaeth pren, ffein a brâf

oedd y bryn, lle tiddodd y pren.

Second Verse.

O'r pren fe ddaeth cainc, ffein a brâf

| This part repeated *ad lib.*

oedd y cainc, Y cainc o'r pren, a'r pren o'r bryn,

Ffein a brâf oedd y bryn, lle tiddodd y pren.

3rd.

O'r cainc fe ddaeth dail,
Ffein a brâf oedd y dail,
    Y dail o'r cainc,
    Y cainc o'r pren,
    Y pren o'r bryn,
Ffein a brâf oedd y bryn,
Lle tiddodd y pren.

4th.

O'r dail fe ddaeth nŷth,
Ffein a brâf oedd y nŷth,
   Y nŷth o'r dail,
   Y dail o'r cainc,
   Y cainc o'r pren,
   Y pren o'r bryn,
Ffein a brâf oedd y bryn,
Lle tiddodd y pren.

5th. O'r nŷth fe ddaeth wŷ, &c.
6th. O'r wŷ fe ddaeth cyw, &c.
7th. O'r cyw fe ddaeth plyf, &c.
8th. O'r plyf fe ddaeth gwely, &c.
9th. O'r gwely fe ddaeth llances, &c.
10th. O'r llances fe ddaeth llancyn, &c.
11th. O'r llancyn fe ddaeth clochy', &c.
12th. O'r clochy' fe ddaeth ffeirad, &c.
13th. O'r ffeirad fe ddaeth eglws, &c.

To   [= etto.] Adv. Again.
"Gobeitho dewch chi 'n gweled ni tô."
We hope you will come to see us again.

Tochleth   N.m.s. A ramshackle bedroom. The word is
hardly to be regarded as an abstract noun,
since it refers more to the room in its confused
state than to the actual confusion.

Todi   [=tydi.] Ref. Pron. Thyself.

Tolio   V. Tran. and Intran. To use sparingly, to
economise.
"Yn ngene'r sach ma tolio."
                       (A proverb).

Tomdills   Coll.n. Daffodils.

Tonc   N.f.s. A snatch of a tune.
"Tonc fach nawr, bois!"

Let's have a snatch of a tune, lads!
Toncen and *toncad* are also used.

Tonis N.c.pl. The yellow races.
This is the word invariably used in speaking of the Chinese and kindred races.

Topi V. Tran. and Intran. To butt, to gore.

Topin N.m.s. Fun, a merry-making.
Topin is frequently used as the equivalent of *neithor* or *nos blân* also.
" Dyna dopin geson ni wth glwed Sheci Shams yn adrodd hanes y plowin' matsh."
Lit.: We had great fun in hearing John James giving an account of the ploughing match.

Toplyd Adj. Inclined to butt, apt to gore.

Topyn-del N.m.s. Pine seed.

Tor N.m.s. A drawback.
" Mae'n dòr fowr iddo fod e mor drwm 'i glwed."
It is a great drawback to him that he is so hard of hearing.

Torad Abs. n. Figure.
" Mae e o dorad taran debyg i Tomos Hafart."
He is of a figure somewhat similar to Thomas Havard.

Torad In the phrase " Ar dorad 'i fogel e," equivalent to the proverb " What is bred in the bone comes out in the flesh."
Literally it means " on the cutting of his navel."

Torad-ty   N.m.s. The plan of a house. Here is a rough sketch of the ground-plan of a typical N. Pembrokeshire farmhouse.

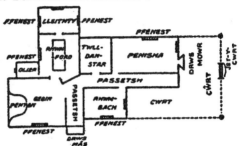

Torcalondid   Abs. n. Heartlessness.

Torchi   V. Tran. To turn up. In the phrase *torchi llewis i gris*, turning up the sleeves of his shirt.

Torgain   N.f.s. The belly-band of the fore horse of a team.

Tori   V. Tran. To utter, to form.
Strictly limited in this sense to the phrase "tori geire," to utter words; especially in extempore prayer.
"Nertha ni, O Arglwydd, i beido rhoi'n meddwl ar dori geire o'th flân Di, yn unig, ond hefyd i weddio a'r yspryd."
Help us, O Lord, not to rely on the mere uttering of words before Thee, but to pray with the spirit.

Tori-ar -sharad   V. phrase. To interrupt one when speaking.

Torri   V. Intran. To become bankrupt.

Torri-'i-enw   V. phrase. To sign his name; lit., to cut or break his name.

Torri'-i-fogel   V. phrase. An expression which, literally rendered, means *breaking his navel*, but which in free phrase would be best equated by the English provincialism "nearly off his head."
"Mae e bron tori-'i-fogel eishe câl myn'd i'r ffair."
He is nearly off his head that he should go to the fair.

Torri'r-llechе   Literally, cutting the rickets. Ricketty children were never taken to a doctor, but to a "wise" woman, who charmed for them. The charm consisted of an incision made on a part of the ear, with the recital of an incantatory formula. This superstition is hardly dead yet.

Torlas   Adj. Grey-black. A sheep whose wool is somewhere between white, and black is called *dafad dorlas*.

Torled   Adj. Squat and all abroad.

Ter   Part. In the phrase *Rhoi tor*—Giving suck, such as a sow or bitch giving suck to its young.

Torred   Coll. n. A litter, applied only to pigs.
"Torred o berchyll."
A litter of pigs.

Torwino   Part. The upturning of the leaves of trees, which occurs with certain winds, and which gives them the appearance of becoming sickly and withery. This is regarded as a sure sign of rain.

Tost   Adj. Sore.
"Wdw i'n dost bob tamed o hana i."
I am sore all over me.

T

Towlad Abs. n. Hindrance, an inconvenience, a set-back.
"Fe fu'r anshawns yn dowlad mowr iddo."
The accident proved a great set-back to him.

Towlu [= taflu.] V. Tran. To throw.

Towlu V. Intran. To hint at.
"Towlu wêdd e fod yn bryd i fi fyn'd."
Hinting he was that it was time I went.

Towlu-cifer V. Intran. To give a day's help, to give a turn.
When one farmer sends a man and a team for a day to help a neighbouring farmer, he calls the act *towlu cifer.*

Towlu-gole Part. Lightning; lit., casting light.

Trade N.f.p. Feet.
This is the plural used in serio-comic or humorous speech: it is never used in ordinary serious conversation.

Trade-bach A term for a new-born babe; a new arrival.
"Fe fydd trade-bach yn y teulu ofon hir."
There will be a new arrival in the family before long. Literally, it means little feet.

Tradfa N.f.s. A course, walk; a place that is frequently trodden upon.

Trad-i-ddwylo Creeping; on hands and feet, all fours.
"Mynd ar drad-'i-ddwylo."
Lit.: Going on the feet of his hands.

Tradins N.pl. Tracks, trails.
"Tradins y defed."
Sheep tracks.

Trad-nos   N.f.pl. Stilts.

Trad-y-brain   Bluebells (Scilla nutans).

Trad-y-gath   N.m.s. Ground ivy (Nepeta glechoma).

Trafel   Abs. n. A difficulty.
"Mi gesym drafel i gâl gafel ar y defed i gyd."
I had a difficulty in finding all the sheep.

Train   N.m.s. A train.

Tramwynt   N.m.s. Draught.
"Paid sefyll yn y tramwynt fan 'na, te wyt ti 'n shwr o gâl anwyd."
Don't stand in that draught, or you will be certain to contract a chill.

Trash   Coll. n. The cuttings of a hedgerow. When farmers trim their hedges, they gather the cuttings together for firewood, or for stopping a gap in the hedge, &c. These heads they call *trash.*

Trawch   [= tarewch.] In the phrase *trawch 'ch pwys lawr*, sit down; lit., put your weight down.

Trawslif   N.f.s. Hand-saw.

Trefa   N.f.s. A quantity of straw ready prepared for thatching purposes. The measure differs in different localities; in the Gwaun it is twenty-four bundles.
"Peder sopen ar hugen dwn
Yn gneyd un drefa gifan grwn."

Trefan   Prop. n. Providence.
"Mae 'n imddibinu ar beth ddarparith y Drefen ar 'u cifer nw."
It depends on what Providence will provide for them.

Trefingar Adj. Loving order.

Tregl N.m.s. Treacle.

Treial Abs. n. (1) Trial, proof, an action at law. (2) Metaphorically, in the plural, *treialon*, for crosses, temptations.

Treialon N.pl. Trials, vicissitudes. The word has no singular in this signification, but *treial*, probation, is used.

Treimplam N.m.s. The largest plane used by a carpenter.

Treio V. Intran. To try, to make an effort.

Trenshwn N.m.s. The old style wooden plate.

Tret N.m.s. A present.

Treto V. Tran. To treat, to give a present to.

Tribe N.f.s. A trivet.

Tribinn Abs. n. Confusion.

Trifer N.m.s. A three-pronged fork, with hooks at the points of the prongs something after the form of those of fishing-hooks. Always made by the local blacksmith and guarded with the utmost secrecy. It had a handle about 6ft. long.

Trigo V.n. Dying, dead. Strictly limited in N.E. Pembrokeshire to the death of an animal, even as *marw* is strictly limited to the death of a human being.

Trigole   N.m.pl. The three marks or paths of a road, viz., the wheel tracks and the horse track. These are to be seen on a road that has been recently metalled.

Trigyn   N.m.s. A pinch of anything held between the thumb and two fingers.

Trillo   Part. n. Rolling. A game so called. Children would form their bodies as near the shape of a wheel as possible, and then roll down the side of a hilly field.

Trin-a
-thrafod   V. phrase. To cultivate.
" Ma eishe trin-a-thrafod y tir ma."
This land requires cultivation.

Trin-'i-sath   V. phrase. A cat clawing a tree.
Other expressions for the same thing are :—
hogi-'i-chledde and *hogi-'i-gwine*.

Trinshwrnwr   N.m.s. A meat eater.
" Trinshwrnwr da yw e."
He is a good meat eater ; i.e., he can dispose of a good quantity of meat at a meal.

Tripls   N.m.s. A cart consisting of only the shafts and pair of wheels ; that is, with the *cisht* off.

Tripwl   Num. Adj. Triple.

Tristo   V. Tran. and Intran. To trust, hope.

Trogan   Part. n. The circular flights of a carrion crow over a domicile or field. It was formerly believed that if a carrion crow flew in a circle several times over a farmhouse, or over a field when cattle were grazing at the time, hoarsely croaking as it flew, serious reverses would soon

fall to the lot of the owner of the field or
cattle. The crow was *trogan* the approach of
an epidemic among the cattle. It was amusing
to hear a farmer of the old type *crá-*ing at
these birds of ill-omen. It was the occasion,
of all others, when he felt justified in using
strong language.

Trongol   N.m.s. A narrow passage between two
houses.

Trei   V. Tran. To soil, dirty.
This peculiar use of the word is seen in the
following expression : —
" Ich chi wedi troi 'ch dillad."
You have soiled your clothes.

Troi-a-triglo   V. phrase. Turning and twisting about ; said
of one that is restless in bed, or uneasy in his
seat.
[Observe : it is not *th*riglo.]

Troilo   V. Intran. To wear away, to rub off, as
of iron or other metal through friction.

Troi'r-ddish   Part. phrase. Turning-the-cup. A method of
fortune-telling adopted by superstitious old
women. After a convivial cup of tea a cup
containing " slop " and tea leaves is turned
around several times and then rested upside-
down, so as to allow the leaves to settle. The
future is then " told " from the arrangement
of the leaves.

Troitan   V. Intran. To go at a brisk pace, to run.
" Ma rhaid i fi throitan hi."
I must go quickly, or in provincial phrase,
" I must foot it."

Troitol   N.f.s. The handle of a utensil, and sometimes used of the foot of a vessel.

Trol   N.f.s.   A trawler.

Troll   N.f.s.   Oatmeal dumpling.
A lump of oatmeal dough put in the broth
to be served with potatoes and cabbage.

Trom   Adj.   Enceinte.
This feminine form of *trwm* is strictly limited
to the above usage, and never understood in
any other sense.   *Trwm* does duty in all other
cases for both masc. and fem.

Trowl   N.m.s.   A wooden straw twister, used in
making straw or hay ropes.
There are specimens in the Welsh Museum.

Trwclo   V. Tran.   To exchange.
" Trwclo cillith."
To exchange knives.

Trwco   V.t.   To exchange.
" Trwca gilleth a fi, 'nei di? "
Exchange knives with me, will you?

Trwcwl   N.m.s.
(1) A small trap.
(2) An old, worn-out cart.
(3) An improvised cart.

Trwel   N.f.s.   A trowel.

Trwmedd   Adj.   Sultry.

Trwnshwrn   N.m.s.   A drenching horn, used in administering physic to animals.
Variants : *trwnshwr* and *trinsher*.

Trwsto   V. Intran.   To thunder.
" Mae'n trwsto 'n ddichrinllid."
It thunders fearfully.

Trwyddl
-draw   Adv. phrase. Through and through, up and down

Said of farmers and their servants when they dine together and live in common.

Trwyn   N.m.s. The point of a rock at its furthest projection into the sea.
" Trwyn yr inys."
The point of the island.

Trwyno   V. Intran. To put in an appearance.
" Ddaru e byth drwyno ma wedin."
He never put in an appearance here afterwards.
Lit. : He never nosed here again.

Trwynsych   Adj. Said of one who turns up his nose at everything.

Tua   N.m.s. A caress.
" Rhowch dua bach i wncwl."
Give uncle a little caress.

Tuchial   Part. Groaning.

Twc   N.m.s. (1) A tuck or a pleat in a garment.
(2) The pain caused by a poultice in " drawing."
The verb *twco* is derived from this noun.

Twco   V. Tran. (1) To tuck clothes.
(2) To dress a babe in short clothes, termed in S. Pembrokeshire *breeching* a child.

Twco   V. Intran. To pain, said of the " tucking " pain caused by a thorn, of spasmodic toothache, &c.

Twcwr N.m.s. A fuller. The last of the Pontfaen *twcwried*, once upon a time so famous, was Benny Tomos, of Felin Twcwr, who died about ten years ago.

Twddiant [= tyfiant.] Abs. n. Growth.

Twlcyn N.m.s. A box used in weighing live pigs. It is a home-made contrivance, into which the pig is driven, and which is lifted on to the scales by means of projecting handles.

Twlsyn N.m.s. A wag, a jolly fellow.

Twll-y -constant N.m.s. The socket in which the heel of a scythe is fixed when attached to a handle.

Twll-y-gwergi A secret hole in the walls of ancient buildings where candles were concealed in the days when they were subject to duty. Many such holes are still to be found in old farm buildings.

Twmbler N.m.s. Wain.

Twmlo V. Tran. and Intran. To tumble, to roll a thing.
" Os na elli di gario'r pwn, twmla fe."
If you cannot carry the burden, roll it.

Twmrewi Part. Lit.: Warm-freezing.
A person sitting in front of a fire on a very cold day, with his front warm and his back cold, describes his sensation as *twmrewi*.

Twp Adj. Stupid.
Twpedd is also used.

Twrch-y -cwed N.m.s. Woodlouse.

Twrchyn N.m.s. A young castrated pig.
Plur. *twrchod*.

Twrne   N.m.s. A turner's place, and perhaps his craft.

Twrpant   N.m.s. Turpentine.

Twaw-clocs   N.m.s. A wisp of dry straw put into clogs to help keep the feet warm.

Twt-baw   Inter. Nonsense!

Tyed   N.m.s. Houseful.
" Ma tyed o blant yn Trehafog."
There is a houseful of children at Trehafog.
Plur. *taieidi*.

Tymowr   N.m.s. The workhouse. The epithet by which this institution is always spoken of.

Tyn   Adj. Diligent, worldly-wise.
" Ma Jôb Blânpant yn dwad mlân yn dda iawn, mae e'n hen griadur tyn iawn."
Job, of Blaenpant, thrives, he is a very diligent fellow.

Ty-to   N.m.s. A straw thatched cottage.

W

Wa   Inter. Ha!
"Fe wharddodd wa! wa!"
He laughed ha! ha! or, he laughed aloud.

Wac   N.f.s. A private path leading to a mansion
or private residence. The word is very rarely
used in any other sense.

Wachal   [= gochel.] Inter. Beware!

Wachlwch   [= gochelwch.] V. Tran.
The plur. only is used as a Verb.
"Wachlwch y tarw."
Beware of the bull.

Wad   N.f.s. A hit.
"Rho wàd iddo!"
Hit him!

Wado   V. Tran. To beat, to drub.

Wagin   N.f.s. Waggon.

Walplad   N.f.s. The top of the wall of a building,
where the beams rest.

Wangam   Adv. Very feeble and able to walk only very
little.
(From gwan + gam).

**Wanieth
-na'u-gily**   Different from usual, out of the ordinary
course.

" Ma dyn yn leico câl pryd yn wanieth-na'u-
gily dy' Sul."
A person likes to get a meal differing from
the usual course on Sunday.

Waplin   N.m.s. Lather, suds.

War   N.s. Track, heels.
" Ma nw ar 'i war e."
They are on his track.
" Ma nw 'n glôs ar 'i wàr e."
They are close at his heels.

Wascod   Waistcoat.
Plur. *wascodi*.

Wath   Conj. Because.
" Wàth nid fi pia fe."
Because it is not mine.

Wawch   Onomatopœic. A sound.
" Rows e ddim wawch! "
He uttered not a sound.

Waw-waw   Onomatopœic. Dog's cry. Bow wow!

We   V. Intran. and Adv. It was; yes.

$\overset{\wedge}{We}$ is the Verbal form and $W\hat{e}$ the Adverbial
in the N.E., but the distinction does not hold
good of the N.W.

**We-dim-bai
-arno**   This is the Demetian equivalent of " it was
kind of him."

We-dim-llai   V. phrase. I felt sure, I thought no less, &c.
" We-dim-llai da fi na fise fe 'n dŵad fel
addewodd e."
I felt sure he would come as he had promised.

Wedjen   N.f.s. Sweetheart.

Wedd N.s. Account.
"Thine data ddim 'i lun ar un wêdd."
My father would not have his photograph
taken on any account.

Weindo V. Tran. To wind.

Weitan Part. Waiting.

Wel-din Inter. Well done!

Welshnot A piece of wood, about the size and shape
of a domino, on which were inscribed the
letters W.N., and which was put in the hands
of a *corryn* by the old-time schoolmaster, to
empower the former to act as "detective of
Welsh." The custom of "Welshnot-ing" is
described in the author's "Renaissance and
Welsh Literature," p. 261.

Wen-sweci N.m.s. A pet lamb.

Wep N.f.s. Awry lip, making a pretence of crying.

Wermwnt N.m.s. · Wormwood.
Variant *wermwd*.

Werwen A spinning term.

Wic-wac N.m.s. The noise made by new boots or
shoes; always regarded as a sign of pride in
the wearer. Time was when the unfortunate
owner of a squeaky pair of shoes was visited
with *discibleth-yr-eglws* in puritan Pembrokeshire. If he cared to retain his chapel member-
ship he forthwith cast the noisy offenders aside:
he literally had to pull off his shoes, because
the ground whereon he stood was—if not holy,
at least puritanical!

Widl   N.f.s.   A whittle, a kind of shawl used for nursing. The story of the red whittles in connection with the French invasion of 1797 is too familiar to need rehearsing.

Widdebol   [= gyfebol.]   Adj.   To be with foal.

Widdig   N.f.pl.   Woodbine.
Sing. *widdigen*.

Wiglwogam   Adv.   Zig-zag.

Winglos   [= wyl nos.]   N.f.s.   Wake, or lichwake; the custom of watching over and performing various ceremonies in connection with the dead.

The Rev. D. Jenkin Evans gives the following interesting account of the old-time *Winglos* in the antiquaries' column of the "Pembroke County Guardian" under date of May 2, 1896 : "Although this old custom of watching and illuminating the chamber of the dead is still practised, it has lost all its most peculiar features, namely, the drawing up of the corpse through the chimney of the house where the death had occurred, before it was conveyed to its last resting place. The process of this extraordinary and mysterious custom was as follows : A certain number of persons would be engaged to remove the corpse from its coffin to a convenient place near the fire, where the pinioning of the dead would be performed. This was effected by tying a rope to the upper part of the body, the other end being afterwards passed up the chimney by means of a long stick or pitchfork. Then a sufficient number of men (possibly according to the weight of the corpse) would be told off and sent to the top of the chimney on the outside of the roof, which they reached by the help of a ladder, for the purpose of hauling the corpse. These—

having first fixed themselves as securely as the perilous nature of the situation would allow—took hold of the rope and signalled to the party inside by crying ' Hir wen gwd !' (words probably referring to the long white shroud with which the body was wrapt), and the party inside answered ' Whare'n barod !' (words equivalent to ' We are ready !'), and slowly but surely up the chimney went the corpse. When it had been brought to the top, it was carefully lowered again, and eventually replaced in its coffin. I am told that the last of such ceremonies in N. Pembrokeshire took place at a cottage on the glebeland known as Old Mill in the parish of Pontfaen."

Willawel N.f.s. The murmur of the wind among the branches of trees.

Wimben N.f.s. A beam in a roof, which is in sight. Uncovered woodwork in the roof.

Wimblath N.f.pl. Laths.
Sing. *wimblathen*.
Latsen is also used.

Wimlwth N.m.s. A fulcrum, a prise. A small stone placed under a bar for the purpose of forcing or raising heavy bodies.

Winci [= gwenci.] N.f.s. Weasel.
Ma tair short o winciod :
(1) Winci rawnog.
(2) ,, frongoch.
(3) ,, fronwen.

Windo V. Intran. To wince, said of a horse throwing up its hind legs.

Windre Abs. n. Pain in the finger-tips caused by intense cold. It is specially applied to the pain caused by plunging benumbed or frost-bitten fingers in warm water.

Wingalchu V. Tran. and Intran. To whitewash, usually with lime, but the word is often used for the act of putting on any colour on walls.

Winiddes [= gwniadyddes.] N.f.s. A seamstress.

Winsh N.f.s. A deep well. The word is transferred by synechdoche from the mechanical contrivance to the water itself.

Winshin N.m.s. A bushel.
" Winshin onest o farlish yw un wedi ffisto 'i ochre, a thinu y streicer rhownd drosto."
An honest bushel of barley is that whose sides have been tapped (to cause the grain to settle down), and over which the round strike has been drawn.
It was a point of honour with an upright corn-merchant, and among the old farmers, to use a round strike, or striker. The niggardly merchant or farmer used a square one, which swept away a larger quantity of the precious grain; hence *yr hen streicer scwar* became a colloquialism for a mean, miserly fellow.

Wirdrwm [= hwyrdrwm.] Adj. Hard of hearing. Restricted here to this sense.

Witneson N.c.pl. Witnesses.
The word is used in the plural only, and in a strictly legal sense. *Tyst* is used in the Singular.

Witsh-flawd N.f.s. Meal moth.

Wltwat Adj. Fickle.

Wmbralo N.m.s. Umbrella.
Gwmbarèl (accent on last syll.) is a variant frequently heard.

Wmbw Onomatopœic. The call of horned cattle.

Wmed-i
-wared Adv. phrase. Up and down.
" Ma nw wedi bod yn whilo wmed-i-wared am yr hwrdd."
They have been searching up and down for the ram.

Wmla [= ymladd.] V. Intran. To fight.

Wmla-cimale N.m.s. A fight with knuckles.
The combatants with closed fists hit each other's knuckles by turns. The one who could endure the ordeal the better was accounted winner.

Wnibeth An expletive, used in various senses. (Accent on last syll.).
" Mae e mor ddwl ag wnibeth."
He is as silly as I-know-not-what.

Wniwns N.m.pl. Onions.
Sing. *wniwnsyn.*

Wp-a-deis Inter. Word spoken to a child in lifting it up.

Wr A particle. Man, lad, fellow.
" Ble chi 'n mynd, wr? "
Whither bound, man?
Particles used similarly are *achan* (masc.) and *les* (fem.).

v

Wrach, y   *N.f.s.* A small tuft of corn, usually plaited in three strands, and about eight to twelve inches in length. The Rev. D. Jenkyn Evans, the Vicar of Pontfaen, gave the following account of the *Wrach* in the antiquaries' column of the "Pembroke County Guardian" for December 7th, 1895:

"The *Wrach* was made of the last corn which was cut at the harvest; and in some districts great excitement existed and much amusement was created amongst the reapers when the last standing was reached. All in turn were allowed to throw their sickles at it, just as boys and girls throw sticks at 'Aunt Sally' in our vanity fairs, and the one who succeeded in cutting the last corn received as his or her reward a jug of home-brewed. In those days, I need hardly say, there were no scythes, much less machines as nowadays, used in cutting corn: our forefathers had only one implement for this purpose—the sickle. . . . As soon as all the corn was cut the *Wrach* was hurriedly made and taken to the neighbouring farm, where the reapers were busy at work. This was generally done by the 'ploughman,' but he had to be very carful to do so without being observed by his neighbours, for if they saw him coming, and had the slightest suspicion of his errand, they would soon make him retrace his steps. But the person in charge of the *Wrach* was ever careful to avoid observation, and when he had crept over fences and stealthily stationed himself over against the foreman of his neighbour's reapers, he watched his opportunity, so that when they were within easy distance of each other, he suddenly threw his *Wrach* over the fence, and if possible, upon the foreman's sickle, crying:

      'Bore y codais i,
      Hwyr y dilinais i,
      Ar ei gwar hi.'

He then took to his heels with all the energy
he possess... , and if he got off without being
caught or cut by the flying sickles of the
frenzied reapers, which were hurled after him,
he was a lucky man. In other instances the
Wrach was brought home by one of the reapers
to the farm house, but it was necessary that it
should be taken into the house without being
wetted. The person who was suspected by those
in the house of having the *Wrach* in his possession, generally had a pretty rough time of
it; sometimes he would be stripped of the
greater part of his clothing, or he would be
deluged with water which had been stored in
buckets and pans for that purpose.   If the
Wrach was brought into the house *dry* and un-
observed, the master had to pay the bearer a
small fine, or oftener a jug of beer 'from the
cask next to the wall' (y gasgen nesa'r wàl)—
a cask which contained the best and strongest
beer, which the master reserved for himself
and a few honoured guests. . . . When the
Wrach had been successfully brought into the
house, it was carefully hung to a nail on the
beam or some other convenient place, in the
hall *(neuodd)* or elsewhere, where it remained
all the year. This custom of bringing the
Wrach into the house and hanging it up still
exists at some farms, though the ancient and
quaint ceremonies just described are now dis-
continued.''

Wrth   [= oddiwrth.] Prep. From.
                "I ni 'n câl llithir wrth John bob wthnos.''
                We receive a letter from John every week.

Wthnos Wes N.f.s. The week of life.
                Saith cifnod bowyd.
                Dwarnode yr wthnos yw :—

(1) Mabandod, o 1 hyd 7 mlwydd ŵed.
(2) Ifenctyd ,, 7 ,, 14 ,, ,,
(3) Gwridŵed ,, 14 ,, 21 ,, ,,
(4) Serch ,, 21 ,, 28 ,, ,,
(5) Anterth ,, 28 ,, 42 ,, ,,
(6) Cifnerth ,, 42 ,, 56 ,, ,,
(7) Gwynŵed ,, 56 ,, 70 ,, ,,
(The holy age).

[Taken down from the mouth of my mother in the year 1907.]

Wy-addo   N.m.s. A nest egg.
(Wy is pronounced wî).

Wyl   [= gŵyl.] N.f.s. A festival, Saint's day.
"Wyl-Beder"—S. Peter's Day.
"Wyl-Gurig"—S. Curig's Day.
(Pron. like English *will*).

Wyne   N.c.pl. Lambs. The equivalent of the literary *wynos*.

Wyt   [= ydwyt.] V. Intran. Thou art, art thou?
Consonantal *w*, pron. wŷt.

WH

Wha!   Inter. Aha!
"Fe wharddodd wha! wha!
He laughed aha! aha!

Whap   Adv. Soon.

Whap-fach   Adv. Presently, shortly.

Whare   N.m.s. Game, play.
The following were the school games of thirty years ago:—
Shiligwt—A kind of tug-of-war.
Ffwtit—Leap-frog.
Cadno—Fox and hounds.
Spei—Hide and seek.
Cipo—Touch and run.
Dandy—Played with marble and pebbles.
Bando—Rustic hockey.
Tom—Rustic bowls.
Ceffile-bach—Little horses.
Bwtwne—Buttons.
Shilingloffan } See-saw.
Lanshabwdi }
Ffalgar (? Trafalgar)—A mock sea-fight. The two "squadrons" ranged themselves on either side of a river, and shot at each other with the *cwm-dwr*. That "squadron" was considered to have lost the day which got the greater dousing.
Bwmbwr—Blind man's buff.
Data-meddw—Drunken father. One of the

bigger lads acted the drunkard, and endeavoured to catch the rest, to whom (if caught) he administered a thorough drubbing.

Whare   Part. Fermenting.
"Ma'r ddiod yn dachre whare."
The beer is beginning to ferment.

Whare   Adv. On the balance; said of the beam of a pair o scales when it indicates perfect balance.

Whare'r
  -amser   Beating time in music.
"Cerddor heb 'i fath wê Lefi Rhinallt; wê dde'n rhoi 'i law tu ol 'i glust, ac yn whare'r amser a'i drwed, a dina lle bidde canu."
Levi Reynolds was an unrivalled musician; he would put his hand behind his ear and beat the time with his foot, and there would be singing!

Whatial   V. Intran. To fritter away time, to loiter.

Whech   N.m.s. A throat disease in young calves.
"Ma'r whèch ar y lloi, ma'n rhaid i ni roi torpant yn i trwyne nw."
The calves have the throat disease, we must administer turpentine to them through the nostrils.

Wheddel   N.f.s. (1) A legend. (2) An instant.
"Ys dŵad y wheddel."
According to the legend.
"Wyddwn i wheddel cyn iddo nharo i "=I had not time to say "Jack Robinson" before he struck me.

Wherwi   V. Intran. To be inflamed.

Whiblen   N.f.s.   Mild home-brewed beer.
Home-brewed beer is made in three degrees
of strength, named : —
Whiblen—Mild.
Tablen—Medium.
Diod—Strong.

Whidels   N.f.pl.   Blisters.

Whiflyd   V. Intran.   To move a little, to budge.
" Alla i ddim 'i whiflyd e."
I cannot budge it.

Whilber   N.f.s.   A wheelbarrow.

Whildrot   Abs. n.   A jog-trot.

Whilen-gnol   N.f.s.   A species of pugnacious blackbeetle.

Whilen-y
-bomp   N.f.s.   The humming beetle.

Whilen-y
-ffordd   N.f.s.   A species of blackbeetle often seen on
the roadside.   There is a superstition that to
accidentally kill one when it crosses one's path
brings ill-luck, and that to kill it anywhere
brings rain.

Whillbawan   V. Intran.   Killing time, dawdling.
" Weithith rhen andras ddim ; tawn i'n rhoi
dwarnod o waith iddo, nele fe ddim ond whili-
bawan a stwffo 'i berfe."
The old villain will not work ; if I were to
give him a day's job, he would only dawdle and
feast.

Whiloges   N.f.s.   A wizened old woman, a fortune-teller.

Whindrew   Abs. n.   A frost-bite.

Whindrewi   V. Intran.   To be frost-bitten.

Whindriff   Adv. Disorderly, in a chaotic manner.
"Fe âth y cifan yn whindriff yn y fan ar iol
i'r hen Ddafis farw, druan."
Everything became disordered as soon as poor
old Davies died.

Whinfforch   N.f.s. A wooden instrument used in conjunction with the whinglog in weeding corn-
fields. A shorter handled one was used in conjunction with the *bilwg* to cut furze.

Whinglog   N.m.s. A long-handled knife, used in weeding corn-fields. It was used in conjunction
with the *whinfforch*.

Whip   Adv. Limp.
"Ma'i fraich e'n whip, mae shwr fod wedi
tori."
His arm hangs limp, it is surely broken.

Whipad   In the phrase "whipaa o fenyn"—as much
butter as a dairymaid holds in her hand in
whipping it.

Whirligegen   N.f.s. A whirligig.
This was made with a stick about six inches
long, with a potato stuck at one end, and a
large hazel-nut bored so as to pass over the
stick at the other end. By means of a thin
piece of string, which was made to pass through
a second bore in the nut and attached to the
stick, a whir'ing motion was produced.

Whirndwp   Adj. and Adv. Ignorant and furious.

Whirnell   N.f.s. A lump on the head, raised by a blow.
Variant *hwrnell*.

Whit   N.f.s. (1) Whistle. (2) The gullet.
(1) " Whit y train."
The whistle of the train.
(2) " Dewcu miwn i'r Hôs and Corn i ni gâl bob o lased i lwchu'r whit."
Come in to the Rose and Crown to have a glass apiece to wet the gullet.

Whit-what   Adj. Unreliable. (Pron. whit-whàt).

Whith   Adj. and Adv. Amiss, and a variety of shades of meaning, to be learnt only from the connection.
" Gwel'd yn whith "—Taken amiss.
" Cwmryd yn whith "—Taken to heart.
" Teimlo'n whith "—Felt very much.
" Drichid yn whith "—To look askance.

Whithrin   N.m.s. A bit, a small quantity.
" Dyw e ddim whithrin o wanieth da fi pun a ddewch chi a'i peido."
It makes no difference at all to me whether you come or not; literally, " Not the smallest bit of difference."

Whithrwydd   Prop. n. and Abs. n. (1) The Old Nick.
(2) Chagrin, vexation.
" Mae e'n rhedeg fel y Whithrwydd."
He runs like the Old Nick.
" Ma Sara wedi gweld whithrwydd fod Dafi wedi 'i thwyllo hi."
Lit.: Sarah has seen vexation that David has deceived her.

Whithwr   N.m.s. A fire " blower," i.e., a long stick with a bore through it used for blowing the fire with.

Whiw-whaw   Onomatopœic. Haphazard.

Y

Yn-nghifor   Part. phrase. Covered over.
"Ma'r wein yn-nghifor o ddwr."
The moor is covered with water.

Yn-i-ben   About his ears.
"Mae e wedi tinu nw yn-'i-ben."
He has pulled them about his ears.

Yn-i-goce   Adv. phrase. In its tumps, said of hay, or
of mats, or of anything that is put in tumps in
the process of being seasoned.

**Yn-mhene'-u
-gily**   Adv. phrase. At loggerheads.

Yn-un-swydd   Adv. phrase. On purpose, for that very thing.
"Mi ddethum yn un swydd i'ch gweld chi."
I came on purpose to see you.

Yn-wlich   Part. Steeping, soaking.
"Odi 'r te 'n wlich?"
Is the tea steeping?

Ynyn   [= yn fy.] Pron. Prep. In my.
"Pan own i'n myn'd i'r iscol
A'm llifyr ynyn llaw,
Heibo Castell Newy
A'r clòc yn taro naw," &c.
(Old rhyme).

Ys

Adv. Till.

" Sano ni wedi gorffod pwrnu tato ys nawr."
We have not been obliged to buy potatoes
till now.

Ysgib-frich

N.f.s. A smoked sheaf of oats administered
to a cow immediately after calving to help it
to cast the after-birth. A pile of damp straw
or fern is put on the peat fire, which produces
a volume of dense smoke, in which the sheaf of
oats is held for a few minutes, and then
hurriedly taken to the cow, wrapped over to
prevent the escape of the smoke which it has
absorbed. The timely administering of the
ysgib-frich has never failed, it is averred, to
bring about the desired result. The custom is
religiously observed to-day in Pontfaen and the
adjoining parishes.

[Ysgub has several variants; ysgib, iscib,
isgub, and escib.]